GENDER
POLITICS
and MTV

GENDER
POLITICS
and MTV

Voicing the Difference

LISA A. LEWIS

TEMPLE UNIVERSITY PRESS ▪ *Philadelphia*

Temple University Press, Philadelphia 19122
Copyright © 1990 by Temple University. All rights reserved
Published 1990
Printed in the United States of America

The paper used in this publication meets the minimum
requirements of American National Standard for Information
Sciences—Permanence of Paper for Printed Library Materials,
ANSI Z39.48-1984 ∞

Library of Congress Cataloging-in-Publication Data
Lewis, Lisa A.
Gender politics and MTV : voicing the difference / Lisa A. Lewis.
p.   cm.
Includes bibliographical references.
ISBN 0-87722-693-8 (alk. paper)
1. MTV Networks.   2. Rock music—History and criticism.   3. Sex role in
television.   4. Women in television.   5. Female musicians.   I. Title.
PN1992.8.M87L49   1990
384.55′54′0673—dc20   89-20169
                                                                 CIP

For Rob

CONTENTS

Contents

ACKNOWLEDGMENTS

SOME GRAND support and encouragement have carried me to the completion of this book. I thank Horace Newcomb for his judicious guidance of my research at the University of Texas at Austin. Joli Jensen and Thomas Schatz, in the Department of Radio, Television, Film, and Amy Burce and James Brow, in the Department of Anthropology, provided valuable readings of early versions of the manuscript. I am grateful to Jane Marcus, in the Department of English for embracing my writing on video with her passion for literature. I thank all those who attended and contributed to presentations of my work at numerous conferences, especially John Fiske, Larry Grossberg, and Mica Nava. I express my appreciation also to those who published parts of my research in progress. Encouragement of these kinds helped drive the project forward.

My warmest thanks go to Pat Benatar, whose support of my work sustained and inspired me the most. I am indebted to the members of her management team at the time of the study, New Star Enterprises, who graciously consented to provide me with pertinent information and services. Kathy Hertz, in particular, made my work easier and certainly more enjoyable.

I thank my family for their interest, especially my cousins and aunts who provided lifelong instruction in female culture. My deepest gratitude goes to Rob Sabal, whose enthusiasm for my work was unmatched.

GENDER
POLITICS
and MTV

INTRODUCTION

IN 1983, the song "Girls Just Want to Have Fun" hit the radio airwaves, and feminists across the United States held their collective breath. Was the lyrical refrain some co-opted response to Freud's famous line "What do women want?" Or perhaps a reactionary eighties backlash to the far-reaching demands of seventies feminism? Was the word "girls" objectionable? Wasn't "wanting fun" a politically unworthy ambition? Some of that breath was expelled with relief as promotion of the song began on Music Television (MTV), the two-year-old cable channel that helped originate distribution of music videos. Cable subscribers across the nation witnessed singer Cyndi Lauper visually interpret the song's lyrics on the video screen. Popular support began to build, and soon women and girls were articulating the song as an anthem of liberation, formulating personal and political scenarios of female empowerment. By January 1985, *Ms.* magazine, the mouthpiece of American popular feminism, had named Lauper one of America's "twelve excellent women."

Readers' letters of response printed in the magazine's subsequent issues approved the choice. Catherine O'Brien, a

House representative in the state of New Hampshire, wrote
the following letter:

> GJWTHF appeared on all my campaign literature as I sought
> public office this past fall. Although few knew what it meant, in
> these discouraging times it reminded me why I had chosen to
> run—to help ensure, through economic and social programs,
> progress for women.
>
> I was therefore thrilled when I saw Cyndi Lauper honored in
> your magazine. GJWTHF—Girls Just Want to Have Fun. I think
> we'll have a lot more fun when we've gained equality (O'Brien
> 1985, p. 5).

Among young and very young women the response to Lauper
was even stronger. Along with Representative O'Brien's letter,
Ms. printed a letter from Julia Burke of Sacramento, California, which focused on Burke's young daughter's attraction to
Lauper:

> My five-year-old daughter pointed out the picture of Geral-
> dine Ferraro among the women on the January cover. She said,
> "I like her. She's the President." She was quite disappointed to
> find out that she ran for Vice President and lost. She was con-
> fused about why none of the Presidents have ever been "ladies."
> I told her that when she gets bigger, Presidents will be ladies
> too. She said, "They'd better." Then we cut out all the women's
> pictures on the cover and even made a pin for her to wear.
>
> Whose picture was on the pin? You guessed it . . . Cyndi
> Lauper's! (Burke 1985, p. 5).

Reading these two letters, it is possible to relive some of the
excitement that Lauper and her song generated for girls and
women, to remember how the singer and her MTV-promoted
song reached across different generations and ages to address
the common desires of women and girls for social recognition
and political power.

This book traces in detail the conditions that put Lauper

and a number of other female musicians of the same time period at the center of cultural politics. It is organized to reveal a historical moment in the making, a moment when business interests aligned to produce a new popular culture product, which in turn provoked a new terrain of ideological struggle over social inequality and subordinate status.

Chapter One considers the commercial and industrial imperatives that led to the creation of the cable television channel MTV. It shows how the goal of producing a commercially successful media product has colored the ways audiences are perceived and addressed. Expanding on the general movement in media industries toward categorizing lucrative audience groups, MTV's originating company sought to target a youth audience, known for its expendable income and liberal consumption patterns, with visualizations of rock music. Although the industrial drive to quantify and predict audience response was manifested in unprecedented amounts of audience research, in the final analysis, interpretation of the target audience was based on "intuitive," ideological assumptions.

Chapter Two explores more fully how MTV's concept origination strategies became dependent on ideological understandings of the target group's tastes and desires. By selecting rock music as the programming resource, and youth as the target audience, MTV brought two complex categories of social assumptions, two "mental frameworks,"[1] into relation. These two interrelated systems of belief, separated for the purposes of criticism, are implicated in attempts to maintain social relations of power and dominance—most specifically, white male privilege. The ideology of rock and the ideology of adolescence express the underlying social goal of maintaining females in an underprivileged position. As MTV's creators sought to produce a new kind of video programming especially for youth, MTV reproduced these ideologies and related social functions by designing a preferred address to male adolescents.

Chapter Three outlines the components of MTV's textual system of male address and analyzes four videos produced to promote male musicians in 1983.

Chapter Four broadens the discussion of MTV's male-oriented address to consider how the social condition of gender inequality has permeated the music tradition of the Western world. MTV, by all the indications of its design, goals, and history, appeared poised to perpetuate, or reactivate, the structures of value and strategies of differentiation that have served historically to define female musicians as inferior. But Chapter Four also marks a turning point in the book. The strategies of dominance identified in this and previous chapters are turned toward the goal of recognizing acts of resistance and political struggle on the part of female musicians (and, ultimately, female audiences). The systematic bias against women in music has not entirely disabled female musicianship; indeed, female musicians have risen to the occasion. Redirecting the spotlight from MTV's reproduction of capitalist and patriarchal structures to the individuals who reside within them begins to reveal the many ways MTV has enabled female musicians and female audiences to turn the channel to their advantage.

Chapter Five introduces four popular female musicians who have suffered to varying degrees under the regime of gender inequality in music and in society generally: Tina Turner, Pat Benatar, Cyndi Lauper, and Madonna. A mini-biography of each concretely illustrates their historically specific experiences of gender discrimination and uncovers the positive role MTV has played in their careers.

Chapter Six analyzes the videos produced to promote the four musicians in the years 1980–1986. A coherent textual system of *female address* emerges, one that operated to challenge MTV's conventions of male address. The videos were infused with symbolic discourse on the meaning of gender, prompting female audiences to reflect on their own experiences of gender inequality.

Chapter Seven and Chapter Eight turn to the issue of how female-address textuality in music video was provoked and fueled by avid female audiences. Chapter Seven lays the foundation for this investigation by concentrating on a primary form of popularity: *fandom*. Fan behavior is treated as a window into the meanings and uses of music and video texts in the everyday lives of audiences. The musicians in this study were wildly popular with female audiences, the most devoted of whom expressed this popularity by imitating the musicians' styles of dress and performance. In the cases of Lauper and Madonna, style imitation became the preferred mode of female fan response. To understand this practice in the specific context of female-address textuality, Chapter Eight focuses on a number of social events involving female fan style imitators during the years under study, particularly 1985. Through imitation, girls acknowledged and used female address to execute their own symbolic expressions of gender experience.

Chapter Nine arrives at tentative conclusions about how realms of cultural production and consumption can become political arenas capable of uniting creators and consumers with similar social interests at stake.

This book is organized as a political analysis, although no single political theory is in evidence. Rather, a number of theoretical perspectives and disciplinary influences are amassed in its pages. Karl Marx's (1972a, 1972b, 1972c) writings provide the study with its most basic analytical impulse. More central is the work of Antonio Gramsci (1971), as elaborated by Stuart Hall (1982, 1983). Hall's application of Gramsci to cultural concerns, particularly the concept of hegemony, underlies the entire analysis herein and is responsible for the characterization of dominance in social and textual discourse as situational and under stress.

The book's analyses of gender relations derives from a variety of feminist scholars and writers whose work has most frequently appeared in the form of an intervention in a gender-

biased field or body of literature. It is unfortunate that female
scholars bear the brunt of enlightening the disciplines about
gender formations. It should not require the experience of
living under oppression to create an agenda for understanding
its operations. Yet after completing this study, I can say that
being female and having experienced life as a female adolescent contributed greatly to my recognition of female-address
textuality. I want to highlight the importance to this study
of feminist writing on girls and youth culture written in a
British context. Angela McRobbie's work (1980, 1983) and her
co-authored and co-edited works (Garber, 1976; Nava, 1984;
Frith, 1978–1979) provided me with my perspective on girls
as a distinct social and cultural group. Her strong intervention into British subculture literature encouraged my critical
entry into the specificity of female youth culture in the United
States. *Gender and Generation*, a collection of essays edited by
McRobbie and Mica Nava (1984) was a revelation and an inspiration. The works in this collection—Barbara Hudson on
femininity and adolescence, Nava on the social regulation of
girls, Valerie Walkerdine on fantasy in girls' lives, and Erica
Carter on girls and consumption practice—have all contributed to my analysis of American girls' social lives, as have
the separately published works of Christine Griffin (1985) on
the everyday lives of school girls and Sue Steward and Sheryl
Garratt (1984) on girls and popular music.

Throughout the book I use the descriptor "girl," in accordance with the British practice, when referring to female-
adolescent audience members, or in my standardized description of textual representations of female adolescents and
preadolescents. I am aware that in the United States, the word
"girl" is often used to denigrate adult women; but I propose
to reclaim the word for young women and employ it in that
spirit, as a reminder of the distinct and special status of young
womanhood. (Similarly, I use the word "boy" when describ-

ing a textual representation of male adolescence.) I invoke the broader gender classification of girls *and* women through the term *female address,* for as the letters published in *Ms.* magazine illustrate, the textual address to girls frequently touched adult women. Perhaps this was because they had once been girls themselves, or, more probably, because the address was capable of enunciating a broader gender experience.

While this book is arranged to illuminate political operations, it is also organized to be a cultural analysis, as it traces an arc of cultural distribution, production, and reception: MTV is started and implemented as a channel of music video distribution; female musicians emerge as professional creators in a music industry that uses MTV as a primary promotion vehicle, and then negotiate their way through the industrial modes of music and video production and credit; female audiences use and interpret MTV and individual musicians' music and video texts, producing culture themselves through fan activity. In service of the book's cultural analysis are theories and methods that media critics have devised to identify and analyze the players and processes surrounding media programming practices. A body of literature has sprung up around the central issue of how audiences can be conceived of as active in determining textual content (although little work has been done on fans and fandom). A modicum of work credits media creators with this role. This book does not perpetuate the exclusive and separate treatment of producers and audiences, but instead asserts that both groups act as agents of textual production and meaning.

My process of coming to terms with the role of the music industry and musicians in MTV's visual medium has been a long one. I have been helped along the way by the work of several music critics, including Simon Frith (1981, 1988), Dave Laing (1985), Iain Chambers (1985), and Dick Hebdige (1982), many of whom are cited in Chapter Two, and Eva

Rieger (1985), whose history of women in music was critical to Chapter Four. Still, the study would have benefited from more consideration of the context of music production and consumption, and the integration of some form of musical analysis into the textual analyses of videos already provided. Frankly, I found very little in the way of useful models for the second endeavor. My discussion of production modes and authorship struggles in the music industry in Chapter Four was, however, aided by fieldwork sessions with Pat Benatar, who graciously allowed me to observe her at work on music and video production stages, and during a concert tour.

I want to emphasize that the history told in this book was not a product of historical reconstruction, but emerged instead as a result of an extended study of contemporary culture in real time. This was crucial to my ability to recognize the emergent qualities, the historical conjuncture, of MTV with female musicians and female audiences. When I began my study of MTV in the early months of 1983, it was in the general context of observing and analyzing a new cultural form. Turner, Lauper, and Madonna had not even appeared on the channel yet. Their appearance on MTV and their emergence into the general culture created excitement and interpretive activity that infiltrated my work. I recorded the musicians' videos, bought their records, attended their concerts, read about them in the press. I participated, in other words, in what Raymond Williams (1977) has labeled their "structure of feeling"—the climate and context of lived experience that surrounded them.

This is to say that the musicians' fans and I participated in the cultural moment of female address in much the same way. According to the criteria of fandom that I outline in Chapter Seven, I generated much of my research data in the same way that fans do. It was the context of academic research that was the distinguishing element, and even that, I would admit, did not (fortunately) distance me in a way that prevented my experiencing the texts and musicians as do fans. I, too, was affected by the musicians' address to women; and studying them was a way of using their texts in my everyday life. I acknowledge a debt to the field of anthropology for its methods of participant-observation and ethnography, which provided me with ways to record and evaluate unfolding cultural events. So much of popular culture is fleeting and, because of its currency, apparently without clear context. Cultural texts and events disappear quickly; their moment of resonance and affect are lost forever. It takes a commitment to participate in the unfolding of culture to appreciate it fully.

ONE

MTV'S INDUSTRIAL IMPERATIVES

ON AUGUST 1, 1981, the Warner Amex Satellite Entertainment Company (WASEC) watched, with dollar signs in its corporate eyes, the start up of Music Television (MTV), its new cable program service. As is the case for all media programming ventures supported by industry financing, the development of MTV was motivated by commercial imperatives of profit, market control, and corporate growth (Meehan 1986). The wiring of the nation for cable television had accelerated in the late 1970s, and there was money to be made by corporations with the resources to address the cable industry's growing need for new and appealing programming. As late as January 1979 there was still no programming designed specifically with a cable audience in mind (Foster 1982, p. 178). However, by the end of the year satellite delivery had proven to be an economical way to distribute programming on a national scale, and three basic cable services were launched: ESPN, dedicated to sports programming; C-Span, which offered coverage of U.S. congressional sessions; and Warner Cable's children's channel, Nickelodeon. Warner Cable moved quickly to form a partnership with American Express, forming the Warner Amex Satellite Entertainment Company, and joined the pay cable market with The Movie Channel. MTV was developed to admit WASEC[1] into basic cable programming, expanding its holdings beyond Nickelodeon, the basic channel it acquired from Warner Cable as a result of its merge with American Express.

Movie programming was an obvious choice for a pay cable operation; films from Hollywood's archives had proven to be popular among broadcast television audiences, and film-going audiences were already accustomed to paying for movies at the box office. The success of two other pay cable channels devoted to screening films, Time-Life's pioneering Home Box Office (the first program service to exploit satellite delivery), and Showtime, owned by Viacom and Teleprompter, had demonstrated the strength of the movie market. But what kinds of programming could fill the many basic channels that cable technology made available and that cable system operators needed in order to build their subscriber lists? More specifically, how did WASEC find its way to the concept of "music television"?

Broadcast television networks, in their attempts to develop new and successful program ideas, have relied on everything from a producer's hunch about an appealing program concept to "scientific" methods of testing audience response. At various times in their history, the networks have looked to big-name actors, successful writers, and particular genres as forms of insurance (Brown 1971; Gitlin 1985). Writing in 1971, Les Brown (1971, p. 135) summarized the consensus about program development, "Whatever else, it must have a suggestion of newness without being so new that its pattern will be alien to what the viewer has liked in the past." MTV's concept originators arrived at the concept of music television by combining such broadcast industry wisdom with new and emerging approaches to media audiences.

Target Practice

Commercial media is driven by the economic need to attract a large audience. But popularity does not necessarily have to come in the form of a complete demographic spread of ages, classes, races, and genders in order for a particular media venture to be financially viable. In a marketplace overrun with entertainment opportunities, capturing a demographic segment of the total potential audience is sufficient as long as that segment has money to spend on the products and services offered by advertisers and cable operators. In the early development stages of radio and broadcast television, this insight remained largely submerged, and program development was less focused on addressing specific social and economic groups. The audience was conceived more as an undifferentiated mass or as family units. Early media backers were too involved with selling radio and television receivers and creating the institutional and financial structures to support the production of programing to concentrate on the composition of the audience. Only later were audience research methods developed in an attempt to forestall program failures and increase profit margins.

Yet as early as the 1930s, radio recognized housewives (who spent large amounts of time at home listening to their radios) as a group with a common consumer interest and sought to target them with soap opera programming. As Robert Allen (1985, p. 133) has pointed out, "The initial economic impetus behind the development of the soap opera form was the need to use daytime broadcasting hours to reach female consumers." Audience differentiation also surfaced as an implicit concern for radio in the years following World War II, when television's viability as a national medium threatened to dissolve radio's dominance of family-oriented entertainment. Radio survived the challenge by redefining its relation to its audi-

ence, originating "formula" programming designed to appeal
to specific "taste groups." The rise of teenage "styles of consumption" in the 1920s, cut short by the economic pressures
of the 1930s, resurfaced in the growing prosperity of post-
war America to make youth an attractive demographic sector
(Frith 1981, p. 182). "Top 40" radio was designed specifically
to take advantage of the new youth consumer market. "It was
aimed at teenagers, who were the fastest growing segment
of the population, had growing disposable income, and had
plenty of time to listen," explain authors Christopher Sterling
and John Kitross (1978, p. 339). The emergence of rock-and-
roll music in the late 1950s and 1960s as the "music of youth"
provided a cultural rallying point for demographics-inspired
media products. The recording industry regrouped around a
youth orientation, and radio became the preferred medium for
rock music promotion and distribution.

    With the entry of television into the consumer market in
the 1950s, costs for domestic entertainment rose dramatically,
making the identification of and programming to moneyed
consumers especially important. Jane Feuer, Paul Kerr, and
Tise Vahimagi have noted (1984, p. 3) that "upscale" viewers
(those with a relatively high income) were of special interest
during television's early years and that they affected the nature
of programming: "The constitution of the audience [was] a
factor during the 1950s 'golden age' of TV drama, when 'up-
market' productions were used to entice the well-to-do to buy
television receivers." Following radio's lead, soap operas were
adapted for television's daytime hours. Shows catering to a
youthful audience were also created, such as "Paul Whiteman's
TV Teen Club" (1949–1954) and the long-running "American
Bandstand" (started in Philadelphia in 1952 and picked up by
ABC in 1957). Beginning with the rock sitcom "The Monkees"
(1966–1968), network television extended its youth-oriented
music programming to fictionalized forms (Shore 1984).

But the 1970s were perhaps the most pivotal years for the development of "demographic thinking" as a principal television programming philosophy (Marc 1984; Feuer, Kerr, and Vahimagi 1984). During these years, the television industry began enthusiastically to base programming decisions on demographic research, hoping to attract sponsors by providing (target) audiences that appropriately "matched" ideal consumer profiles for given products or services. The 1969 network ratings war between NBC and top-rated CBS is most frequently cited as the catalyst for the industry's refinement of the notion of the target audience into a "scientific," finely honed system of viewer profiles:

> Although [Michael] Dann [chief programmer at CBS] claimed victory in terms of NUMBERS of viewers, [Paul] Klein at NBC claimed a DEMOGRAPHIC victory on the basis of a greater percentage of young adult viewers, the "quality demographics." Although CBS had the majority of the top ten rated shows, their appeal was primarily to a rural audience consisting of the undesirable populations of children and adults over 50. Moreover, CBS was losing out on the urban audience for its owned and operated stations. Thus in programming the 1970–1 season, CBS accepted Klein's interpretation, replacing Dann as programming chief with the soon-to-be legendary Fred Silverman . . . a man who swore by demographics and audience measurement procedures (Feuer, Kerr, and Vahimagi 1984, p. 4).

The emphasis in NBC's challenge rested on targeting the most active consumer, a complicated viewer profile that brought together demographic categories of age and geographic location (the two prime considerations according to Feuer, Kerr, and Vahimagi) and, more implicitly, class, race, and gender: "Specifically it was discovered that young, urban adults (especially females) aged 18–49 were the prime consumers of the types of goods advertised on TV" (Feuer, Kerr, and Vahimagi 1984, p. 3). What would come to be known as

"quality demographics" was worked into a bona fide programming strategy under Fred Silverman's stewardship.

The move toward the "scientific" targeting of audiences by
network television is generally regarded as a move away from
the mass-audience approach, which had operated as something
of an industry paradigm up to that time. Although the television and radio industries had recognized the isolated appeal
of certain program types for certain audience sectors in the
early years of program development, they were still oriented
toward attracting sheer numbers as measured by ratings services. But over time, competitive pressures among television
networks and radio stations, coupled with increased diversity
in the entertainment field, made audience targeting a clear
commercial advantage.

Cable television's arrival with force on the entertainment
scene in the late 1970s positioned it perfectly to take advantage
of demographic thinking, although many of the new companies anxious to make a killing with cable program services did
not recognize the trend. Bob Pittman, who ran The Movie
Channel for WASEC, was the driving force behind the use
of "target audience" as a guiding principle for his company's
origination of a new basic cable channel concept. Pittman, who
was twenty-nine years old during MTV's concept planning
stage, was precisely in the age group occupationally schooled
in demographic thinking—in his case, on the job as a radio
program director. His allegiance to audience demographics
and research as a basis for concept origination was a tribute
to Fred Silverman's program development practice, although
with MTV Pittman ultimately went further in the concept's
creative implementation. Levy (1983, p. 33), who interviewed
Pittman for *Rolling Stone*, described him in these terms: "His
meteoric career has been characterized by a penchant for market research and a willingness to discard traditional 'wisdom'
in favor of pursuing the 'real meaning' of the data compiled by

phone calls, sales-trend analyses and surveys of the Mood of the Nation."

"Traditional wisdom" directed television program developers to base new programs on formulas, on whatever had proven to be popular in the past. The networks' reliance on audience ratings contributed to the recycling of program formulas by assessing the popularity of programs after the fact of their production. But the emerging demographic approach suggested a different strategy to Pittman. He called for selecting the audience, not the programming formula, first, an approach he later described as developing a "product for people," not "learn[ing] formulas" (Spotnitz 1989, p. 30). Pittman and the team of young executives organized under the capital support of WASEC discovered that no cable channel was targeted specifically to the demographically desirable post-war "baby boomers," aged twelve to thirty-four, the most affluent consumer group (Wolfe 1983, p. 43). This discovery provided an opening for the creation of a channel that could hold appeal for this particular age group. Members of the selected target audience were tested with customized surveys about their media preferences at the early stage of concept origination, with the idea that popularity was a phenomenon to be created, not merely measured after the fact. Marshall Cohen, in charge of WASEC research at the time, believes MTV to be the most researched channel in U.S. television history (Levy 1983, p. 33).

Cultural Practice

Bob Pittman was himself, at twenty-nine years of age, a member of MTV's chosen target group. While he recognized the targeted audience of twelve to thirty-four year olds as a desirable consumer group, he went a step further to identify them as a "cultural" group. It was this second step, involving Pittman's subjective experience of his own generation rather than "scientific" testing methods, that led directly to the concept of MTV. Pittman believed that the target group's members, while relatively diverse in age, were culturally united by the circumstance of their historical synchronicity with the two proven and popular entertainment attractions of the era —television and rock and roll. He described MTV's potential audience as "television babies who grew up on TV and rock and roll" (Levy 1983, p. 33). Growing up with the two media had clearly been formative in his own life. He had worked in the music business through radio and television from the time he was fifteen years old. Pittman was distressed that his generation's two favorite activities—watching television and listening to music—were mutually exclusive. He had undoubtedly witnessed consumers who watched television with the sound turned down while they listened to music in an attempt to reconcile the incompatibility of the two entertainment forms. Pittman's solution was to put specially designed images to rock music tracks, to create "television for music." He had a hunch that a cable channel devoted to such a programming endeavor could be financially successful.

In keeping with WASEC's commitment to audience research, the concept of MTV was tested among representatives of the demographic target group. The research, overseen by Cohen, corroborated Pittman's "cultural" interpretation. Eighty-five percent of the people polled in the target group said they definitely could become excited over a cable channel that merged television and rock music (Levy 1983, p. 33). The tests provided quantifiable evidence of the concept's viability and were used to gain the cooperation of those needed to launch it—advertisers, cable operators, record companies, and even the press (Levy 1983).

Pittman's evaluation of the cultural significance of rock music and television for the target audience was not systematic, but it did have saliency because it approached, albeit in rough and approximate fashion, the methodology of qualitative analysis.[2] It emerged from his lived experience of culture, his informal participant-observations of the meaningfulness of popular media for his generation. But quantitative, not qualitative, methodology was the order of the day in the age of demographic reasoning. The development of research to make Pittman's "gut-level" response systematic was not a priority, and even Pittman's own rhetoric devalued cultural analysis in deference to demographic thinking.

Demographic research may categorize consumers well, but it is less adept at providing information that takes into account their social context. The concern with dividing audience members into categories often renders researchers blind to the sociological richness of group affiliation. Social differences of age, generation, class, ethnicity, and gender are defused into politically neutral categories, mere taste indices. Viewers are classified in strict consumerist terms, according to features that function more as indeterminate variables than human characteristics. The complexities of the audience's social makeup, the highly charged interactions of social differences among audiences, and the specificity of their textual preferences can be obscured. Without this more complete understanding of the target group and the reasons that rock music had achieved cultural significance, MTV would ultimately falter in its interpretation of the audience's symbolic desires and create a narrow and biased textual address.

Demand and Supply

Armed with a viable concept, WASEC faced one of the biggest problems encountered by all new cable programmers: how to obtain and pay for programming. Production economy is at the core of the commercial imperative to minimize costs and maximize profit, and with up to twenty-four hours of available time on each channel, cable programmers must ensure that their idea for specialized programming is financially feasible. The large number of cable channels devoted to extant program material, syndicated television programs and movies, attests to cable programmers' difficulties in coming up with and paying for sufficient original programming to fill their schedules. The WASEC group solved this problem with a decidedly innovative approach, although one that incorporated a proven method of program supply. In the manner that a radio station receives complementary records from the record companies (remember Pittman had worked in radio), MTV would obtain free video clips of song soundtracks. They would make record companies into television program suppliers.

The timing for presenting such a plan to the recording industry as a whole could not have been better. The music business was in a slump. Audiences were swimming in a sea of entertainment choices. The years 1976–1978 had been good years for record sales, but 1979 became known as "the year of the Platinum Goose's downfall" (Sutherland 1980, p. 96). The retail record business reported a loss of $400 million in three years, from a gross of $4 billion in 1978 to a 1981 level of $3.6 billion (Loder and Pond 1982, p. 69). Sales of hit albums had been off 30 percent to 65 percent since 1977 (Hickling 1981, p. 52). Best-selling albums were no longer able to command the market they had in years past. The sales slump, as could be expected, had an adverse effect on the record companies' employment figures as well. In two years, a thousand people directly employed by U.S. record companies lost their jobs. CBS Records, one of the largest record companies in the world, had the most startling statistics. Of the company's salaried staff, 15 percent (including its nine vice presidents) were terminated, nine of nineteen branch offices closed. All together, three hundred CBS employees lost their jobs (State of the Industry 1981, p. 36).

A form of "catch-22" began to plague the recording industry. Sluggish sales meant less money to spend on advertising new releases, and the absence of advertising helped ensure low sales figures. In its review of the industry's health in 1981, *Rolling Stone* quoted Ben Karol, the owner of the King Karol retail record chain, on the subject of record company promotion: "It doesn't look good at all. The direction from the top, from manufacturers like Warners and CBS, is very negative. They've virtually stopped promoting new records, they hardly have any budgets for advertising, and there are very few meaningful releases due. You can predict the results" (Henke 1982, p. 51).

The record industry was starving for a new, economical, and efficient mode of promotion to make its product stand out from the pack. It was still relying on the two historical mainstays of record promotion: radio play and concert performance. But in a visually saturated entertainment arena, those strategies were beginning to look outdated.

Pittman pitched the idea of teaming up on a video program service to the record companies by showing them the channel's advertising rate card. In exchange for supplying video clips, each company, he argued, would be receiving millions of dollars of television exposure for its single releases on MTV. Neither radio nor concert tours could provide the simultaneous national exposure offered by MTV. All but MCA and Polygram Records were convinced from the outset that the channel would amount to free advertising time (Levy 1983, p. 34). The record industry agreed to supply video promotion tapes of contract musicians' songs, and MTV was rolling in programming even with its twenty-four-hour, round-the-clock format (Wolfe 1983).

WASEC was to fulfill its promise to the record companies of a new and improved promotional vehicle. MTV exceeded even WASEC's own expectations as to the channel's ability to affect record sales. Six weeks after MTV went on the air in selected test markets such as Tulsa, Wichita, Peoria, Syracuse, Grand Rapids, and Houston, record sales rose for certain musical artists who were being given heavy play on the channel. Retailers in these areas received requests for music that was not even getting radio airplay in their communities. By 1983, an A. C. Neilsen survey commissioned by WASEC showed MTV to be influencing 63 percent of its viewers to buy certain albums. For every nine albums bought by MTV viewers, four purchases could be directly attributed to the viewing of the record-company-produced music videos (Levy 1983, p. 34). Lee Epand, vice president of Polygram Records, one of the companies originally reluctant to turn over free copies of promotional videos to MTV, finally admitted that the cable channel had proved to be "the most powerful selling tool we've ever had" (Levy 1983, p. 78). Jim Mazza, president of Capitol Records and EMI Records, told *People Magazine*, "If it weren't for MTV, the music industry would still be floundering" (Wolmuth 1983, p. 96). In 1983, CBS Records, after having been forced to lay off employees in 1981, was enjoying its best-selling album ever, Michael Jackson's *Thriller*.

What had begun as a practical approach to securing cheap (free) programming within the parameters of MTV's concept ended up being a factor that determined MTV's program content. By getting record companies to supply videos, MTV ensured that the videos would look like advertisements for record company products. Among other things, this meant musicians would appear in the videos, and songs used on the soundtracks would promote single releases. The music industry was, after all, operating from the same commercial imperatives as the cable television industries.

Format Radio for Television

Although Pittman professed that MTV was not created on the basis of formula programming, he did rely heavily on radio as a model for MTV's format (Haney 1983), drawing on his own background as a radio program director. WASEC committed $1 million to the production of animated ID-segments to build an identity for the channel and provide transitions between video clips and commercial breaks (Wolfe 1983, p. 44). Freed from the costs and worries of producing programming, the company was able to sink much of its capital and intellectual resources into on-air promotion of the channel itself, an efficient use of money and personnel. WASEC hired personalities called "veejays" (after radio disc jockeys, or "deejays") to introduce individual videos and serve as spokespersons for the channel. The record-company-produced videos were not played according to a schedule, as with television programming where regular time slots and similar program blocks are prime objectives. Instead, in the manner of radio, MTV used a playlist to order the video clips. From the channel's concept-origination stage, Pittman had isolated rock and roll as the music of preference, and this mandate was narrowed further into a music formula in accordance with the practice of radio formating. As a former radio program director, Pittman was intent on selecting an identifiable "sound" for MTV. *Rolling Stone* declared the "sound" to be "AOR," an abbreviation for "album-oriented rock" (Levy 1983), otherwise known as "progressive" music and defined by John Hasling (1980, p. 94) as "current music that is relatively avant-garde and experimental . . . the type of music that is often played at rock concerts."

Despite the use of radio formulas, MTV declared demographic reasoning to be MTV's primary operating mode. As Pittman outlined it, all videos were to be given at least a trial run on the channel and would be subject to "the quick yank" only if viewer response proved low, as ascertained by MTV's own research department's constant data collection. The practice of soliciting audience input was itself worked into a public relations vehicle for the channel; WASEC's *demographic* think-

ing was presented as evidence of its *democratic* commitment
to viewer participation. On-air promotions continually represented MTV as the creation of the audience rather than as a
product of corporate strategy and greed. Viewers were featured in spots, repeating the rehearsed line, "I want *my* MTV!"
Demographic thinking was applied by Pittman to his concep-
tion of the record companies' role in MTV as well. Before the
channel went on line, Pittman assured the companies that it
was not MTV's intention to undertake the role of gatekeeper
over popular music taste. "We'll play anything that fits the
video production genre that's coming from a major record
company," he promised the industry in an interview conducted
for a WASEC publication (Kitay 1981, quoted in Wolfe 1983).

As a whole, MTV's concept added up to an exceptional set
of commercial strategies. It brought rock music and television
together in a new form designed to capture the most desirable group of consumers for cable operators and advertisers.
It minimized costs by getting those with a vested interest in
rock music, the record companies, to supply programming by
encouraging them to think of the channel as their personal
advertising vehicle. The concept was sheer genius from the
standpoint of commercial viability. What was unforeseen was
the number of ideological contradictions that would be set
into motion as a result of the industry's pursuit of its commercial imperatives.

TWO

THE MAKING OF A PREFERRED ADDRESS

MTV WAS conceived for a specific target audience—a youth audience—the buyers of rock and roll records. Only after the desired audience was identified did development of suitable programming begin. MTV's concept originators found themselves in the difficult position of having to interpret the symbolic interests of a perceived audience group, guided by a demographic profile, consumer lifestyle research,[1] and the vague content directives implied in the MTV concept. In his initial delineation of the concept, creator Bob Pittman had specified the use of television images to interpret rock music soundtracks, but the question still loomed: "Which images?" A specific system of representation had yet to be formulated.

In actual production practice, demographic thought is realized according to what David Marc (1984, p. 32) has referred to loosely as an "ideological template." Producers interpret audience research according to their own conceptions of what appeals to certain audience types, relying on "knowledge" about the targeted constituents that is taken for granted by society. These ideological assumptions become a gauge used to manufacture a signification practice. But knowledge is always socially constructed and tied to the interests of those who exercise power within the social system. Producers can become unwitting collaborators in the reproduction of social relations of inequality and can create ideologically biased television discourses.

Muriel Cantor's study of the content selection process for children's television, a form of specialized programming, revealed the ideological underpinnings that form producers' attempts to interpret a specific target audience:

> Certain of the producers' conceptions of their audience are more often stereotypical than they are thoughtfully drawn. . . . Many times the product to be advertised will determine which sex is the target for the program. If the toy is meant for boys, the show will be an adventure, western or space-fantasy. Girls are reported to prefer comedy and rock and roll groups (1974, pp. 110–111).

Cantor's (1974) description embodies Marc's (1984) "ideological template" at work. Ideology, quite explicitly, plays a role in the content selection process described. Stereotypes are an ideological shorthand for the biases generated by a social system in which preferred meanings about audiences are constructed and naturalized. Gender difference becomes a marketing variable that prompts advertisers to produce sex-specific toys, and provokes producers to fashion program narratives that reproduce socially promulgated gender ideologies. In a similar vein, MTV's production mandate, to develop a televisual address that embodied the cultural significance of rock and roll and that would appeal to a youth target market, meant activating ideological assumptions about rock music and youth.

The Ideology of Rock

In choosing rock music as MTV's focal point, Pittman evoked the specific, pre-existing ideological discourse of rock and roll. While on the surface "rock music" is a neutral label that distinguishes a particular kind of music, it also comprises a set of ideological assumptions about music creation and social life. Rock emerged as not only a musical genre, but a system of discourse through which the effects of the commercialization of music and the industrialization of music production can be negotiated, and by which social inequalities can be activated in a cultural arena.

In an ideological division reminiscent of the high culture/popular culture distinction, rock discourse forged a hierarchy within popular music by creating a structure of value against which "pop" music could be devalued. Rock was made to stand as a higher form of popular music, as *the* representative of art and artfulness. Rock criticism developed to assert rock's new position of importance, with *Rolling Stone* leading the formulation of an evaluative standard in the popular arena. The academic community contributed to rock's elevation by initiating university courses devoted to the sociology of rock music. Enthroned as the more progressive style of music in the early 1970s, rock succeeded on ideological grounds despite the greater popularity of mainstream pop music (Chambers, 1985).

Pop music was negatively defined against rock's professed artistic superiority. Pop's reliance on formulaic musical structures and on conventionalized repetition in form and lyrical content was subjected to aesthetic standards of uniqueness and complexity borrowed inappropriately from high art culture. It was maligned as the creation of the commercial music industry, and therefore deemed trivial and unworthy of critical attention. Pop musicians were denied the status of artists because of their association with extreme popularity and commercial success. Audiences for pop music were chided for being less sophisticated and more susceptible to the record industry's persuasive salesmanship.

Simon Frith (1981, p. 1) has described the rise of rock music discourse as "a last romantic attempt to preserve ways of music-making—performer as artist, performance as 'community'" in the face of the commercialization of music. Rock discourse aligns itself with the romantic scenario of the struggling artist, a scenario that finds expression in the circulation of stories of the ways in which rock musicians have "paid their dues." True rock musicians are thought to have earned the right to an elevated status because they have worked harder, experienced the pain of little recognition, and honed their craft by logging time in small music venues. This "model of self-improvement," as Dave Laing (1985, p. 60) termed it, serves the project of devaluing pop music artists by allowing rock musicians to be "pitted against the 'instant' nature of many teenybop artists, *apparently* with little performing experience and *apparently* manipulated by a producer or a manager" [emphasis added].

Rock's ideology of artistic superiority was complemented by an ideology of authenticity, or what Laing (1985) has called an "ideology of sincerity." Accordingly, rock was considered to be the more genuine form of popular expression, an outgrowth of people's experience of their socially subordinate status. In contrast, mass popularity for pop music was interpreted as a sign of industrial manipulation and not of cultural production. By setting itself against both industrial control of music and consumer support of industrially produced music, rock discourse made strategic use of the pessimistic theory of media manipulation associated with the Frankfort School.[2] And as Frith (1981) has pointed out, rock discourse appropriated folk music discourse, which had already articulated the concept of musicians as purveyors of ordinary people's experiences and sentiments.

The contradictions of rock discourse become readily apparent upon examination. Rock discourse's anticommercial stance encourages a position of political opposition to the capitalist organization of cultural production, yet at the same time it denies the extent of capitalist control over its own creations. Rock songs, like pop songs, are created under the rubric of industrial production and distribution. Both generate profit for record companies. Rock music is dependent on consumer support even though commercial success is not among the criteria by which rock ideology expresses authenticity. And although rock discourse defines pop music as inauthentic expression, by virtue of its popularity, pop music can be said to speak to and for an audience. Such a position, however, requires a theoretical shift away from the Frankfort School critique toward a perspective that accepts audiences as interested cultural subjects whose designation of certain persons and groups as popular is a sign of selection and active participation.

In an attempt to uphold the distinction between genuine popular support and commercial popularity, rock music discourse eschews promotion. Pop music, as a consequence, is associated with artifice, salesmanship, and an objectionable commitment to promotion. Similarly, the notion that musicians possess an "image" is antithetical to the rock sensibility because it opens up the issue of industrial creation. Rock discourse attempts to reconcile the promotional impetus of all popular culture forms, including rock music, by using the concert tour as the music's primary promotional vehicle. A concert tour localizes the promotion of rock singers and bands, and combats the impression of distance associated with national advertising campaigns. The rock concert works well as a communal event for fans and provides musicians with a stage not only for the performance of their music, but for their assertion "in person" of the ideology of authenticity. As described by Laing (1985, p. 64), the ideology is enacted in vocal performances "not by how skillfully a singer can SIGNIFY or present an emotion . . . but by the listener's idea of how far a singer 'really feels' what is being communicated." Bands are strategically defined as the musical unit of choice because bands are more readily to be defended as creative collectives, less suseptible to the rigidity of industrial labor relations and creative hierarchies imposed by the record industry. Pop music is not associated with bands in the same way as rock music and tends to be linked with textual forms of promotion, including publicity photos and television exposure. Although the history of rock music is bound up inexorably with television promotion and publicity—Elvis' appearances on "The Ed Sullivan Show," rock artists' performances on "American Bandstand" —the struggle to maintain a difference between rock and pop is accomplished partly by giving more weight and value to concert tours for rock musicians and less to mediated forms of promotion.

By creating a standard of difference, a structure of value around rock music, rock discourse became useful to the goal of elevating white-male musicianship and creating an idealized vision of white-male spectatorship. Its allegiance to art and folk values and its denouncement of commerciality and popular pleasure were made to conform to gender ideologies, and were fashioned into material strategies for oppressing female musicians and female audiences. Enforcing a division between rock and pop meant female musicians could be relegated to pop music categories and, as a result of the association, devalued as artists. Fans of pop music could be judged incapable of appreciating aesthetic complexity. By denying the expressive potential of pop music and its ability to function as authenticating discourse, female participation in music was undermined and political articulations kept at bay. Rock music cultivated an address to male youth. Rock concerts became circumscribed as a male-youth leisure practice. But rock's ideological devotion to male discourse was not an entirely new or original proposition. It was a product of many historical precedents to devalue and exclude the musicians and audiences of subordinate social groups, especially women and blacks (as discussed more fully in Chapter Four). And because rock was defined as an expression of youth, it relied on social assumptions about what it means to be young.

The Ideology of Adolescence

Pittman has stated that he designed MTV to "mirror the issues of people moving from adolescence to adulthood," what he calls the "essence of rock" (Levy 1983, p. 76). The sense of journey and transition that Pittman's description evokes is characteristic of the ideological terms in which adolescence is typically regarded. In the United States, adolescence is viewed as a distinct stage of life that lasts from the onset of puberty to the full assumption of adult roles (Zemon Davis, 1965); and the *process* of maturation is a key demarcating concept. Adulthood is considered to be an achievable state, arrived at through a series of biological changes (sexual maturity) and the social assumption of roles and responsibilities (social maturity). These roles and responsibilities are largely defined in terms of participation in the social units of productive work and the nuclear family, two central oppressive structures of capitalist life.

As a result, youth are positioned within a transitory, social "space," and are accorded varying degrees of flexibility and freedom. While passage rites and conformity pressures are constructed to keep the range of play limited and ensure movement toward adulthood, there is a certain amount of social tolerance for leisure activity, sexual exploration, and displays of rebellion against parents and other social authorities. Such practices have come to constitute the accepted ideological frame for "normal" adolescent behavior, but only within other dominant social parameters of class, gender, and race. For example, poverty and racism attenuate adolescent license by first making adolescent employment an economic necessity, and then making gainful employment difficult to find. Gender, as a limiting parameter, establishes a field of difference that makes adolescent privilege more available to male youth.

Adolescence and gender are brought into a particularly charged relationship by the fact that adolescence is activated in individuals as a result of biological maturation. Gender itself is a system of social differences based on biological difference. It is not uncommon in psychological accounts of adolescence to find discussions of gender difference—the fact that biological changes happen at different ages for girls and boys leads many psychologists to point out different levels of emotional and sexual maturity. But very little work has been done on how the social conditions of gender difference, the social system of gender inequality, are manifested at the time of adolescence.

As their bodies mature, children are called upon to publicly display their adoption of the heterosexual norm and the nuclear family configuration that economically and ideologically supports the nation. This affects boys and girls in different and specific ways. For female adolescents, biological transformation and social transition collapse around the notion of reproductive function. Girls' new physiological capability is translated into the social role of mothering. As Katherine Dalsimer (1986, p. 10) pointed out, adolescence has been linked so inexorably to ideological conceptions of gender that much of the literature produced on female adolescence frames its discussions in terms of a transition from girlhood to motherhood. Feminists working in the fields of psychology, sociology, and the study of youth culture have just begun to suggest how girls' experience of adolescence is made distinct as a consequence of their gender status. In voicing this opinion, they have flown in the face of their respective literatures' tendency to define adolescence as a uniform social experience.

Barbara Hudson (1984) has described adolescence as a system of discourse that fundamentally incorporates assumptions and definitions of *male* experience, activity, and desire. Adolescence and masculinity are united ideologically to support a social system of male privilege. Socially sanctioned retreats from parental surveillance and the constrictions of domestic life, aggressive attention to leisure practices and associated peer activities, pursuit of sexual experiences, and experimentations with social roles and norms—things typically associated with adolescence—embody the very activities and attitudes that help boys to assume their privileged position in the patriarchy.[3] Toward this end, boys learn to feel comfortable in public space, adjust to competitive pressures, network with their male peers, build a familial support system, and prepare for risk-taking in future work endeavors. However, the social authorization given to such practices is directed specifically to boys, and does not extend as fully to girls.

As Hudson (1984) described it, adolescence is unproblematic as a "masculine construct," but becomes the source of contradictory expectations when applied to female adolescents, who are subject to conflicting gender discourses—most notably the discourse of femininity. The femininity discourse exists as a set of expectations designed to restrict girls' behavior and choices, especially at the time of adolescence. Hudson's (1984, p. 42) fieldwork in schools and social service settings in Britain revealed that authorities activate the contradiction in their contact with girls by asking them to "develop 'masculine' characteristics of independence, political and career interests" as well as "a personality style of caring for others, looking after children, being gentle and unassertive." Female adolescence, in Hudson's terms, is about negotiating two contradictory discourses: adolescence and femininity.

The American writer, Susan Brownmiller summarized her own conscription into the femininity discourse at the time of adolescence, recalling the experience of contradictory impulses:

As I passed through a stormy adolescence to a stormy maturity, femininity increasingly became an exasperation, a brilliant, subtle esthetic that was bafflingly inconsistent at the same time that it was minutely, demandingly concrete, a rigid code of appearance and behavior defined by do's and don't-do's that went against my rebellious grain. Femininity was a challenge thrown down to the female sex, a challenge no proud, self-respecting young woman could afford to ignore, particularly one with enormous ambition that she nursed in secret, alternately feeding or starving its inchoate life in tremendous confusion (Brownmiller 1984, p. 14).

Angela McRobbie (1980) pointed out the consequences of gender discrimination on youth cultural expression—how it mediates against girls' participation in the street culture of boys. For boys, leisure is a privileged arena provided for the "sowing of wild oats" and experimentation with roles and dangers before beginning a lifetime of work. "The street" is a major site of sociability and escape, the formation of subcultures, rebellious play, male bonding, and female pursuit. But herein lies the problem for adolescent girls, for they are subject not only to expectations based on their age, but, overwhelmingly, to expectations assigned to their gender. Both women and girls experience the streets as dangerous and fearful places. The concept of "sexual geography" described by Rayna Reiter (1975) in her study of male and female use of public space in southern France can be applied to the United States as well. Females are expected to use streets as the route between two interior spaces, whether places of employment or consumption activity. The social consequence of street loitering or strolling is the label, "prostitute," and the coding of one's body as available to male pursuit. Women's level of comfort on city streets is tenuous at best—rape and harassment are constant threats that structure their street behavior. A girl learns the gestures of deference early: to avoid making eye contact, and to "shrink" her body so as to take up as little space as possible.

Thus, leisure practices that involve public space are often considered to be inappropriate for girls. Subcultural youth groupings, many of which are allied in part by musical preferences, are usually off limits to girls. Leisure time is itself subject to a division along gender lines. Middle-class and lower-class girls in the United States grow up in a culture in which women's work in the home is a constant, yet devalued, activity, and work outside the home is still underpaid and limited in scope. In the many instances in which women work outside the home, household labor becomes an even more relentless form of double duty. As teenagers, girls encounter the expectation that, like their mothers, they will assume the role of invisible worker at home, even as they are encouraged to seek higher education and a career.

The social authorization of adolescent license produces great tension over what limits should be placed on leisure time and activities, and on how much experimentation and rebellion should be tolerated. Here again, gender difference is a determining factor. Michael Brake (1985, p. 23) has described the discrepancies in the ways male and female youth are articulated as social problems: "Males have usually been involved with illegal activities such as theft or violence or vandalism, and females with sexual misbehavior." The perception that girls are somehow "less delinquent" than boys has generally resulted in a greater provision of social programs for male youth (Nava, 1984). Prostitution is considered to be the predominant mode of female delinquency, a form of behavior that is less visible than many male delinquent activities and easily misidentified. Girls who engage in street loitering or walking, so called "normal" behavior for boys, can become associated with delinquency and even find themselves institutionalized.

In effect, girls are excluded from much of the leisure activity, social-bonding practices, and subculture formation that critics of male youth culture identify as important arenas for the negotiation of social contradictions. Girls' leisure activities take different forms as a consequence of gender inequality or, perhaps more aptly stated, as a result of female resourcefulness and the will to resist subordination. Yet typically, girl culture is described in terms of a negative relation to male street culture and a functional relation to female gender oppression, rather than as a distinct cultural form in its own right. For example, Frith (1981, p. 229) acknowledged the existence of the girl culture modes of dance and dressing up, but only as a manifestation of their socially objectified position: "All this female activity, whatever its fun and style and art as a collective occupation, is done, in the end, individually, for the boy's sake. It is the male gaze that gives girls' beauty work its meaning." But, it is precisely the "fun and style and art as collective occupation" that speaks to the expressiveness of girl culture, the complementary world of leisure and social bonding it creates for girls. Girls' preoccupation with creating "looks" through dress and make-up has many meanings when viewed within the context of female friendships and imaginative play. To reduce these activities to an overdetermined desire to please boys is to reproduce the male bias in cultural criticism. In contrast, McRobbie (1984, p. 145) described dance as an activity of control, pleasure, and sensuality for girls—an activity that offers girls "a positive and vibrant sexual expressiveness and a point of connection with other pleasures of femininity such as dressing up or putting on make-up."

The "M" Stands for Male

MTV was designed to be a visual arena for rock music; therefore, finding ways to interpret rock ideology visually became its implicit agenda. But in its clear intent to use rock and roll for purposes of commercial gain, MTV's concept was fundamentally at odds with the anticommercial stance of rock discourse. MTV had successfully convinced the record companies to start making what amounted to television advertisements for rock-music singles and brought together program and advertisement as never before in American television. From the perspective of rock ideology, MTV was an insidious creation of the marketplace and the most serious threat yet to rock's ideology of authenticity. *Rolling Stone* hinted at the implied ideological crisis in its 1983 review headlined, "Ad Nauseam: How MTV Sells Out Rock and Roll" (Levy, 1983). MTV was not only perceived as a violation because it engaged in rock-music promotion but because its involvement in promoting rock music with television texts recalled practices associated with pop music. MTV blurred the boundaries that had been erected between rock and pop music. It eroded the consensus on rock's difference and superior value, and thereby undermined rock's ability to serve as a venue for social inequality in popular music culture.

WASEC tried in various ways to combat this basic contradiction in MTV's concept. Demographic thinking was elevated from an industry development and operations strategy to a textual address in spots such as the "I want my MTV" campaign. By asserting a parallel between demographic research and democratic rule, the company hoped to establish in rock audiences a belief in the channel's sincerity of motivation. A more sweeping compensation strategy was the foregrounding of another element of rock discourse, the ideology of (male) adolescence. With rock's ideology of authenticity under fire because of MTV's promotional impetus, one way of reassuring audiences that the channel was true to rock discourse was to represent textually its implied male ideology. MTV was put in the position of illustrating what previously had never even been spoken—rock's white-male bias.

The attempt to embody rock ideology visually resulted in the early exclusion of black music and black musicians from

MTV. But rock discourse had already undergone something of an ideological crisis over the suppression of its original debt to black musicians, and the rock establishment was quick to wage a publicity war against the channel's treatment of black artists. In 1983, at the peak of the bad press over MTV's alleged racism, during an interview with veejay Mark Goodman musician David Bowie (who is white, but draws on black music in his work) inquired about MTV's policy on the airing of black music videos:

> BOWIE: There seem to be a lot of black artists making very good videos that I'm surprised aren't used on MTV.
>
> GOODMAN: We have to play music we think an entire country is going to like. . . . We grew up in an era where the Isley Brothers meant something to me. But what does it mean to a seventeen-year-old?
>
> BOWIE: I'll tell you what the Isley Brothers or Marvin Gaye means to a *Black* seventeen-year-old, and surely he's part of America (Levy 1983, p. 37).

Goodman's statement that MTV's playlist must appeal to the tastes of an entire nation was an attempt to cover the channel's demographic partiality with democratic rhetoric. The economic rationale underlying the statement is MTV's dependence on its successful proliferation in cable markets, the majority of which are located in white suburbs. But the response also reveals the extent of MTV's ideologically naturalized view of its youth audience as upscale and white. Not until the phenomenal cross-over success of Michael Jackson's album *Thriller*, which represented a realignment of commercial and ideological positions, did MTV broaden its format to include more black music. By then, in a form of cultural red-lining, black-artist videos were being distributed on the newly established cable channel, Black Entertainment Television (BET).

The ideology of (male) adolescence surfaced in the choices

WASEC made in compiling MTV's continuity segments. When it came to designing the sets, from which the veejays would announce upcoming videos and read music news segments, male-adolescent leisure interests were most clearly in focus:

> The furnishings, according to one of the providers, are "the kinds of goodies a fifteen-year-old would want in *his* bedroom"—stuff like stereo equipment albums, wooden boxes, videogames and vaguely nifty doodads on the wall, including gold records donated from the likes of Men at Work, Loverboy, and Journey (Levy 1983, p. 33) [emphasis added].

Although the bedroom setting was more in keeping with the cultural arena of female adolescents—a place to hang posters of pop stars, have sleep-overs, dance to records, try on clothes and make-up, talk on the phone—girls were not considered in the set design.[4]

The selection of veejays was made on the basis of how well the personalities enacted the ideological divisions between rock and pop. Sue Steinberg (then Pittman's executive producer) described the selection of veejay Nina Blackwood as a decision based on her "young-looking, sexy, hip" image (Levy 1983, p. 34). It was Steinberg's prediction and hope that Blackwood would make "the young boys . . . go nuts" (Levy 1983, p. 34). Girls' penchant for intense fan behavior was acknowledged in MTV's selection of male veejay Mark Goodman. Steinberg described him as the "teen-idol type," stating, "We hoped young girls would write letters, start fan clubs" (Levy 1983, p. 34). Both choices reproduced the ways in which women and girls are positioned by the adolescent and rock discourses. In the case of Blackwood, a woman is sexualized in accordance with male-adolescent prerogatives. In Goodman's case, the female music fan is coded as obsessive about stars and images, but uninterested in musical artistry.

Guided by MTV's reproduction of rock and adolescent ideologies, as well as their own sense of music consumers, the record companies developed a male-oriented textual address in their music videos. Consequently, the channel soon came under heavy fire for airing videos with violent and sexually suggestive images in a public fury that outpaced the dismay expressed over MTV's exclusion of black music: "What possesses those pot-gutted, hairy-backed, bat-decapitating 43-year-old spandex-and-studs idiots to use some gorgeous, pouting, 16-year-old professional model (and part-time topless dancer) to play the 'girlfriend of the lead singer' part in their videos?" (Sommer 1985, p. 9) In part, the charges constituted a convenient rallying point for the moral panic of politically conservative parent groups. They also reflected the diffusion of concern over sexist textual operations, voiced by feminists in the 1970s, into the popular consciousness of the 1980s. The charges of sexism, however, were never related directly by opponents of MTV to the channel's reliance on the notion of target audience, or to the privileging of male adolescence in its interpretation of the targeted group. This is alarming given the defense offered by MTV spokespersons that MTV's texts and policies were the result of its need to cater to a youth audience. Pittman consistently responded to allegations of sexism by naturalizing the highly ideological category of adolescence that MTV's format attempted to reproduce: "It's not the Barry Manilow channel. . . . Some songs are unhappy. Some have a dark message. It's the essence of rock. It mirrors the issues of people moving from adolescence" (Levy 1983, p. 76). Pittman's response illustrates the disparity between MTV's rhetoric (that it was enacting an address to a broad demographic category of youth of both genders) and its textual practice (the representation of male adolescence). It also reveals how problematic the social complexities that underlie certain demographic and ideological categories can become for producers of televisual content.

THREE

MALE-ADDRESS VIDEO (1983)

MTV'S PREFERRED address to male adolescents was executed in individual music videos by making the image of "the street" an over-arching sign system for male-adolescent discourse. To invoke this attachment of young males to the street, male musicians were shown loitering on sidewalks, strolling along avenues, and riding in cars. These representations of street-corner activities served to valorize leisure, the arena in which adolescent boys carve out their own domain. Even when the physical image of the street was absent from a video, it remained an implied presence, for as a sign system it summarized perfectly the male-adolescent quest for adventure, rebellion, sexual encounter, peer relationships, and male privilege. The videos evoked male-adolescent discourse by representing boys' privileged position with respect to their female peers. Drawing on the connection between male-adolescent license and adult-male rule, the male-address videos activated textual signs of patriarchal discourse, reproducing coded images of the female body, and positioning girls and women as the objects of male voyeurism. Both the image of the female peer (the adolescent girl) and the more mythical (for boys) image of the adult woman were prominently featured. When girls appeared, they were not represented as equal

participants in the symbolic system of the street, but functioned as devices to delineate the male-adolescent discourse.
Male-address videos empowered male-adolescent viewers by
providing them with a symbolic equation between the representations of the street and the female body, and their own
privileged access to public space and patriarchal prerogatives.

Four videos from 1983 serve as specific examples of MTV's
preferred male-adolescent discourse. As a group, the videos
execute male address in distinct and particular ways, with differing levels of implied self-consciousness about the discourse
they construct. They contain a limited range of approaches
to female representation, and none can be said to present a
female point of view on adolescence. The year 1983 is significant because during this year male-address appeared to be on
a strong footing as the preferred textual practice, but, as will
be described in later chapters, female-address video was on the
verge of coalescence.

Tender Is the Night

In Jackson Browne's *Tender Is the Night*, the world of the
street is developed as a boy's physical and spiritual haven. The
video opens with Browne, who plays the protagonist, walking
alone at night down a long urban alley. A lengthy photographic
shot builds suspense and gives viewers time to contemplate the
direction of the narrative line, the video's unfolding point of
view. The boy is at ease, self-absorbed. The late hour and the
secluded location are not threatening to him. As a male, he
commands the street; as an adolescent, he revels in it. Unlike
a woman or girl, he is unafraid; unlike a female adolescent,
he is not excluded from the aura of the night streets. The
corner of an X-rated movie marquee becomes visible in the
frame. Its presence in no way alters the boy's route, nor does
it make him wary, as it might a girl or woman. This is where
the protagonist wants to be, where he feels he belongs.

The boy arrives at the section of street designated visually as "the strip." The production's design and photography add to the street's overall allure, refracting and blurring the neon lights on its wet surface. Colored light washes over cars that cruise the street with deliberate slowness. Lovers are out in full force. The scene glorifies the strip as a symbol of male adolescence, representing the ritualized activities of "stepping out" and "cruising" and the privileges of sexual pursuit and leisure. The video depicts the world of the street as organized by pleasure, spontaneity, free agency, and male desire. The vision is further developed in scenes that oppose the image of street life with images of domestic life. The camera peers in the protagonist's kitchen window to witness him quarreling with his live-in girlfriend (played by Browne's girlfriend, Darryl Hannah). The girl functions as a sign of the adult roles and responsibilities against which adolescence is posed—commitment to a monogamous relationship and a work routine. The couple's quarrel represents not merely an interpersonal conflict, but an enactment of the boy's adolescent rebellion. While he appreciates the "tender" lovemaking that lies at the core of his sentiment for the girl (presented visually in a sensual montage sequence), he balks at the socially prescribed outcome of sexual intimacy—the expectation of exclusivity and the restrictions of marriage. When his relationship with the girl moves toward this "adult" configuration, he wants out. It is the whole culture of the street (of adolescence), the freedom and sexual exploration it affords, that the protagonist finds ultimately more "tender," more physically and spiritually rewarding.

Out on the street, as the video illustrates, girls are easily available, and on less demanding terms. Spontaneous associations spring from car cruising, and even the girls who appear with other boys are not committed to exclusive relationships (as the flirtatious face of one female passenger in a car driven by a boy suggests). The protagonist's cast-off girlfriend is forced to resume her position within the male-adolescent discourse. Leaving home after the quarrel, her possessions in hand, she ends up on the street and immediately comes to the attention of a boy who is out cruising in his car. She becomes the object of another male adolescent's spontaneous, commanding, yet fleeting desire. The exchange between the boy in the car and the girl on the street recalls the transaction between a trick and a prostitute; he stops and calls out to her, she approaches the car, they talk, and she gets in.

Sharp Dressed Man

An expanded version of the prostitute motif is elaborated in ZZ Top's video *Sharp Dressed Man*, in which sexual experimentation in adolescence is linked symbolically to the assumption of adult-male power. The band's members, who wear beards and are themselves too old to play male-adolescent protagonists, assume the collective role of adviser to the male lead. They direct the boy in male-adolescent discourse, guiding him from an innocent and impotent childhood toward a sophisticated and powerful adult-male image.

The boy's innocence and ineffectuality are represented by his service job as a car attendant at an exclusive nightclub, a representation that concurrently emasculates working-class males. He observes male privilege from afar, symbolized by the cars and women of club members. His desire to have what they have, to be what they are, is manifested in his expression of desire for a woman who arrives with one of the members. Magically, the band appears on the scene, rock-and-roll shamans, to lead him to the fulfillment of his desire. They produce the keys to a ruby-red car (the band's trademark), dangling them enticingly before the boy like a symbol of male-adolescent license. Out of the car, step three scantily dressed, "hot" women, their erect nipples visible through their blouses. A photographer immediately takes their picture, affirming their status as objects of the male gaze. As fantastic creations of ZZ Top, the three direct their attentions to the boy. The band members recreate the mythical avuncular role, initiating the boy into manhood by leading him to experienced prostitutes. Sexual experimentation is not only sanctioned but is presented as a fundamental step toward the boy's maturation into manhood.

Only by living out the male-adolescent discourse, by shirking his responsibilities as an employee, going off into the night with a flashy car and lusty women, does he qualify for the previously unattainable woman, and for life as a potent male. Interestingly, the woman who is the boy's object of desire is presented in a visual mode that was developed by female-address videos to reveal female sexual exploitation.[1] Inside the club, she appears bored by and disinterested in her date, is subjected to his roving hands and accelerating harassment, until finally she pours a drink in his lap and leaves. But this is not the woman's story, and the details of her character only serve to further the narrative of the boy's transition to manhood. From the moment the woman makes eye contact with the boy in the parking lot, she is destined by the narrative line and ZZ Top's omnipotent direction to become increasingly dissatisfied with her date and more desirous of the boy. Her rejection of her date is required by the discourse of male adolescence, which asserts the boy's privileged position by showing him attracting a woman who "belongs" to another man.

Sexy and 17

Stray Cats' video *Sexy and 17* establishes male-adolescent authority by making the band's members into juvenile delinquents who disrupt the site of social authority most salient for adolescents—the school. The sign system of the street remains an implied presence. The boys challenge their teacher by wearing street attire in the classroom—black leather, T shirts, sunglasses—nostalgic emblems of male-teen culture from the fifties. The school boys use rock and roll to promote a disreputable image, playing instruments in the hallway and singing, "Hey man, I don't feel like going to school no more!" The prestige the display wins among their peers is demonstrated as the song provokes their classmates to a dancing frenzy.

The central enactment of male-adolescent discourse involves the boys' perceptions of female adolescents. The video reveals the fundamental confusion over who girls are, what they do, what they think about, and what they want that tacitly permeates the male-adolescent experience. Friendships among girls form a strong social network during their school years, with some friendships even lasting into adulthood. Boys often see girls in groups, and this configuration becomes the subject of speculation and a sphere of conflict within male culture. Male-address videos filter girl friendships through the ideology of male adolescence by including images of girls in groups but then visually suggesting that the configuration is intended to facilitate male sexual experimentation. In both *Sharp Dressed Man* and *Sexy and 17* groups of girls are treated in this way.

Girls' involvement with their looks and make-up is also given the status of a fetish in *Sexy and 17*. Female beauty culture is presented as male-inspired and lacks the resonance it attains in female-address videos. "Little Marie," the main object of the protagonist's affections according to the lyrics ("my little rock-and-roll queen"), is photographed in pornographic style as she showers, puts on make-up, and paints her toenails in the "privacy" of her bathroom and dressing room. A close-up shot of her face turned toward the (male) spectator emphasizes her painted lips and eyes. The camera tilts up the length of her legs to reveal her provocative costume—high heels, one fishnet stocking, and bikini panties. The lyric lines, "It's a little bit obscene, got to let off a little steam," attempt to reposition the blatant objectification of the girl within the parameters of normal male adolescence. The song's refrain, "She's sexy and 17," claims the video's voyeuristic stance for all men, not just boys, while at the same time privileging male adolescence as a time of unbounded sexual exploits.

Part of what imbues the boys in *Sexy and 17* with authority is their ability to play rock and roll on stage and make girls dance and feel sexual desire for them. The boys play as a band after school in a scene that allows Stray Cats to perform while maintaining a narrative presence. The fictional band's popularity with the girls at the nightclub comments on Stray Cats' own motivations for playing music—their desire for a cadre of female fans. "Little Marie" jumps up boldly to dance, in a narrative moment that offers female audiences the possibility of exploring female-adolescent pleasures. But as is typical in male-address videos, male pleasure and power take priority, and "Little Marie" is reduced to the role of a groupie, with her pleasure defined in terms of the male point of view. While modes of female adolescence are manifested in her defiant dress and expressions, and in the intensity of her involvement with music and dance, all of these elements are finally made subservient to male discourse. Her independent absorption in dancing alone to rock music is undermined as the protagonist steps in and establishes a firm male lead, throwing her into twirls and twisting dance moves while he remains controlled and essentially motionless.

Beat It

Michael Jackson's video *Beat It* presents a contradictory and conflicted portrait of male-adolescent discourse and addresses boys' own doubts about destructive and violent behavior, the discourse's most extreme manifestation. Its representation of an ethnic-male point of view threatens to expose the discourse's racial prejudice, perhaps even open it up to a female sensibility. However, the video is designed to appropriate (white) male-adolescent discourse for black males and leaves the discourse's gender bias intact. By exploring the contradictory recesses of male discourse, *Beat It* approaches a female point of view; but because this is not its main concern, the address to girls is largely mitigated.

In the video, two street gangs (whose numbers include members of real Los Angeles gangs) converge on a warehouse for a stylized fight scene. The textual system of the street, a sign of male-adolescent unity, has broken down under the scrutiny of an "authentic" ethnic environment. Instead, Jackson's street is the site of territorial disputes and male competition. Danger is present, and the potential destruction of the fictional gang members is a clear possibility. The gang members themselves are studies in (and provide lessons in) black-male affectation. Expertly they control their body language, attitude, and overall appearance; their faces are drawn and intensely serious. Their every gesture is calculated and aggressive—a flipped cigarette, snapped fingers, slaps on the back, exaggerated gaits. Each boy dresses "thickly," in leather: hats, headbands, chains, insignias, jeans; as a group they are individually, yet cohesively, styled. Together, they create tremendous presence, an air of indomitable power. The song's lyrical content, in the context of the narrative, is addressed to viewers who feel that they are outside the gangs' powerful community: whites, boys who have been unable to command gang membership or who are the objects of torment by gangs, and all girls and women.

> They told you don't you ever come around here,
> Don't want to see your face,
> You better disappear,
> The fire's in their eyes,
> Their voice is really clear,
> So beat it, just beat it.

Jackson does not play a gang member, but has a complex and contradictory role in the video. His words to the audience invoke the many issues of power and powerlessness, authority and lack of authority, blackness and whiteness, and maleness and femaleness. As the video's narrator, he tells viewers how to feel about the gangs and their slow convergence on one another for a violent showdown. As a character, his intervention in the action determines its crucial resolution. Yet at the video's start his character is presented visually as weak and ineffectual. He lies on a bed in his bedroom. His thin, nearly scrawny physique is in marked contrast to the gang members' size and weight. Appearing within domestic space, lying across his bed, Jackson has none of the street presence of the gang members, and is linked visually to the feminine. Lying on the bed, "speaking" about the gangs' threats, the boy appears to be a victim. But as he rises from the bed, his anger swells, and he begins to assume a position of strength and superiority. The lyrics he speaks to the camera begin to analyze the gangs' psychological and social motivations, relating their terrorism to the discourses of masculinity and adolescence, and to the social reality of black urban existence.

> Don't want to be a boy,
> You want to be a man,
> You want to stay alive,
> Better do what you can,
> You have to show them
> —that you're really not scared.

The transition to manhood, the lyrics imply, is bound up with the necessity to display courage, force, and an ability to dominate. The lyrics, juxtaposed with the intensely male affectation of the gang members, serve to create a context for their actions. The line "You have to show them that you're really not scared" creates an ambiguous address. The "you" addresses those who are afraid—according to the narrative, those who fear gang violence. But because fear is an emotion that defines female existence, it may be easily appropriated by female audiences. The "you" also refers to the gang members who fight and allows the video to explain their violent behavior within the context of (black) male ideology, even to suggest that despite appearances and dictates, they too live in fear. Such ambiguity opens the video to a number of viewer perspectives and creates a critical space for evaluating the male-adolescence discourse as represented in the gang members' rule of the street.

Yet as the video unfolds, male-adolescent discourse is upheld through Jackson's actions, costuming, and attitude as the protagonist. He goes to the gangs' "hang-outs," the pool hall and the diner, to head off the confrontation. He knows their turf and is not afraid to enter. Once inside, his anger, which remained contained in the bedroom scene, is unleashed. He begins to dance aggressively with clenched fists and kicks, the implied violence that the gangs themselves practice. His own style statement functions to give him an air of command and charisma, thus aligning him with the gang members and particularly with their leaders. Although the color of his red leather jacket can be seen as a sign of his association with the feminine (blood, menstruation), its fabric and styling are the same as the gang members' jackets. He goes to the warehouse ostensibly to stop the gangs from fighting, to intercede in the male-adolescence discourse; but once there, he becomes their new leader. Both gangs begin to move to his dance, the new rhythm he establishes, just as previously they had followed the rhythm of their respective gang leaders. He succeeds in interrupting the fight, but in the process forms an even larger, more unified gang. He effectively eliminates the violent male competition that had threatened to undo the male-adolescent discourse, and thus preserves the discourse itself. The black-male adolescent fantasy of rising above the threat of the gang, even of joining their ranks, is also satisfied.

For girls who identify with Jackson's articulation of fear, there is greater ambiguity. Aside from Jackson's own androgynous nod to female viewers, the only female representation in the video is of one gang member's adoring girlfriend, whose head is yanked back by the hair so that he may kiss her before leaving for the fight. Compared to *West Side Story*, from which the video's visual motif of gang warfare appears to have been lifted, *Beat It*'s portrayal of female participation in and around male-adolescent discourse is practically nonexistent.

The four videos described move from the uncritical, naturalized male-adolescent discourse of *Tender Is the Night* to the overtly symbolic treatment of male adolescence in *Sharp Dressed Man* to the nostalgic, comic portrayal of juvenile delinquency and the confused, somewhat vicious representation of female adolescence in *Sexy and 17* to the more serious, fractured vision of male adolescence in *Beat It*. Other male-address videos on MTV in 1983 executed the address differently, selecting other "workable" representations, but in the end all were united by a central focus on articulating adolescence within the context of male-adolescent experience and sexual desire.

FOUR

CONDITIONS OF CULTURAL STRUGGLE

MTV PROVED to be a significant intervention in rock ideology and in the ideology of adolescence that tacitly supported it. Although MTV's concept and format guidelines were designed to profess the channel's allegiance to rock, its corporate origins and commercial motivations (made manifest in the use of the advertising model for the channel's programming design) were a signal to rock aficionados that MTV was operating in ways that were contrary to rock ideology. In light of this built-in contradiction, MTV developed a textual system of male address to underscore its commitment to rock ideology and avoid alienating a rock audience. But in so doing, MTV gave visual form to rock's male bias. It careened toward the most damaging repercussions of rock ideology—the exclusion and devaluation of female musicians and female audiences—and revealed a design intent on perpetuating the social condition of gender inequality.

Although it is commonly believed that the careers of musicians are born out of natural ability or the dedicated pursuit of a training program, in actuality some people, as a result of their social position, have greater opportunities to develop their talent. Music is not and has never been free of the social conflicts and contradictions that characterize society as a whole. Music developed as a cultural arena in complicity with hegemonic[1] relations of patriarchal rule. Public consent for gender inequality in the larger realm of social life was generated in part through the creation of gender inequality in music. As a consequence, female musicians were discriminated against over time simply because they were members of a subordinate group. Gender differences in music prevented women from expressing themselves fully and from making deep emotional connections with other women through music.

"Every Good Boy Does Fine"[2]

For much of human history, women and girls have been denied access to musical education and the full range of musical creation. Early educational institutions reserved musical training primarily for male students. The early denial of training opportunities for girls and women was described by Jane Bowers and Judith Tick (1986, pp. 4–5) in the introduction to their anthology on women and music history: "During most of the fifteenth and early sixteenth centuries, women had virtually no access to the two kinds of training that constituted the principal means of acquiring a thorough music education —study at a cathedral school or apprenticeship to a master player."

Eva Rieger (1985) traced the exclusion of women from music making to the origin of official institutions of music. In the middle ages, churches made it an official practice to bar women from participation in liturgical rites, effectively creating a gender boundary to "high music" culture. Nuns were allowed to engage in music making in the isolated environment of the convent, ensuring a separate and devalued form of female participation in religious music. This exclusionary history in church music is ironic in light of the fact that in recent years churches are often the first place a musically inclined girl sings before an audience. The secularization of music and fragmentation of religious power over time have given women the opportunity to perform in church choirs. This has been the pattern of female-musician repression. When total exclusion of women is impossible, a separate sphere of creation is established and then systematically devalued. Only when devaluation occurs in social arenas that make use of music are female musicians offered a place within them.

Rieger (1985) also described the early cultivation of an ideology separating the activity of performing music from the activity of composing music. Artistic value was attached to composition, and the superior training programs, which were open exclusively to men, privileged the writing and conducting of music. Set against composing, the interpretation of music through performance was valued less, as were performers themselves. Female musicians were far more likely to become music performers than music composers because "women have always only been allowed a first foothold in those areas where creativity was considered to be of secondary importance" (Rieger 1985, p. 136). The ideological division between composition and performance served to devalue women's role in music making and cast doubt on female creativity. The fabrication of a male superiority in music creation was made even more credible through assertions that women had a "natural" creative deficiency. The ideology of creative composition was effective in eliminating many female musicians from music history. Before modern recording techniques were developed, performance was an ephemeral creative form. In contrast, music compositions were written, and thus could be passed down through generations of musicians. Even today, the ideology of creative composition and uncreative performance, generated centuries ago, persists in contemporary popular music criticism and is dredged up for use in subordinating female musicians. Female vocalists who do not write their own songs or play instruments are often considered to be of lesser talent, and in the logical extreme, not to be musicians at all.

Female musicianship was damaged as well by successful attempts to blend women's music making with female social roles. With the formation of the bourgeoisie in the eighteenth century, new and powerful associations were forged between bourgeois women and the home and family. Michelle Rosaldo (1974) has observed that in societies in which the domestic/public split is highly elaborated, gender inequality is greater,[3] and as the ideology of female domesticity began to take hold among the bourgeoisie, musical niches for women became more defined. Musical training for girls found a focus in the simultaneous support of class distinction and gender difference. Piano playing and singing were articulated as appropriate forms of female musical expression because they were most easily incorporated into the bourgeois woman's role in the family: "It was important to a man's prestige that his wife could entertain his guests with music, and of course a musical education for his daughter served as a good investment for an advantageous marriage" (Rieger, 1985, p. 141). Not until the beginning of the twentieth century were female musicians allowed to play in orchestras, and then only as harpists "because the harp was considered to be a 'feminine' instrument" (Rieger 1985, p. 135). The female-vocalist niche still pervades contemporary music culture. And as Sue Steward and Sheryl Garratt (1984) have pointed out, the choice to play a musical instrument, and the decision of which instrument to play, still involve ideological attitudes about gender. The standards developed around female beauty, they suggest, turn young women against horns and other brass instruments because playing them can cause cracked or bleeding lips and "ugly" facial contortions. The technology associated with popular musicianship—electronic instruments, amplifiers, mixers—discourage girls, who are not socialized to know basic mechanical and electrical operations.

Historically, the devaluation of music making by women converged with women's newly defined service role in the family. Musical performances by women were treated as a service to be provided for parents, husbands, and children—not as a source of pleasure for the musicians themselves, and certainly not as a career direction or means of making money. The relegation of female music making to a service function in the home was followed by the devaluation of amateur musicianship. Men's music making was disassociated from women's music making by upgrading the category of "professional musician" and downgrading amateur efforts. Prior to women's influx into drawing room entertainment, men had been accustomed to performing music in the home; amateur musicianship was defined positively and valued. But as music in the domestic setting became more solidly entrenched with bourgeois female roles, professional standards were established and amateur status was devalued. Amateurism became associated with inferior musicianship, in part because of its association with female domestic space (Rieger 1985, p. 143). This link between amateurism and female musicianship worked to women's advantage in the 1970s when punk music emerged in Britain to present a radical challenge to the standard of pop music professionalism. Punk's advocacy of "defiant amateurism" (Swartley 1982, p. 28) undermined the devalued status of the amateur musician, granting women unprecedented access to musical information and audiences. Although punk emerged essentially as a working-class male subculture, Dick Hebdige has made the point that punk included a minority of female participants who aggressively tried to carve out a specifically female form of expression, in sharp contrast to the usual subsuming of women by subcultural phallocentricism: "Punk propelled girls onto the stage and once there, as musicians and singers, they systematically transgressed the codes governing female performance. . . . These performers have opened up a new space for women as active participators in the production of popular music" (Hebdige 1983, pp. 83–85).

Historically, as women persevered and became professional musicians despite the disincentives, they were often subjected to an enforced distance from family and home life. Although, as an apparatus of gender difference, the family serves to oppress women, it is also a source of pleasure that is not easily rejected. Rieger (1985, p. 144) narrated stories of rigid controls against marriage for those few women who ventured to make music a career: "Many opera house directors made celibacy a condition of employment. Marriage could be interpreted as a breach of contract and grounds for dismissal." Social expectations of wives at the time—to be the exclusive caretaker of the home, children, and husband—helped ensure that a professional career outside the home would clash with domestic life. For all the literary and cinematic representations of women as obstacles to male artists' creative impulses, it seems that *husbands* also adversely affected female musicians' careers throughout the eighteenth and nineteenth centuries.

The association of women's music with domestic life and the role of service to the family was refined for the female music professional into a practice of sexual favors in the public domain:

> Women singers could permit themselves more freedom than most women because they lived outside bourgeois norms, but they were often dependent on the men who determined their careers. Although they sometimes received quite large fees, the real beneficiaries of their artistic productive capacity were the impressarios, the opera house directors, the financial backers and the patrons. Many men arranged a concert in return for sexual favours and there is evidence that even newspaper critics expected sexual benefits in return for favourable reviews (Rieger 1985, pp. 145–146).

Women who operated outside the nuclear family, where they would have been under the jurisdiction of one man's domination, could expect to be treated as every man's servant. For female musicians it was not only a source of humiliation, but a way of undermining their ability to obtain the rewards and recognition of serious musicianship. The *practice* of sexual favors in early music history gave way to an *ideology* of sexual favors in contemporary popular music culture. Female musicians may be suspected still of sleeping their way into record company contracts, even when they are legitimately signed and clearly talented.

In the context of female-musician devaluation, rock-music discourse arose to construct pop music as a modern day musical niche for women. The female-vocalist niche, which for centuries has been effective in narrowing musical opportunities for female musicians, is wedded to the pop-music niche, thereby doubling the effect of devaluation. The rock band is preserved as a bastion of male-musician camaraderie, a replication of the "team" mentality that is generally at the core of men's work and play. Female musicians are sometimes channeled into solo artistry, even when they arrive on the record company's doorstep with their own band. The historical coding of certain instruments as inappropriate for women places female musicians at a disadvantage in the rock world, where electric guitars and drums are archetypal signifiers. Rock's designation of the concert tour as the preferred mode of promotion produces an effect similar to the early barriers against marriage for female musicians, imposing separation from families and husbands or lovers. Female musicians who enter pop music are tied to commercial manipulation, excluded from the ideology of authenticity, and viewed as speaking for no one. For when female musicians are allowed the credibility of speaking for an audience, particularly for girls and women, gender inequality is fundamentally threatened.

Making their way through history, female musicians have

suffered an unconscionable assault on their creative potential and spirit. They have been excluded from music education, relegated to certain musical forms and popular culture arenas, made to choose the role of wife over the roles of music professional and artist, defined as amateurs, and coerced into unwanted sexual encounters in order to enter and succeed in the music profession. But social conditions of inequality have a way of opening wounds that do not close. Certainly, music production and distribution have changed in form over time; today, popular music is highly commercialized and industrially organized, tied to concepts of audience, division of labor, corporate ownership, and promotion. These new conditions have in some ways enabled female musicians to overcome past repressions; but in other ways, they have merely changed the terms of gender discrimination.

Authorship and Production in the Music Industry

There has been a marked historical tendency to assign authorship of creative products to a single individual. Janet Wolff (1981, p. 11) has argued that the inclination descends from the nineteenth century romantic notion of the artist and incorporates two historical developments: the rise of individualism and the rise of industrial capitalism. The early preference given to composer over performer as the creative source of music was a manifestation of this practice. In this case, the ideology of individual authorship converged with the practice of female-musician devaluation to rob female musicians of recognition for their creative contribution.

The romantic ideal of the lone creator has been more difficult to sustain in the age of industrial music production. The commercialization and industrialization of music has dramatically changed the way in which music is created. Music production is organized around the segmenting of creative processes and a hierarchical form of collective production that involves more creators and more stages of creation. To make music within the music industry, musicians work with a number of people—songwriters whose songs are chosen for their repertoire (in the event the musician does not write the material); producers of albums; engineers of songs; record company officials who dictate release dates of albums and singles and handle marketing and distribution; and, most recently, directors of video promotion. The separation of individual creators into categories of creative work is a function of the industrial mode of divided labor and helps industry maintain control over production. It is important to the record industry that each music product leave an identifiable creative trail in order to facilitate the management of wage–labor relations and to support the status of the song as a distinct commodity (Laing, 1985).

The tension between artist control and industry control is active and ever present in popular music production. Musicians must constantly reconcile their artistry and craft with their record company's main objective, the accumulation of capital. This unstable condition has generated a new ideological value structure that retains the ideology of romantic artistry but expresses opposition to industry involvement in music creation. Musicians are considered to be either authentic *authors* of their music (and positively valued) or *puppets* of the industrial system (and devalued). The historical preoccupation with what constitutes creativity in music making is met with a new question, "What constitutes *'creative control'* within an industrial mode of production?" Musicians are evaluated against the ideological standard of whether they control their own creations or allow their creations (and by extension, themselves) to be controlled by industry interests. The evaluative standard is ideological because it suggests that musicians under contract to record companies need not be affected or changed by contact with commercialized music or the industrial mode of production, both of which, of necessity, they cannot entirely escape. In a similar scheme, rock ideology reasserted romantic artistry by forging a politic of opposition to industrial control and commercial imperatives.

The simple dichotomy suggested by the author/puppet evaluative standard assimilates easily with the historical logic of female-musician devaluation. The early practice of sexual favors, later refined into an ideology of sexual favors, associated professional female musicians with manipulation by their male superiors. This converged neatly with the notion of industrial puppetry; if female music makers were prone to sleeping with bosses to get work, or with reviewers to obtain positive reviews of their music, it was a small step to the accusation that they allowed themselves to be manipulated by a male-run record industry. As commodity culture developed, advertising campaigns made use of female images to sell products, thereby implicating women in capitalist sales schemes. The creation of pop music as a female niche reinforced the position by linking female musicianship to overt commercialism. Thus, female musicians are particularly vulnerable to the charge that they operate within the record industry merely as instruments to sell records. This colors the ways in which female musicians are promoted and leaves them disproportionately subject to the accusation that they are products of industry control rather than deserving and talented artists.

The music industry has reformulated authorship in terms of a system of credit whereby numerous individual creators are named and credited with a specific piece of creative work from the set of segmented music processes. This system of assigning credit represents only a small modification in the model of individual authorship in that it maintains the focus on the individual rather than the collective. Because no consensus for collective authorship has emerged to counter the historical focus on the individual author (despite the collectivity of modern production), authorship discourse has become increasingly conflicted and contradictory under industrial capitalism. Authorship may be interpreted as the exclusive domain of the performer, songwriter, producer, or other individual, depending on the ideological benefit accomplished by the assignment. The persistence of an ideology of individual authorship allows the creative role to be assigned strategically according to political interests. Authorship, as a result, has become a primary arena of struggle and negotiation.

Some of that struggle appears in the form of consumer confusion over how to assign authorship. In today's age of mechanical reproduction (representation and promotion), performers are better known and song writers less well-known than their historical predecessors, which creates a tendency for music fans to associate the song with its singer. Unaware of how segmented music production really is, the public will often assume that the performer is also the composer of the music. This tendency is advantageous to female musicians who are likely for historical reasons to assume the role of performer. Yet, the valuing of composition over performance is still an active element of authorship ideology. Fans who do attend closely to album liner notes (to the industry's system of credit) may discover that a performer does not write his or her songs. The discovery may confuse them, for if only one author is possible, then who should it be? Fans may feel compelled to resurrect the residual ideology of creative composition and give primary artistic credit to the songwriter, and not to the performer.

The music industry conceals the dynamics of creative control by controling the terms of authorship assignment and reducing authorship to a matter of who receives official credit as songwriter or producer. In actuality, authorship is accomplished through a process of negotiation among creators, between creators and the industry that employs them, and between creators and the audience that popularizes them and buys their music. The multiple layers and complexities of the industrial modes of production and distribution create a veritable field of possibilities for musicians who desire to communicate a personal musical vision and control their own music products. Creative control is not wholly dependent on the performer writing his or her own music. Although songs are, on occasion, written by the performer, they may also be written for the performer, rewritten by the performer, written with the performer (co-written), or selected by the performer. Each of these strategies involves the performer at some level of authorship activity. And, in cases in which performers have no involvement in composition, and may not be given a choice of which material to perform, it is still possible to make a song one's own through the act of performance. Vocal or instrumental renditions can personalize the song's expression, as can a stage act or video that includes a distinctive repertoire of movement, talk, and appearance. Collaborative participation in songwriting, the exercise of free choice in song selection, the practice of customizing songs, and the strategic intervention by the musician in a song's lyrics or arrangement are all legitimate, if unrecognized, indicators of authorship. Musicians "work the system" in a variety of ways to accomplish their personal objectives.

One of the most effective strategies musicians employ to negotiate authorship within the industrial system of divided and segmented music production is to initiate or participate in collaborative associations. By design, the division of labor and segmentation of production help record companies manage workers and capital efficiently; but for creators, the division of labor and production can mean isolation and an environment unconducive to creation. Many musicians have discovered that they can offset the negatives of industrial production and maintain their commitment to artistry by crossing the lines of divided labor and stepped production through collaboration. Although the division of labor favors distinct job assignments, the industrial fact of collective production enables creators to form close working alliances. Collaboration is the informal, interpersonal, democratic method of creating music that resides beneath the more obvious, formal system of divided labor and authorship crediting.

Musicians may negotiate with their record company for the right to choose the people they want to work with, thereby ensuring productive and pleasurable collaborations, or collaborations can emerge from the record company's personnel assignments if individual creators can discover ways to connect creatively and personally. Hence, creative control is not dependent wholly on individual production or even on the negotiation of contractual rights of approval. Individual production is impossible anyway given the level of industrialization in popular music production. And rights of approval, are difficult to attain under the hierarchical system of corporate management, particularly for new artists, although such rights are a possibility for musicians with an established track record. The importance of building a track record creates a role for the audience in the authorship negotiation process. By registering their popular support, audiences create the climate necessary for the musician to be able to negotiate creative control from the record company.

While musicians may affect their final music product by collaborating with titled workers along the pathway of production and promotion, they do not usually receive credit for such involvement from the industry or from the press. Informal interactions and interpersonal exchanges that occur within the industry are not easily uncovered or measured, and creators who participate informally and collaboratively may not be rewarded fully for their labor. Collaboration generates compensation and recognition only if it can be translated into official forms of credit. For female musicians, whose creative input is by assumption often in doubt, informal methods of collaboration can even function as an institutionalized system to suppress authorship. Female musicians may collaborate informally with titled workers throughout the production process, but never receive a sanctioned credit. Without official commendation as song writers, record producers, or video directors their collaborative efforts go unrecognized and unremunerated.

Gender may erect barriers to female participation in collaborative efforts. The ideology of sexual favors can subtly taint relations of professional exchange between men and women, making opposite-sex collaborations difficult. There is also the danger that within an overwhelmingly male-occupied music industry opportunities for collaboration spring from male networks or buddy systems, making them more accessible to male creators. Denying collaborative associations to female musicians cuts them off from one important outlet of individual initiative and pushes them closer to the pole of industrial control, where they can more easily be defined as puppets of the system. On the positive side, women are socialized to develop interpersonal skills, and therefore have great collaborative potential.

The Historical Conjuncture with MTV

MTV, by giving preference to male-adolescent discourse, reactivated the ideologies and practices of female-musician exclusion, devaluation, and derision. But there were also a number of ways in which MTV enabled female musicians to win the industry backing and audience recognition denied them historically. In the years immediately preceding MTV's start date, the conditions of gender inequality in music were increasingly unstable. In the early and middle 1970s, the women's movement directed women to pursue their female creative visions within and against male-organized arenas. Toward the end of the decade, punk rock encouraged amateur female musicians to perform and to seek professional music careers. But in 1979, just when new female musicians were breaking into or preparing to break into professional musicianship, the recording industry took its notorious financial nose dive as the combined effects of a sluggish national economy, home-taping technology, and entertainment diversification began to be felt.[4] Poor economic conditions threatened to curb for the foreseeable future the music industry's awards of new contracts to "risky" musicians. This translated into dim prospects for female musicians.

MTV turned those prospects around. With the start of MTV, record sales increased dramatically and the recovering music industry was in the mood to take some chances. MTV made a point of emphasizing new bands in its playlist, and the works of many new and unknown bands and vocalists, including female musicians, were offered to audiences for the first time. MTV piped musicians and music discourse into the home, reaching female audiences who might otherwise have missed out on male music culture. The channel's preferred male address confronted girls and women textually with the fact of their exclusion from the dominant discourses of adolescence and rock music and made many of them into grand supporters of the female musicians who had begun to carve a space for female creativity and subjectivity in music by means of their MTV promotions. By lending their popular support, female audiences helped to catapult a number of female musicians to star status virtually overnight. Seldom has success and advancement come so big and so fast as on the coat-tails of MTV. In 1982, the Go-Gos became the only all-female vocal and instrumental group ever to make the "Top 10" record charts. Their first album, *Beauty and the Beat*, was also the first album by an all-female band to hit "Number 1" on the charts. That same year, *Ms.* magazine ran an article, entitled, "At Last . . . Enough Women Rockers to Pick and Choose." Although a few female musicians gained recognition as instrumentalists, the real success story was in the category of vocalist, where women had traditionally excelled. Cyndi Lauper's 1983 debut album, *She's So Unusual*, remained among the Top 30 albums for over sixty weeks. (The life of a single is generally considered to be about twelve weeks.) Lauper's album produced four hit singles in the Top 5, a new record for a female singer. One year Tina Turner was a woman without a record deal, but the next year she had a top hit single and also won the top Grammy award for 1985. Turner's popularity and industry recognition was in poignant contrast to her nearly life-long attempt to succeed as a professional musician. A 1985 *Rolling Stone* "Reader's Poll" ranked Cyndi Lauper first in the category for "New Artist," second to Tina Turner in the "Female Vocalist" category, and while a distant third to Bruce Springsteen and Prince as "Artist of the Year," she ranked higher than Michael Jackson. Madonna sold 3.5 million copies of her album *Like a Virgin* in just fourteen weeks. The record went "triple platinum" before its artist had set foot on a touring stage, even though concert tours had been the principal promotion device before MTV. Pat Benatar, signed in 1978, was busy performing on concert stages both before and after the start of MTV. She observed a clear shift in female concert attendance after the channel began to distribute female musician images into the home:

> When we first began, most of our concerts were probably 80/20 male-oriented. There were very few women. Very few women used to go to concerts no matter who was playing, male or female. I saw that really change about 1982. It became like 60/40, and the next thing I knew, it was 50/50, then 60/40 the other way. Now there are more women in the audience than men (Benatar, 1987).

While the symbolic content of MTV's videos worked against a subjective position for female musicians and female readers, its formal conventions and narrative structures tended to favor the vocalist. The female musician niche became a position of advantage. In music video, the vocalist lip-synchs the song's lyrics while being featured visually as the musical performer, and sometimes also appears as an actor in the video's narrative scenarios. Backup singers and band members (if they appear at all) may act out parts, but the camera follows and provides the majority of the close-ups to the vocalist. In the videos' narrative sequences, the soundtrack provided by the vocalist can operate like a narrator's omnipotent voice-over to guide the visual action. Sometimes, she literally puts words in the mouths of other characters (sometimes male) through the use of a common music video device whereby a selected lyrical phrase is lip-synched as if it were dialogue. Appearance in a video offers musicians a greater range of visual performance than that afforded by the concert stage. Eye-contact and facial gestures, available to only the closest concert-goers, are accessible to all video viewers. Any role playing on the concert stage is limited to costume changes and the use of props. In video, role playing is greatly facilitated by the pre-association of television with characterization. Staging can be made intricate by using locations, sets, and interactions with other actors. In other words, the gamut of devices available to television productions is opened up to musicians in music video. By commanding their own visual performance in the videos, female musicians began to use the medium to overturn the staid standard of female representation and enlist audiences in authorship activity. Creatively, MTV presented female musicians with a new layer of production practice, thus opening another site for their authorship strategies and new possibilities for collaboration and contract negotiations. As a promotional medium, it helped female musicians move beyond the still photographic image and define themselves through movement and action. MTV's ability to affect sales and generate popularity also enabled them to begin building track records.

MTV's intervention in rock ideology served to blur the lines of distinction between rock and pop, thereby disabling the underlying structure of value that had functioned to pigeonhole female musicians and female audiences. Playing against the new ambiguities in classification and value, female musicians spread their music across musical and ideological boundaries, appropriated what was valued in rock, and asserted the merits of pop. The new instability of rock discourse provided an opportunity for commercially inspired music to be redefined as artistic and worthy, and for fandom to be rearticulated as authentic cultural response. Female musicians and female audiences were able to avoid taking the fall for the industrialization and commercialization of music and to concentrate on their subjective desires and needs.

MTV created the conditions for cultural struggle by establishing a new, effective promotional device for music artists, industries, and audiences and then representing the musicians, music, and music consumers in narrow and biased ways. In Stuart Hall's (1982, p. 81) terms, the rock and adolescent discourses that came to dominate MTV became "the primary framework or terms of an argument" and, as he cautions, in struggles over meaning "changing the terms of an argument is exceedingly difficult, since the dominant definition of the problem acquires, by repetition, and by the weight and credibility of those who propose or subscribe it, the warrant of 'common sense.'" While the ideologies of rock and adolescence and the pattern of superior male musicianship and privileged male audience interpretation had achieved a level of naturalization, their internal contradictions began to be laid bare by the practices of MTV. With female musicians and female audiences united as agents of cultural struggle, change became possible.

FIVE

FOUR FEMALE MUSICIANS

THE CAREERS of the four female musicians discussed in this chapter—Tina Turner, Pat Benatar, Cyndi Lauper, and Madonna—illustrate the conditions of music creation for women and point to the specific areas in which conflicts have occurred and improvements have been effected. As the biographies of the four musicians unfold, we get a sense of the historical path of female musicianship and its conjuncture with MTV. Each musician shows an increasing sophistication about issues of representation and self-presentation, develops greater confidence about asserting her right to creative control and credited participation in music-making ventures, learns to use professional collaborative associations and negotiate her way to having both a personal and professional life.

Tina Turner and Pat Benatar had professional careers in music before the start of MTV, with club and concert stages as their primary performance and promotion sites. Before MTV, Benatar's record company had produced video performance pieces and, as soon as MTV made national distribution possible, the company made extensive use of video. Turner's comeback as a solo artist was accomplished in conjunction with her exposure on MTV. Cyndi Lauper and Madonna became commercially successful as a direct result of MTV promotion. Audiences saw these artists and their music videos on MTV before or concurrent with radio airplay of their songs.

Tina Turner
"I look down and I'm there in history." [1]

Born Anna Mae Bullock, Tina Turner began her formal singing performances at the Baptist church in the town of her birth, Nutbush, Tennessee. After moving as a teenager to St. Louis, Missouri, Ann began to attend nightclubs, where she was exposed to music as a form of public entertainment and began singing with Ike Turner's band (Turner, 1986). The church choir singing experience was a socially sanctioned activity and took place in an environment suitable for female musical performance. The experience of frequenting and later singing in nightclubs was anything but suitable. Nightclubs were outside the domestic boundaries imposed on young women, and women who attended clubs were considered to be interested only in carousing with men, and not in listening to music. Musicians who played the clubs cultivated "wild and loose" reputations, in keeping with the image of nightclub life. For Ann, going to nightclubs at sixteen and seventeen years of age meant violating social taboos and her mother's teachings. Joining Ike Turner's band did not mean getting into music—it meant getting into trouble.

In her autobiography, *I, Tina*, Turner described her mother's reaction to finding out about her club singing, something she had hoped to keep secret to avoid the consequences:

> She hit me a backhand lick to the side of my face. . . . She said, "So you been singin' with Ike Turner"—and the way she said it sounded like a banner headline: PISTOL-WHIPPING IKE TURNER. Because that was the reputation he had—if there was a fight,

Ike would pistol-whip you, right? Here some guy would come, looking for his wife, maybe, and ready for a decent fight, and Ike would go whunk-whunk-whunk—get him with the butt of his gun. . . . But I hadn't done anything wrong. I felt I was a good girl. I went to school. I did all the housework at home (Turner with Loder 1986, pp. 56–57).

Ann's maintenance of appropriate female behavior—going to school, doing domestic chores—was insufficient to cancel her "bad girl" activity—singing in a nightclub with disreputable musicians. Her mother wanted her to be a nurse, a career consistent with the female social role of service, and she forbid her to sing in the clubs. But for Ann, the only avenue to professional musicianship was stage experience, and she persisted despite the social costs.

Ann's opportunity to sing with Ike Turner's band might never have presented itself if the club scene had been less informal and encouraging of amateur talent. When Ike Turner performed, people in the crowd were often brought onto the stage to play with the band. This was not so much to discover hidden talent as it was a way Ike and his band members had devised to flirt with girls and women. Thus, Ann did not go through formal auditions. As the story goes, she assertively took advantage of an open microphone to perform for Ike and the audience simultaneously (Turner 1986, pp. 55–56). Ike was genuinely impressed with Ann's voice and invited her to sing with the band on a regular basis. This opened up a musical training situation available historically only to males: Ann became an "apprentice to a master player"—Ike Turner—who knew the music business inside out (Bowers and Tick, 1986). Unfortunately, Ike preferred the role of master to the role of teacher. Ann's musical association with Ike Turner was marked not by collaborative exchanges or artistic investigations, but by a dictatorial rule enforced with physical threats and abuse.

She was pressed into performing songs written by Ike, at times even having their vocal renditions dictated to her. He insisted that she sing with sexual overtones, in too high a key, and in an overly loud voice: "Ike always had me screaming and screeching" (Turner 1986, p. 85). Her costuming for stage performances was largely a feature of his direction and taste. Even her name was changed to Tina Turner by Ike (without consultation) for record tracks and stage performances. As told in Tina's autobiography, Ike chose the first name "Tina" because it reminded him of the white jungle goddesses who appeared in the matinee movies of his youth. He constructed her image in conformance with the standard of female sexual representation developed by the Hollywood cinema. Her new last name, "Turner," was a sign of ownership, not marriage (Turner 1986, p. 75).

Ike made it impossible for Tina to achieve an independent professional status as a musician during her association with him. This is made evident in her description of how she came to tour with Ike and became part of the "Ike and Tina Turner Revue":

> I said, "I cannot travel with you, I cannot sing these songs." [Songs Ike wrote about other women, which Tina did not enjoy singing.] So he said, "Okay, we'll make some allowances, give you a certain amount of money," I said okay. That was the trick. So we started traveling, and that's when I got involved. I didn't plan it, because he said he was going to pay me, and when he didn't, I was afraid to ask for the money because I was living with him (Collins 1986, p. 52).

By initiating an intimate relationship with Tina, Ike Turner clearly believed he had successfully precluded a professional association and ended her right to compensation or collaboration. For sixteen years, Tina performed with him onstage and on record tracks, receiving very little monetary remuneration, and with the expectation that she would be available sexually for Ike alone (while he continued to have sexual relations with other women). Frustrated by his musical limitations and, undoubtedly, his secondary status as a black man and a black musician, Ike Turner played out in the personal arena the capitalist strategies of hierarchical management and low wages, and the patriarchal strategies of male domination and female devaluation, using their techniques and ideas "in miniature" to control the career and psyche of one of the world's most talented female vocalists.

It is no coincidence that the truth about Tina Turner's association with Ike Turner surfaced at the time when recognition of female musicianship was on the rise, and Turner herself was looking for a way into the world of professional rock music. Indeed, Turner's career reactivation in the mid-1980s was predicated on the revelation of her oppressive past, which exposed the link between the patriarchal system of male privilege and the suppression of her musical abilities. A promotional blitz that publicized the details of Turner's years as a battered wife and musical slave to her ex-husband and partner was timed with the 1984 release of her first rock solo album, *Private Dancer*. The album's most successful single, "What's Love Got to Do with It?" was promoted heavily on MTV. Turner's autobiography, published in 1986, compiled much of the information given to the press at the time of her 1984 musical releases and stands as a permanent record of a particular historical era for (black) female musicianship.

The personal anecdotes of Tina's abusive marriage served to provide an interpretive context for the songs on the album, making them into autobiographical statements to the audience. Stanzas of "What's Love Got to Do with It?" may not have been written by Turner,[2] but an authorial voice is created for her as a consequence of fans' attempts to reconcile the song's text with extra-textual information about the singer's personal history:

> It may seem to you,
> That I'm acting confused
> When you're close to me.
> If I tend to look dazed,
> I read it someplace,
> I've got cause to be.

Gender experience became the context of authenticity that Tina needed to make the transition from rhythm and blues and cabaret performances to commercial rock music. Quotes by Turner in the press, such as, "I've never sung anything I couldn't relate to," (Mehler 1984, p. 21) lent additional credibility to autobiographical readings of the songs she performed.

None of the album's songs are credited to Tina Turner. She did not write the songs, at least not according to the industry definition of songwriting. Yet she was an important collaborator on several songs. For example, "I Might Have Been Queen" was written expressly for her. Jennette Obstoj, Rupert Hine's songwriting partner, met with Tina and "listened as Tina narrated her life story, from the cotton-field years back in Nutbush through Ike and the 'Revue'—the whole saga of pain and oppression, right up to the present and her interest in Egypt, her belief in other lives" (Turner with Loder 1986, p. 216). Her life story was then used by Obstoj as a basis for writing the song's lyrics.

Turner's strength in musical interpretation entered into the creation of the hit song "What's Love Got to Do with It?" When Tina first saw the song, offered to her by her manager's friend and compatriot Terry Britten, she was concerned that it sounded like a pop song. The song's tone was disturbing in light of her efforts to redefine herself within a rock aesthetic.

Her new manager, Roger Davies, who was present when she confronted Britten with her objections, described their process of collaboration on a new rendition:

> Tina walks in and says, "I don't like your songs." "Good start," I thought. She says, "They're not rough enough." Terry says, "Well we can just change 'em around a bit." Then he starts fooling around with them on his guitar—and he's a terrific guitarist. Tina starts getting excited. She says, "Well, I have to have them in a higher key." No problem—he fastens a capo onto the guitar and just slides it up the neck (Turner with Loder 1986, p. 216).

Tina confirmed the story and reported on her reaction to "What's Love Got to Do with It?" as it was presented originally, and the contribution she made to its reworking:

> The song was this sweet, little thing. Can you imagine me singing like Diana Ross or Barbara Streisand, trying to sound velvety and smooth? I really fought. Eventually, we roughened it out instrumentally and I added some [rock] phrasings, and we changed the song's attitude and got a hit. I have input, not just in song selection but in treatment too. I'll never be a musician, but I know what's right (Mehler 1984, p. 20).

Turner's self-deprecating assessment of herself as a non-musician is in accordance with the historically constructed myth that positions performance outside of creative practice. The false distinction between performance and composition as it relates to creative contribution is clearly still in operation, not only in how female musicians are viewed in the press, but in how they view themselves. The actual practice of song construction, as Turner describes it, reveals musical rendition to be not only a creative authorship practice, but a politically powerful one. Also suggested in Turner's description are the informal aspects of song production and their devaluation by the industry. In keeping with standard industry practice, the final songwriting credit for "What's Love Got to Do with It?"

awarded to Britten and Graham Lyle, does not account for Turner's participation in the song's selection or her reworking of its tone.

The authorial arena available to Tina during the Ike and Tina days was in performance, both vocal interpretation (when Ike allowed it) and onstage delivery. Her singing and dancing were two areas of expertise that enabled her to survive the difficult years after her departure from Ike and the "Revue." As Tina described it, "I was depending on my performances. If you're a good performer you can always work in the business" (Turner with Loder 1986, p. 213). When she began work on a solo career in the 1980s, she turned to these areas as the means to carve out a recognition of her authorship and allude to her new efforts at creative control. Vocal rendition became a means to translate songs into her personal vision, performance a means of rebuilding an image and audience rapport. In video, Tina discovered a promotion vehicle that capitalized richly on her ability to convey nuances of facial expressions, body gestures, and movement.

Part of the credit for Turner's musical direction in the 1980s belongs to the manager she selected, Roger Davies. He encouraged her to pursue rock music despite the bias against female rock musicians and oversaw promotions and contract negotiations that were in her interest both as a musician and as a woman (Turner, 1986). Although Tina admitted in her autobiography, after leaving Ike, "I felt in the back of my head that I might need a boyfriend–manager," it is a sign of her personal and political development that she "realized [she] would have been stepping back into the same old situation" (Turner 1986, p. 206). Instead, she chose a manager with whom she could discuss and plan collaboratively the changes that she needed in her career and wanted to make.

Tina Turner's early career with Ike Turner has come to epitomize the changes in the ideological paradigm and social condition of female musicianship. Her comeback demonstrates that female musicians need not rely on intimate relationships with men to produce professional popular music, but can trust in their own talent. It dispels the notion that female vocalists are sexual figureheads—that while they may sing, they are inept creatively and conceptually. The history of female musicianship embodied in Tina Turner's autobiography and songs has enabled audiences to reevaluate the past and make changes in the present and future.

Pat Benatar
"Those cooperatin' days are over." [3]

Pat Benatar was born Patricia Andrzejewski and, like Tina Turner began her singing career with performances in church choirs around her home town of Lindenhurst on Long Island, New York. Although a full decade separates the births of the two musicians, churches remained one of the few acceptable places in which girls could gain experience in musical performance. Benatar has explained, "As a kid, I sang at any choir, any denomination, anywhere I could . . . because churches were one place where you could really put your full heart and power into singing" (White, 1988).

Growing up in the 1950s and 1960s, in a white (albeit working-class) family, Patricia received a musical education, but within the narrow confines of a classical musical training program. Her school teachers enrolled her in special voice classes, and in 1970, at age seventeen, she began operatic voice training in preparation for admittance to the famed Juilliard School of Music. Although her mother had sung in the chorus of the New York City Opera, she ended her career when Pat was born, an example of the residual ideology against combining a musical career and family life. Dissatisfied with the training regimen and lifestyle expectations of classical musicianship, Pat dropped out of the program and turned away from singing. Enacting sex-role expectations, she married, took her husband's name, Benatar, and moved with him to Virginia. For two and a half years, she lived the life of an army wife and worked as a bank teller until she began to examine her alternatives, to come to terms with her own popular-music influences and her desire to be a rock musician (Pond, 1980).

Pat and her husband, destined for eventual divorce, moved to New York City in order to begin Pat's popular music "training" on the nightclub circuit. What she recalls most is learning just how many obstacles are placed in the path of women who want to sing outside pop music: "People tell you, 'Janis Joplin died. Give it up'" (Pond 1980, p. 15). Despite the bias against female rock performers, she retrained her operatic voice to sing rock and roll—because she was female, her early musical training had guided her toward the vocalist niche. As a girl, she had not had access to the informal training ground of the "garage band," which introduced male counterparts of the same generation to playing in a rock band. Rock's unsavory reputation made it an inappropriate musical form for girls, and her parents had not permitted her even to attend rock concerts as a teenager.[4] Therefore, as she developed into a rock musician, Benatar performed as a vocalist and not as a member of a band, rock's privileged musical unit.

In New York City, Benatar played clubs and cabarets and "ate beans and rice," until an open audition won her a regular gig at Rick Newman's club, Catch a Rising Star (Pond 1980, p. 15). Newman became her manager and continued in that role for ten years. On the strength of her club performances and, as always with capitalist-culture industries, her perceived marketability, Benatar was signed in 1978 by Chrysalis Records. The contract came in just under the wire before the record industry slump in 1979 and three years shy of the start of MTV; it made her one of very few professional female rock musicians. She had transcended the classical training program of her youth and the odds against a woman's gaining professional status in rock music. But the start of her music career was also the beginning of a new set of problems because of the challenge her presence represented to the male-defined world of rock music.

Benatar entered the recording business as a vocalist and solo artist; but with the backing of a record contract, she moved quickly to build a band that would operate as a collaborative unit to complement her rock sensibility. Two members, Neil Geraldo (hired to play guitar for the first album) and Myron Grombacher (a drummer brought on for the first tour) were to form, along with Benatar, the collaborative core for one successful album after another. But to the record company, she was still a female singer, and they promoted her as such. They withheld information about Gerlado's active role in her music (Pond 1980, p. 15) in order to downplay their contract vocalist's commitment to creating with a band. In 1987, after seven albums' worth of collaboration with Geraldo and Grombacher, Benatar reflected on the contradiction created by being marketed as a female vocalist while working creatively as a member of a band: "The only mistake that we made was that we should have been a band. We should have called ourselves something, because that's really what it is. The common joke among us is that Myron, Neil, and I are Pat Benatar" (Benatar, 1987). In her own mind, the name "Pat Benatar" came to stand *not* for her individual musical persona, but as a tag for the band.

There was also considerable pressure from the record company to present a sexual image that would sell to the presumed-to-be-male audience for rock music. In music video promotion tapes produced two years before MTV introduced its national televised distribution network, Pat was directed to shake her body and move in "sexual" ways—to "be hot." In hindsight, she attributes her inability to resist such manipulative direction to the ideology of niceness she had been taught as a girl. Her clothing and stage movements, which had not provoked a gender-charged response in her New York club dates, began to be turned against her in photographs shot for promotional purposes and used in publicity efforts. The clothes she wore and her gestures on stage were interpreted according to the standard of female representation that operates to code women as sexual objects of desire. Benatar has commented on this distortion: "I was trying to be aggressive, but not necessarily sexy" (Gans 1983, p. 13). Controlling the mode of female representation had proven to be an effective strategy to deny female subjectivity, and representation, not surprisingly, became one of the prime arenas of struggle over Benatar's right to participate in and affect male music culture.

As a rock musician, Benatar operated within the ideology of authenticity that places having an image outside the bounds of true rock musicianship. Her musical history was in harmony with rock ideology—she had paid her dues in New York nightclubs, had allowed her rebellious edge to surface in her singing, and she was producing rock albums within a rock band structure. The preoccupation with creating an image in promotion and publicity caught her by surprise because, as a professional rock musician, she had not expected to *have* an image. She has described the experience as going from "being absolutely oblivious about my image to having this sex-goddess bitch bullshit slammed in my face" (Gans 1983, p. 13).

In the pre-MTV days of her career, Benatar seemed to be mired in a constant furor over her representation. She was accused of complicity in her own manipulation because she chose to wear the clothing and affect the gestures that were seized on as sexual by the music press and select audiences. She was made over and over to answer these charges in publicity interviews, a technique that distracted readers from serious consideration of her music and her popular appeal. She responded in earnest that her choice of clothing was not a calculation on her part to sell her sexuality, that her clothes were chosen more for function than meaning,[5] and she tried to sidestep female stereotypes by stating that she didn't even *like* clothes (Lunch, 1985). An example of these efforts is her explanation of her leg-wear: "I wore tights onstage because they were comfortable. I didn't realize that when I put my leg up, people went crazy. I was just putting my leg up" (Pond 1980, p. 14).

Rolling Stone, in its coverage of Benatar, used the standard of female representation as a strategy to deny her full accep-tance into the canon of rock music. In 1980, on the heels of her second successful album release, the magazine ran its first cover story on Benatar. It was a conflicted piece, seemingly celebratory about her arrival on the rock scene, but slyly bent on undermining her place in rock (Pond, 1980). The story is entitled "Pat Benatar: This Year's Model." The word "model" evokes the paragon of female representation embodied in the fashion model, an ideological safeground the article wished to activate in light of the challenge Benatar's musical success represented to rock. The inclusion of the phrase "this year's" summons up the idea of a manufactured image with only tem-porary currency, an association that discounts her authorship and her potential as an enduring figure in rock music.

Accompanying photographs, taken by *Rolling Stone*'s then chief photographer, Annie Leibovitz, are insidiously com-plicit. Both the cover photo and the photo that accompanies the article are concerned with emphasizing Benatar's sexuality and her gender difference, not just in relation to the magazine's readers, but in relation to her band. Benatar and Geraldo had begun a personal relationship after he joined the band, and the ideology of sexual favors surfaces in both the photographs and text to question subtly her musical authority. The cover photograph shows Benatar posed with Geraldo in a sexual embrace. She is looking, open-mouthed, at the photograph's spectators. Further enticing the reader is the stance Benatar assumes in playful resistance to Geraldo's nibbles on her neck. Her tight, black, Spandex–clad legs are spread wide to reveal that her genitals are placed directly over Geraldo's crotch. A thin red strap of fabric trails between Benatar and Geraldo, a manipulative photographic metaphor for an erect penis. The image recurs in a second photo, in which Leibovitz has positioned Benatar's boot heel in front of Grombacher's crotch in a manner that again alludes to a protruding penis. This photograph comments symbolically on Benatar's main ideological infraction—her intrusion into the male domain of the rock and roll band. The male members of the band mug for the camera and display gestures of athleticism and physical prowess. They do not appear with their musical instruments, but are united instead by their presentation as men. Grombacher, in sweatpants and without a shirt, shows off his bicep muscle. Bass guitarist Roger Capps does push-ups. Geraldo holds Benatar aloft as if lifting weights, while rhythm-guitarist Scott St. Clair Sheets looks on with an agreeable grin. The composite image makes a fetish of male camaraderie, strength, and phallic power, and leaves Benatar (held prone and off the ground) outside its boundaries.

Steve Pond's text for the article quotes Benatar voicing her displeasure with the way she is generally represented in promotional material and in the press, an underlying theme of the review, which is ironic in light of the magazine's own photographic spreads. *Rolling Stone* reports her statements that fault her record company for sponsoring undesirable images,[6] not out of genuine concern for the special problems faced by female musicians, but to bolster the argument that Benatar is a puppet controlled by the record industry. She is allowed to raise the *issue* of her manipulation, but only as a pretext to proving that her career is essentially a *product* of manipulation—in other words, that she has no legitimate claim to musicianship. In this way, the text echoes the second photo-graphic representation by asking whether Benatar's male band members are the musical prop for her image.

Pond's description of the male band members' appearance reveals the double standard that informs rock discourse, the nonchalance with which male rockers' attire is approached, and their freedom from many issues of representation that female musicians must face:

> Geraldo stands downstage in jeans and a red shirt, leading the group and looking like a typical street punk; rhythm-guitarist Scott St. Clair Sheets stands unobtrusively off to the other side in black leather pants and striped red shirt; short-haired bassist Roger Capps resembles an old rockabilly singer in straight-legged black pants and outdated sunglasses; and drummer Myron Grom-bacher, a carrot redhead in battle fatigues, jumps around and shakes the drum set that his roadies have to weld down every day (Pond 1980, p. 14).

Scott St. Clair Sheets can unobtrusively wear black leather, which is among the most sexually coded clothing for women. Grombacher's jumping and shaking is merely an item of musi-cal eccentricity, not an occasion for a sexual metaphor.

Benatar made an attempt to direct attention away from her image and sexuality in the years immediately following these criticisms. She reduced her movements on stage, cut her hair short, and wore pants and jackets. But the flak over her image persisted. By 1983, she ended her efforts to deflect the criticism and in an interview in *The Record* spoke with new understanding about its misogynic source:

> If a woman goes on stage looking too good, either she's slutty or she can't possibly have any talent, or she has no brains. . . . I went through this other phase, thinking, "Fuck them—I'm not going to wear anything that'll make me look like that in pictures anymore." . . . Now I'm comfortable. Now it's "fuck everybody —you don't like it, don't look at it. This is it!" (Gans 1983, p. 13).

Bolstered by Chrysalis Records' insistence on selling Benatar as a solo artist, *Rolling Stone* also took a stab at destroying any idea that Benatar was a full, contributing member of her rock band. The story's text worried over Geraldo's intense involvement in Benatar's musical sound and song selection process in a tone that questioned whether he shouldn't be getting the credit for Benatar's music. The article avoided considering the band as a collaborative unit in order to concentrate on undermining Benatar's authorship. The personal relationship between Geraldo and Benatar became the fuel to fire the ideology of sexual favors—to activate the historical memory of the practice of sexual favors that destroyed the credibility of female musicians in previous eras. *Rolling Stone* began the story by positioning Pat in the role of domestic servant. The tour bus is used as a metaphor for the American suburban home, with Pat as the happy homemaker—doing dishes and picking up after the boys in the band. Thus, the article invoked the sexual division of labor within the family as a means to imply ideologically that Benatar held a secondary status within the industrial division of labor as well. What was lost on *Rolling Stone* is how Geraldo and Benatar's intimacy has always contributed to their successful collaboration, and how Benatar's reinterpretation of the band as a family (as opposed to an all-male team) made it possible for her to sustain the rigors of touring.

In the early years of her career, Benatar was interrogated in the press about her creative control over the music. "They were so desperate to prove that I was a puppet," she remembered, "That I was the vehicle for everyone else's genius" (Benatar, 1987). She was put in a bind as she tried to describe the contradictory process of collaborative music production in which informal creative exchanges and a system of formal crediting coexist. The more informal side of collaboration was represented in her description of the process of recording the music:

It's hard to say who does what, in the end. . . . We do it all; I work on the arrangements with them, and everything. I'm not the prima donna who comes walking in after the tracks are cut and says, "Am I in the right key? Where do I start? Point me towards the microphone." I'm in there day and night, just like the rest of them, doing the same thing they're doing every day (Gans 1983, p. 13).

But as she attempted to give credit to Geraldo, who because of her solo career has gained little recognition, she fell into the trap of devaluing the informal aspects of collaborative work: "He has to physically write down what goes where. If you had to rate it on who does what, Neil would get 95 percent of the credit. But we figure everything together—sometimes amicably, sometimes not" (Gans 1983, p. 13). If, as Benatar suggested, they "figure everything together," she has accorded Geraldo an exorbitant amount of credit. The issue underlying such an assessment is the ideological valuation of (written) composition versus the (invisible) interpersonal decision-making that flows from the creative collaborative process. It is a tendency Benatar repeated in her discussion of making the video for "Love Is a Battlefield."

In a video address tagged onto one of her commercially available music-video compilation tapes, Benatar gives Director Bob Giraldi "all of the credit" for coming up with the video's concept. But her description of the process leading to the concept's origin exposed its true collaborative nature:

I wanted to do something in the street—that's the feeling I got. The song is basically a love song, but I wanted to turn it around so it wouldn't be between a man and a woman relationship. I wanted it to be some kind of a twist—so it would be about young people and the problems they go through. I wasn't sure what. I know I wanted it to be in the street and I wanted it to be with a lot of kids and dancing. When we spoke to [Giraldi], he came up with the runaway idea (The Making of "Love Is a Battlefield," 1985).

Benatar's initial impulse to reverse assumptions in the song's lyrical content and rely on the visual motif of the street defined the elements that are the foundation of the video's ability to speak to female audiences.

By 1983, coinciding with the release of the *Love Is a Battlefield* video, there was a shift in the press toward a greater consideration of Benatar and the band as a collaborative unit (Gans, 1983). Benatar has responded to the change with hindsight:

> When I look back on that time of our lives, I think about how nothing has really changed. Everything is really the same as it always was. They were so desperate to prove that I was a puppet, that I was the vehicle for everyone else's genius. Nothing has really changed, I mean, we've all always worked together (Benatar, 1987).

Before the start of MTV, Benatar sold lots of records, but was less successful at managing her visual image. But video promotion introduced the possibility of using narrative lines and formal juxtaposition to create a context for the female musician's image. With the pivotal release of the video *Love Is a Battlefield* in 1983, Benatar began to secure the multidimensional and active visual presentation that had been missing from her early photographic representations. By the time of the video's production, Benatar's track record was also putting her in the position of having more control over her own representation. Still, she retained her historical vantage point:

> The new girls [Lauper and Madonna] talk about how they don't let anybody manipulate them and they can't understand why some of us did it. It makes me smile because I think, well, that's great to walk in after we did all the fucking dirty work. I mean we were there when people were still slapping you on the ass (Benatar, 1987).

Cyndi Lauper
"I want everything and I want it now!" [7]

Cyndi Lauper is the same age as Pat Benatar and they grew up in close proximity in the New York City boroughs of Brooklyn and Queens. Lauper's family background, like Pat's, was working class; however, Cyndi's parents divorced when she was five, and she was raised by her mother and an extended family of maternal aunts and grandparents. Cyndi's mother worked long hours as a waitress in order to support Cyndi and her two siblings. The predominance of women in her early life initiated Lauper into the realm of female cultural activity and the injustices of gender-based oppression:

> I think the reason I am the way I am comes from watching my mother and grandmother and the women in my family and in the neighborhood. It's funny, in a neighborhood, you see the women as teenagers, and then you see them grown with children—all in the span of your being from five to ten. And you see them take on the same look in their faces that you saw on your mother's. And this is the life of women, you know? (Loder 1984a, p. 19).

While Benatar was encouraged by her teachers and the example of her mother's short opera career to think in terms of a musical profession, Lauper found her way to music through participation in girl culture. She bought and listened to pop records, sang harmonies with her sister while doing the dishes, and, like thousands of other girls in the mid-1960s, went crazy over the Beatles. School was not a positive experience for Lauper and did not encourage or focus her creative energies. She was abused emotionally and ostracized in Catholic schools, then discouraged by the New York public school system, and she finally dropped out of school altogether (Loder 1984a, p. 17).

Cyndi's love of eccentric clothing, which was to become her trademark as a professional musician, was also a prod-

uct of girl culture. She moved from dressing up Barbie dolls
to dressing up herself. Her mother was a sharp dresser and
"clothes talk" was a female bonding activity enjoyed by her
extended family. The women took great pleasure in immersing
themselves in popular culture trends, using their knowledge
of movie stars, for instance, to create imaginative scenarios to
lessen the burden of harsh female lives: "[My mother] looked
like Susan Hayworth for a while. My aunt looked like Polly
Bergen. They said I was going to look like Sandra Dee, but
then I grew up and looked like myself" (Meldrum Tapes, 1986).

Although Cyndi identified with female culture, she re-
solved not to fulfill female sex-role expectations. In search of
another life, she left home alone, traveled, worked odd jobs,
took art classes, and looked for artistic mentors. Her quest for
independence and recognition began to reveal the oppressive
side of pop ideology, the cultivation of belief in the possibility
of "being discovered" that serves to support female passivity:
"I used to pray all the time that I would change into this or
that. But you can't" (Loder 1984a, p. 19).

Cyndi returned to New York City, determined to work at
singing and to make singing work for her. She took a series of
jobs in various types of bands, singing various kinds of music
—from disco to rock and roll. Singing "covers," songs written
and sung by others (Patti LaBelle, Janis Joplin, Rod Stewart,
Mick Jagger), taught Lauper the difficulty of singing material
designed for another vocalist. Only when her voice failed after
performing too many covers did she seek a vocal teacher for
actual training in music. Singing covers also fueled a desire
to create her own songs. She was developing beyond being a
consumer of music to being a music creator.

Lauper's first crack at a record company contract came in
1979 when Polygram Records offered to sign her. Through her
manager, Lauper had met a songwriter named John Turi and
had begun to write songs with him; they formed a band called

Blue Angel. The hitch was that the record company was not interested in the band, only in its vocalist. But Lauper refused categorically to cut the band loose. She identified with the discourse of rock that held that band members, like buddies, stay together to the bitter end. And as it turned out, the end was bittersweet. After six months of holding her ground with Polygram Records, resisting what *Rolling Stone* writer Kurt Loder termed "all efforts to lure her from the band and into a solo career," the record company agreed to pick up the band (Loder 1984a, p. 60). The first, and only, Blue Angel album was not successful commercially. Polygram Records cut them off, their manager sued, and Lauper was forced into bankruptcy.

Reflecting in a video interview on her decision to fight for the band, Lauper turned suddenly to face the camera and quipped: "I must say, I was in there slugging it out for the guys" (Meldrum Tapes, 1986). The comment was an apology to female audiences, to the feminist sensibility. It was as if, in hindsight, she understood that her desire to save the band was a product of her female socialization in self-sacrificing behavior and service to men. She appeared to feel troubled that she limited her own potential as a professional musician in order to help male musicians achieve.

After the breakup of the band and a cooling-off period, Lauper decided to pursue a solo career after all. She began shopping for a new manager, but was disheartened by talk of contract stipulations and by half-hearted commitments. She made the difficult decision to go into business with her new boyfriend, Dave Wolff, who was himself a musician manager. They took their time making the decision because of the social prohibition against combining professional and personal lives, and because of the tensions and entanglements that can arise from business partnerships between persons who are involved with each other romantically. The move might have left Lauper open to the accusations that flow from the ideology of sexual favors and undercut her attempt to secure creative control over a first solo album. But as Lauper tells it, the unwillingness of the other managers she spoke with to commit to an intense effort on her behalf was a deciding factor for the professional union with Wolff. The possibility of collaborating on her career management with the person who had a personal stake in her success overrode concerns about interpersonal dynamics or appearances. Unlike Tina Turner and Ike Turner, Lauper and Wolff made a pact not to let their personal and professional goals interfere with each other (Meldrum Tapes, 1986). Wolff appears in a number of Lauper's videos, underscoring for fans and critics his collaborative working relationship with Cyndi. The press has not been overly preoccupied with Lauper's intimate relationship with her manager, a sign of the growing acceptance of professional collaboration with intimates and the gradual demise of the ideology of sexual favors.[8]

Wolff introduced Lauper to CBS Executive Producer Lenny Petze. He in turn set up a meeting with Producer Rick Chertoff (Loder 1984a, p. 63). Chertoff showed Cyndi how to create within the industrial mode of music production and was willing to share with her his practical knowledge of creative authorship strategies. Lauper's art school background, and the preferred discourse of rock, had produced in her a great attachment to the idea of individual authorship even though she had tended toward writing partnerships because she did not play an instrument. Stung by her experience singing covers, Lauper had a "burning desire to be an original" (Meldrum Tapes, 1986) and was initially taken aback when Chertoff brought out the bag of songs he was peddling,[9] unwilling to accept the idea of song selection as a viable authorship strategy. "I wanted to write songs, so it was a compromise" (Meldrum Tapes, 1986). Most of the songs, she determined to be too "pop" in the terms articulated by rock discourse—formulaic, predictable, and commercial. And when Chertoff played Robert Hazard's song "Girls Just Want to Have Fun," Lauper's rancor increased tenfold, for the song violated her feminist sensibility as well. She thought it was sexist and refused to consider it, "he played me "Girls . . ." and I said, well I ain't doing *that* song . . . because it wasn't what it ended up to be" (Meldrum Tapes, 1986). Chertoff introduced Lauper to the practice of authoring songs by rewriting them, a strategy that did not usurp the industry's allegiance to its system of credit, but which, nonetheless, enabled Lauper to make the song her own:

> [This] is something that I'll never forget that Rick did for me. I was so headstrong and so set. It was basically a very chauvinistic song. He said, "But wait, think about what it *could* mean, just think about it for a minute, forget all this other stuff, and think about what it could mean." I said, "Well how could I do that? Look at this and look at that." He said, "So change it." So that didn't occur to me that much and I would get very aggravated all the time because I'd say, "Well why should I put all the time into this song when I could be putting the time into my own." That was very real, I felt resentful alot of times. But when I worked it out, and when we got it to happen, it was magical (Meldrum Tapes, 1986).

Hazard's original version of the song was fashioned as an inflated male fantasy of female desire with lyrics that read:

> My father says, "My son,
>   what do they want from your life?"
> I say, "Father, dear we are the
>   fortunate ones.
> Girls just want to have fun."

But Lauper's alteration of the song's lyric text resulted in a custom-made vehicle for the expression of her views on gender inequality:

> My mother says, "When you gonna
>   live your life right?"

"Oh, Mother, dear we're not the
    fortunate ones.
And girls just want to have fun." [10]

The change was subsequently used as a cornerstone for the
song's video interpretation, with Lauper's own mother in a
leading role. The video's design affirmed Lauper's appropriation of Hazard's song and became a means of extending her
authorship. The appearance of Lauper's mother also encouraged an autobiographical interpretation of the song's text,
much as Tina Turner's lyrics functioned to refer to her life
experience.

The credits on the inside jacket of Lauper's debut album,
She's So Unusual, gave Hazard songwriting credit for "Girls
Just Want to Have Fun," an indication that he was duly com-
pensated. In the informal liner notes, Lauper thanks Hazard
"for letting me change your song." Essentially, Lauper traded
in official credit for writing the song for the right to be its
author, and as it turns out, initiated a commercial success that
translated into dollars down the line. Hazard was put in the
somewhat embarrassing, although financially rewarding, position of accumulating royalties from the sale of a song that no
longer expressed his creative vision. He maintained his ownership, but was no longer the song's author. While it is not
uncommon for song writers to remain all but invisible in the
wake of a vocalist's rendition, the case of "Girls" represented
an extraordinarily political intervention by Lauper, one that
clearly worked to her benefit.

Chertoff and Lauper worked together well enough to collaborate directly on song writing. Cyndi provided an account
of their co-writing of the second single release, "Time after
Time," a ballad about a girl whose ambition for herself causes
a rift between her and her boyfriend. The account portrays the
rich texture of the collaborative process and is worth reproducing in its entirety:

I was looking through the *TV Guide* and I saw all these old
movie titles and I started writing them down and one of them
was "Time after Time." I was in the studio with [Rick]. We
started to work and he said, "Well, what do you want to do?"
And I said, "Just play [the piano], just play." He started playing
a chord and then went to another chord. I said, "That's really
great, a great sound," and we just went back and forth and I just
started singing. It got to the point of . . . [she sings] "Time After
Time." I had that title so I just used it as a working title for that.
But then all of a sudden . . . the music and the title started to
feel like something, a little on the electric side. You know what
I mean? . . . Like you could feel it in the air. So we kept writing.
We got the melody, then we had to get the words. I did a little
and he did a little of the melody, it's always back and forth.

We had ended the session. . . . I had a long conversation with
him. He had just broken up. . . . He had a relationship that wasn't
going well and I knew them both. We started talking about the
difficulties of being a strong woman in a relationship—a very
strong woman, which can be overpowering. . . . It's hard to explain. Actually, maybe not. Maybe I should just say it. My whole
life, before I met David was always the same thing. I knew what I
wanted to do and what I wanted to be. I'm a very strong person
in that respect. I survive everything. . . . I had a lot of relationships that were always the same thing. I was moving too fast, I
was growing too much. I would have to stifle myself a little because it would be very intimidating. It had happened in their
relationship. I started to tell him about what it was like and he
told me what it was like. And then we started to write about the
remorse side, the real emotional side of it.

He started writing: "Flashback," "Warm nights," "Almost left
behind," and it made me almost cry. And "Suitcase of memories"
was out of his mouth. And then I say, "Time after Time." Then
I took over and told my dream, my vision. . . . "Sometimes you
picture me walking too far ahead, you're calling to me and I can't
hear what you said 'cause I'm . . . so . . . then you say go slow and
I fall behind" (Meldrum Tapes, 1986).

The account begins to describe the interpersonal and informal side of collaborative work. Songwriting may follow, as
it does in this instance, from a conversation between friends,
an intimate exchange of feelings. In order to depict accurately
the impetus behind the writing of "Time after Time," Lauper
found that she had to become personal and disclose her gender experiences if she was to represent the sentiment that gave
birth to the song. Chertoff was content to let their collaboration become an authorship vehicle for Lauper, a way for her
to discover her own statement. In the spirit of collaboration,
he backed off from his point of view in order to allow Lauper
to develop her female vision of the song's chosen theme. Lauper received songwriting credit, while Chertoff took his in the
form of a producer credit.

Lauper negotiated creative control over her representation
by becoming heavily involved in her own promotion. Her participation in the production of the video for "Girls Just Want
to Have Fun" was substantial, although again it was acknowledged only informally. In Michael Shore's (1984) day-by-day
account of the making of the video, Lauper's name appears
over and over as a contributor at virtually every stage of production. It was Lauper who picked the video's producer, Ken
Walz, and its director, Edd Griles, based on her prior experience of working with them on a video for her band Blue Angel.
Lauper suggested the video's concept, picked location sites in
New York City, brought in choreographer Mary Ellen Strom,
and found extras to appear in the video. The construction
workers, who serve as pivotal symbols in the video's snake-
dance sequence, were real workers whom Lauper coaxed into
the on-camera action. Shore (1984, p. 171) described her coach-
ing other passers-by whom she drew into the scene: "Cyndi,
who appears to be doing as much directing as Griles or anyone else, runs them through their paces several times while
waiting for the new chorus-line members to return to the loca-

tion." As the description eloquently demonstrates, the division of labor suggested by the official title of "director" did not preclude Lauper's collaborative accomplishments. Lauper's involvement in the shoot continued as she suggested the antique boutiques where campy items used in the creation of interior sets were purchased, and spent hours splatter-painting furniture for the bedroom scene. Her input even extended to post-production work; she screened rushes, approved the rough cut, and checked in on the progress of the time-consuming special effect that appears midway through the video. In his diary-style chronicle, Shore was attentive to Lauper's many initiatives and interventions, and even included snatches of interviews that allowed her to voice her intentions:

> Finally, there is the artist herself: Cyndi is not just a pretty face onstage, a pretty voice on record. She's an experienced actress as well. . . . Cyndi plays an unusually large creative role in the conceptualizing and staging of the video itself, from start to finish. . . . says Cyndi . . . "I know what I want and don't want—I don't want to be portrayed as just another sex symbol" (Shore 1984, p. 167).

Although many rock critics interpret the success of the new "video musicians" as indicating a shift toward the valuation of looks and visual image over musical talent, Pat Benatar's difficulties with representation should demonstrate that female musicians have always been subjected to this criterion. If anything, video has brought male musicians under the kind of visual scrutiny that female musicians have always had to tolerate. Lauper's self-consciousness about representation, her ability to use visual language to overturn staid images, create song authorship, and build a musical career are indicative of new directions in female musicianship and the important role played by music video. Her success has come to stand for the new attention to and opportunities for female artists, the opening up of the narrow codes of representation imposed on the image of the female musician, a widening of the avenues of song authorship, and expanded participation in the multiple facets of music production and promotion.

Madonna

*"It doesn't matter who you are,
It's what you do that takes you far."* [11]

Madonna Ciccone grew up outside Detroit, Michigan, in a large Italian-Catholic family headed by her father, who worked as an engineer in the auto industry. Her mother died of cancer when Madonna was six years old; her father remarried the family's housekeeper two years later. Both events, Madonna has remarked in interviews, left her with a sense of abandonment that fueled a fierce desire for attention, eventually driving her to pursue stardom (Connelly, 1984). But the desire for attention was not only a product of psychological trauma, it was also a result of the social system of gender inequality that denies recognition to intelligent and talented girls and women. Lacking a sympathetic mother, the rule of the patriarch in the family intensified in the form of her father's strict enforcement of Catholic morality. The presence of her numerous brothers demonstrated to Madonna the double standard that formed his parenting routines: "I had a traditional Catholic upbringing, and I saw the privileges my older brothers had. They got to stay out late, go to concerts, play in the neighborhood. I was left out" (Phillips 1987, p. 24).

Born in 1958, Madonna is five years younger than Pat Benatar and Cyndi Lauper. She entered adolescence during the heyday of the women's liberation movement in the early and middle 1970s, and her desires and actions are representative of the pressures brought to bear on gender definitions at the time. The movement's rhetoric called on girls to be career-oriented and to seize equality by pursuing the male vision. But opportunities lagged behind rhetoric and the mixed signals caused considerable conflicts for young women poised at the start of life. The pathway to personal achievement had to be paved from within the confines of female lives.

Madonna recalls discovering at an early age the proven female attention-getting strategy of flirtation: "The power of my femininity and charm, I remember it was just something I had, that I'd been given. . . . From the age of five I remember being able to affect people that way" (Fissinger 1985, p. 34). But pleasing does not ultimately lead to self-development and equal treatment. To achieve as a woman takes the will to violate expectations of female service. As she grew into adolescence, Madonna accepted the role of "bad girl" in an effort to accumulate experiences and focus her yearning for recognition. She rebelled against her father's rule, despite her desire for his attention, and pursued male-adolescent privilege despite its alienating effects on her peers: "Boys didn't understand me, and they didn't like me because I wasn't stupid, and I *was* blunt and opinionated, but I was a flirt at the same time. They took my aggressiveness as a come-on. They didn't get it" (Fissinger 1985, p. 36). Years later, she would equate her treatment by adolescent boys in junior high school with her treatment by press reviewers.

Barred from the leisure activities of her brothers and male-adolescent peers, Madonna adopted dance as her primary mode of expression and took ballet classes regularly. Dance provided a socially accepted mode of channeling her desires for control and pleasure. Dance meets social requirements by making the female body into an object of admiration, but, as Angela McRobbie (1984) has argued, it also produces a number of benefits for girls themselves. The discourse of the prima-ballerina, as represented in fiction designed for girl readers, introduces girls to the idea of career commitment and the hope that rewards and recognition are available to girls who work hard. Madonna credits her dance training with teaching her the discipline needed to handle the rigors of her music and acting careers (Stanton, 1985). As she became successful, she borrowed from the discourse of dance to characterize her achievement for critics and fans, saying, "I had a dream and I worked hard and my dream came true" (Stanton 1985, p. 60).

When Madonna was a girl, the discourse of dance converged with her allegiance to the discourse of pop. Pop ideology was attractive because it provided the fantasy of stardom, a symbolic solution for her female-adolescent craving for recognition. The rhetoric of the women's movement helped instill the sense of possibility and the drive to make over the fantasy into a career direction. Committing to dance was the first available step. But the odds against succeeding in a dance career, and the increasingly restrictive regimen imposed by a classical ballet training program, reportedly led Madonna to consider combining dance with music creation, and to relinquish a four-year dance scholarship after only a year and a half at the University of Michigan in favor of the New York City dance-club scene (Connelly, 1984; Fissinger, 1985).

In New York, Madonna's musical training was first fostered by a boyfriend's garage band. She sang, learned to play guitar and drums, and wrote songs with Dan Gilroy and his brother, who lived and practiced their music in a rented synagogue in Queens. They formed a band together, Breakfast Club, but Madonna was not given the opportunity to sing as much as she wanted, and she soon left the band to start her own. Schooled within a garage band, rock's primary training ground, Madonna sang rock and roll in her new band, aided by black rhythm-and-blues musician Steve Bray, an old boyfriend from Michigan. A manager signed the band, but balked when she began to veer away from rock toward funky, urban (black) dance music. Finally, Madonna quit the deal and, along with Bray, started writing dance music and attending dance clubs at night with demo tape in hand, trying to charm and entice club deejays to play it. She found a willing prospect in Mark Kamins, a respected deejay at the club Danceteria. Kamins played the song and, taking note of the audience's response, helped her produce an improved version. He took it to Sire Records, which offered Madonna a recording contract in 1982[12] (Connelly, 1984; Fissinger, 1985; Bego, 1985).

The string of events in New York before Madonna's "big break" became the subject of much scrutiny in press accounts of her rise to fame. Early articles focused on Madonna's sequential sexual relationships with Gilroy, Bray, and Kamins, the three men who figure in her development stages (Connelly, 1984; Fissinger, 1985; Skow et al., 1985). In a reversal of the ideology of sexual favors, the articles positioned Madonna in the role of an exploiter who sleeps with men as a calculated measure to steal their musical knowledge and contacts. *Rolling Stone's* first cover story on Madonna in 1984, (titled with the sexual innuendo "Madonna Goes All the Way") raised the issue directly: "She's an unqualified success. But did she exploit people to get there?" (Connelly 1984, p. 81). The implied accusation punishes Madonna for her apparent inversion of the female role of service, for putting men in the position of serving her career rather than the other way around. The extent of Madonna's success and the three men's relative lack of success at the time made it difficult to sustain the usual interpretation of women as the vehicle of male talent and control. Instead, it was the men who began to take on the color of victimization as frustrated reviewers lamented the ideological crisis Madonna's ambitious progress created. Madonna herself resisted the efforts to create a new ideological model to deny the value of her accomplishments. *Time* magazine was obliged to convey her feelings on the matter in its 1985 cover story: She resents suggestions that she slept her way to the top . . .

because the idea that she couldn't make it to the top on drive
and ambition alone is insulting (Skow et al. 1985, p. 76).

Rolling Stone's story also examined Madonna's career path
for evidence of her violation of rock discourse. The centerpiece
of the biographical account was her choice of Reggie Lucas,
an experienced producer, to produce her first album, and not
Bray or Kamins. The choice of an experienced producer over
inexperienced ones is the prerogative of a professional, a sign
of Madonna's mature assessment of her needs at the time, yet
because it violated the loyalty imperative of the rock discourse
(as well as the practice of female service to men), the decision
became a point for criticism.

Madonna, in fact, embodies *not* rock discourse, but pop
discourse. Rock's ideology of authenticity demands an absence
of image or, in other terms, correspondence between public
image and personal subjectivity. But image and representation, Pat Benatar's nemeses, are Madonna's playground. She
revels in self-promotion, in the creation of an image or images,
in being a personality, a celebrity. She accepts artifice as an
integral feature of music production and promotion and is
comfortable with textual production. Madonna breaks with
the preferred ideology of rock by equating image-making and
acting, image and character: "For most people, music is a very
personal statement, but I've always liked to have different characters that I project. . . . The problem is, in the public's mind,
you are your image, your musical image, and I think that those
characters are only extensions of me" (Gilmore 1987, p. 87).
Revealing image to be a construction does not entirely dis-
able the capacity of image to function as a personal statement
of the musician's subjectivity. Symbolic practices can yield authentic expressions. Madonna has verified that the characters
she creates spring in part from her own experiences. And it is
her ability to represent gender experience symbolically in the

characters she creates that provides points of identification for a female audience.

Predictably, Madonna's association with pop music was interpreted as an alignment with industry control and was used, at least at the beginning of her career, as an excuse to undermine her authorship. Perhaps the best illustration of how the puppet metaphor circulates in the popular arena has been provided by Madonna herself, who described in an interview how she first encountered it:

> I was making this movie, *Desperately Seeking Susan* [in 1984]. One of the drivers that took me to the set every day was this kid, and one day he said to me, "I have this bet going with my friend, he told me that all the music you do was done by someone else and they picked the songs and did it all, and all they needed was a girl singer and you auditioned and they picked you. And Madonna isn't your real name and all of it is fabricated." And I said, "WHAAAAAATT?? Are you out of your mind??!" But that's what his friend told him, and it suddenly hit me that's probably what a lot of people think. It hit me (Fissinger 1985, p. 36).

Although Madonna's revelry in pop discourse made *Rolling Stone* defensive at first, the magazine did decide to place her photo on the cover of issues in four consecutive years (1984–1987),[13] implementing a shift in attitude toward a reevaluation of pop and the disintegration of the rock/pop dichotomy.

Madonna's image constructions, which she develops in her video promotion, zero in on the most controversial and conflicted images of women: bad girl, virgin, pregnant teen, glamour queen, and stripteaser. There is a sexual edge to all of her "characters" and this, again, resulted initially in the interpretation that Madonna was operating in collusion with the industry and with patriarchal ideology to reproduce the standard of female representation. But gradually, Madonna's manipulation and critique of the codes of female representation began to be acknowledged in the press, having already been recognized by female audiences. Her appropriation and resignification of the standard of female representation was a fundamental upset to the standard's ability to function as a strategy to thwart female musician authorship and subjectivity. The story of Madonna's exercise of creative control over her own representation began to be a subject of discussion in feature articles, and the discovery of her authorship over her image(s) eroded the tendency to portray her as a puppet of commercial manipulation.

By laying claim to symbolic self-determination, Madonna prompted a backlash, a reassertion of patriarchal entitlement to modes of female representation. The publicity industry proved to be its messenger, reacting to her assertions of control over representation by stalking her in an attempt to take unauthorized photographs. Madonna herself has equated the unsolicited picture-taking with male acts of aggression against women, with the violation of her body, and seems to appreciate the ideological stakes that are at issue:

> It's not even the taking of pictures that bothers me, it's the element of surprise I always encounter every time they jump out of the bushes or jump from behind a corner. . . . They're always scaring me. . . . Every time they jump out to take a picture, the way they take them—it's like they're raping me (Stanton 1985, p. 63).

When nude photographs of Madonna (taken when she was modeling for artists to support herself in New York) were published by *Playboy* and *Penthouse* in September 1985, it was her lack of control over the situation that Madonna found most disturbing: "The thing that annoyed me most wasn't so much that they were nude photographs but that I felt really out of control—for the first time in what I thought to be several years of careful planning and knowing what was going to happen" (Schruers 1986, p. 60).

Madonna entered the music business with definite ideas about her image, but it was her track record that enabled her to increase her level of creative control over her music. By negotiating authorship through informal collaborations, she was gradually able to parlay unofficial collaborative liaisons into a sanctioned credit as producer:

> On my first album, the demos we made were not as close simply because I didn't have as much direct involvement with the production of my album. I didn't know enough to speak out. It wasn't until my first album [*Madonna*] was three-quarters of the way done that I realized, hey! I know a lot more about this than I'm allowing myself to speak out about. So I started going backward and stripping the songs down and making them more sparse. Until then they'd been layered with a lot of stuff. Then when we got into the second album [*Like a Virgin*], I had a lot more confidence in myself and I had a lot more to do with the way it came out soundwise. I really worked side by side with Nile Rodgers. . . . Nile was very open with me, he gave me the feeling we really were collaborating and I felt free to say what I wanted (Stanton 1985, p. 66).

By her third album, *True Blue*, the reports place Madonna more firmly in control. Bray, her collaborator on a number of songs, is quoted at the studio during the production of the album: "If you just talk in the hallway for more than twenty seconds, you hear, 'You guys! Get in here'" (Schruers 1986, p. 60). Pat Leonard, with whom Madonna writes and produces, describes the confidence and daring in her musical decision-making: "We'll do something and I'll say, 'Let's go to the next chorus and repeat it,' and she goes, 'Why? Where do these rules come from? Who made up these rules?'" Leonard applauds her musical sensibilities: "If you listen to what she says, it instantly becomes a 'Madonna' record—her instincts

just turn it into that, no matter what producer she's working with" (Schruers 1986, p. 60). Madonna's proven ability
to create songs that become hits has facilitated her involvement with record producing and promotion. It has enabled
her to negotiate authorship in the form of official credit for her
album sound (the producer credit), to penetrate the discourse
of rock, and to be treated by the music press as an author.

SIX

FEMALE-ADDRESS VIDEO (1980–1986)

FEMALE ADDRESS emerged on MTV in the form of female-musician videos designed to speak to and resonate with female cultural experiences of adolescence and gender. Two interrelated sign systems developed as the textual practice of female address; I have defined them as (1) *Access Signs*, and (2) *Discovery Signs*.[1] *Access Signs* are those in which the privileged experiences of boys and men are visually appropriated. The female musicians appearing in the videos textually enact entrance into a male domain of activity and signification. Symbolically, they execute take-overs of male space, effect the erasure of sex roles, and make demands for parity with male-adolescent privilege. They rework the ideological stance of male privilege into a redress of grievances for girls by appropriating the richness of signification that the image of "the street" holds for boys and men. In this way, female-address videos challenge the gender assumptions at work in MTV's preferred male discourse. *Discovery Signs* refer to and celebrate distinctly female modes of cultural expression and experience. These signs attempt to compensate for the devaluation and trivialization of female-cultural experience by presenting images of activities that are shared by girls alone. By representing "girl culture," the videos set a tone that celebrates female resource-fulness and cultural distinctiveness. The enjoyment of clothing and distinctive personal style is reclaimed for girls and articulated richly as a symbolic vehicle of female expression. Modes of female-adolescent fun and leisure and girls' peer associations are enacted visually, as are female methods for creatively negotiating the specific difficulties that are a result of being female at the time of adolescence.

The coexistence of access and discovery signs in female-address videos creates a complex political text for audiences to consider. Access signs argue for equal rights and recognition for women and girls by invoking images of sex-role reversals and gender utopias. Discovery signs, which rejoice in female forms of leisure and cultural expression, and female sources of social bonding, attest to the value of women's culture, particularly culture as defined by female adolescents. Girls in the audience are encouraged to understand that access to the privileged realm of male cultural experience and representation is partly a matter of discovering their own cultural agency.

The textual analyses presented below are organized along a timeline to accent their historical, emergent quality. Twenty videos are examined; all are from the period before and after the coalescence of female address in 1983, and they constitute most of the videos produced through 1986 to promote the four female musicians under study. Two Pat Benatar videos are discussed first. Produced just prior to MTV's start date, they typify the mode of female-musician promotion before the emergence of female address.

1980–1981: Before MTV
You Better Run; I'm Gonna Follow You

Pat Benatar's video repertoire reads like a history book of music-video representation and, significantly for this chapter's concern, reveals the emergence of a female-address sensibility. Benatar's first video, *You Better Run* (1980), and her second (released in quick succession), *I'm Gonna Follow You* (1980), had yet to benefit from the formal innovations of MTV, but do depend textually on a formula of male address to present their female performer. *You Better Run*, a performance video, features the band playing their instruments under the gaze of wildly active cameras, but the major attraction is the female singer, Benatar herself. The camera leers at the vocalist, as if demanding a performance from her. Benatar compliantly pouts and shakes for the camera, frequently touching her hair and body. There is a hard and defiant edge to her presentation, yet the performance seems geared primarily to the male spectator. While the sign system of male address that MTV would help conventionalize is not yet in place, codes of female representation from art portraiture, television, and cinema are evident in the video. Seven years after shooting the video, Benatar recalled vividly the direction she received, and how it determined her representation:

> We were dancing and we were starting to tape and [the director] says to me, "Come on, I want you to get out there and shake your ass, I want you to be *hot*." And I went, like "fuck off," and so the attitude that comes across on the video isn't . . . it has nothing to do with what I'm doing. It has to do with the anger at this human being who had infuriated me *so much*. And, hey it's tough shit. They're spending $150,000, baby, you better shoot (Benatar, 1987).

At this early point in her career, Benatar had not yet built the successful track record that would enable her later to select the directors of her videos and decide the mode of her visual representation.

I'm Gonna Follow You moves away from rock documentary conventions by eliminating shots of Benatar's band and featuring her alone in stylized settings. Significantly, it adopts the street as its primary interpretive motif, following the lead of lyrics such as, "You don't know these streets like I do." In so doing, it foreshadows MTV's use of the street as a central meaning system and its subsequent appropriation by female-address videos. But *I'm Gonna Follow You* had not discovered narrative and formal devices for integrating social context into its visual statement, nor was it concerned with constructing a "woman-identified" system of address.[2] Benatar is photographed alone, posing passively in a sequence of street locations. The image of the street does not offer any particular understanding of her character or her condition, nor does it substantiate the lyrical assertion that she "knows these streets." Her frequent changes of clothing contribute primarily to the impression of a passive model's pose, not to a stylistic statement that supports a message.

1982–1983: Emergence
Shadows of the Night; Lipstick Lies; She Works Hard for the Money

Two later Benatar videos, *Shadows of the Night* (1982) and *Lipstick Lies* (1983), come closer to the vision of female address and can be considered to be early versions. Neither video addresses directly the female *adolescent* viewer, but both tend instead to focus on representations of adult working-class women. *Shadows of the Night* asserts a stance of access from its beginning, placing Benatar in the role of a "Rosie the Riveter" character from the days of World War II, who fantasizes about direct and heroic (male) forms of participating in the war—namely, clandestine military action. Formally, the video presents Benatar as a character rather than a musical performer, allowing for the construction of context through the addition of narrative and the logic of character development. At the video's start, Benatar's "Rosie" is shown at work, cutting machine parts in a factory that has an all-female workforce. Gazing at a poster of the fighter plane that she is presumably working on, the reality of her repetitive work gives way to fantasy. She transforms herself into a fighter pilot who is receiving, along with her male cohorts, instructions for a special mission to sabotage Nazi war plans. What follows is a miniature war movie in which Benatar acts as the heroic protagonist.

As we have seen in Michael Jackson's video *Beat It*, the sign system of the street encompasses male competitiveness and paramilitary organization (gangs)—qualities and formations that are precursory to adult-male roles of soldiering and military leadership. In its representation of war *Shadows of the Night* alludes to one logical extension of the sign system of the street: military service. The video's nostalgic World War II plot and the exaggerated romanticism of the female protagonist's heroic actions place in the foreground the way in which war movies represent male heroism, an empowering representation that Benatar's character seeks to appropriate.

After receiving instructions, the fighter pilots fly off in their planes and land in German territory. Covertly, they enter Nazi war headquarters and plant several sticks of wired dynamite. While making their escape they are discovered, and the Nazis give chase, but too late to prevent the aviators' retreat into the air. The Nazis pursue them in another airplane, and in an exchange of fire that makes use of newsreel footage, the German plane is destroyed by the Benatar commandos. Back at Nazi headquarters, the Nazis act out their exasperation in a comical tongue-in-cheek style, just a few feet from the ticking bomb. Moments later, their fortress explodes, and Benatar and her fellow pilots make a successful escape, fully victorious. At that instant, the adventure story dissolves back to Benatar's "Rosie," who repeats her manufacturing task until the video fades to black.

Access signs are articulated elaborately by the adventure story's appropriation of the right of women to participate experientially, psychologically, and representationally in the heroic actions reserved for men. The use of the "Rosie the Riveter" characterization recalls a significant moment in women's labor history, when many homebound women were tapped to join a predominantly male labor force, but the accompanying fantasy sequence exposes the marginalized role such work represented ideologically. Glory lies in the consumption and use of military equipment, not in its production. The close adherence to classical Hollywood cinema conventions in the video's fantasy sequence references the romantic image that has been created for male war adventures. By presenting a female character as the heroic protagonist, the segment breaks with the "rules" of female representation and opens a space for stories of female adventuring. Discovery signs that tap into female sensibilities and activities are developed more subtly. Utopian fantasy is drawn on as a female source of pleasure and a means for presenting scenarios that illustrate both problems and their solutions. The fantasy framing device used in *Shadows of the Night* is used with more potency in the pivotal *Love Is a Battlefield* video, as the runaway teenage girl (played by Benatar) imagines a world in which girls and women move freely without fear of harassment and have the power to avenge gender inequity.

The video *Lipstick Lies* is also organized around the issue of female fantasy and desire. Again, Benatar plays a factory girl, a modern day "Rosie the Riveter," continuing the theme of female working-class experience. At the end of a long workday, the factory girl chums around with other female workers, drinking beer and playing pinball in scenes that combine access signs of male leisure activity with discovery signs of female friendship. The video's representation of females engaged in male leisure activities and peer camaraderie is important because it reverses the codes of male adolescence. The video's main action revolves around the Benatar character's attempts to resolve her need to escape her working-class tedium and consummate her desire for upward mobility by leading a secret life after work. The video steals a narrative fragment from the movie *Flashdance* (itself precursory to female address in certain aspects) in which a handsome boss from a higher social class lusts after a female worker from afar. In *Flashdance*, the girl strives for upward mobility by turning her passion for dance into a position with a recognized ballet company, eventually winning her boss on his own (class-determined) terms. In *Lipstick Lies*, however, Benatar's character attempts to effect the class cross-over through alterations in her style and appearance, guided by her fascination with fashion models, whose portraits she cuts from magazines and hangs on her walls. The references to fashion approach the discovery signs of later female-address videos, but are far less celebratory. The video's juxtaposition of the song's lyrics, "lipstick lies" and "a victim of your fantasy," provide vague admonishments instead against the tactic of style manipulation. Within the video's narrative, the girl's dress-up activities do facilitate (for a while) her movement within the world of the upper class. But at the video's end a reversal unites the factory girl with a boy from her own class who shares her fantasies, and who has himself been masquerading in a tuxedo, believing her to be a member of the elite class.

The video's representation of stylistic affectation explores the way in which female style manipulations are tied to dissatisfaction with the material conditions of female lives and begins to suggest how style might be a useful tool to effect change. But this effort is undercut somewhat by the class-mobility theme. The protagonist's efforts to rise above her class position by "passing for rich" is predicated on her ability to attract a male benefactor, the classic female ploy of "marrying up." The video's resolution, in which she falls in love with a boy from her own class, marks her effort as a failure, and reveals the ineffectuality of female tactics. The storyline allows the boy (who has also attempted to use style as a vehicle of class mobility) access to the female discovery sign of style manipulation, further interfering with its ability to speak for women. Overall, the video's connection of female style affectation and class mobility proves to be a far less powerful combination than the linkage that would be made between style and gender inequality by female-address videos the following year.

One more early version of female address that bears mentioning is Donna Summer's *She Works Hard for the Money* (1982), which falls into line with the early Benatar video representations of female working-class experience. The video traces the daily routine of a single mother as she struggles through four jobs—scrub woman at an office building, waitress at a diner, seamstress in a factory sweatshop, and mother of two children. The zealous repetition of female labor on the screen is accompanied by a fantasy sequence in which the protagonist's lifelong ambition to be a dancer is revealed. Its strategic placement in a scene with her two unruly children clarifies the context of her failure to fulfill the goal as a sacrifice made for love and family. The woman, played by an actress and not by Summer herself, fantasizes about dancing, not as a route to upward mobility (the *Flashdance* version), but as an expression of bodily pleasure and artistic ability, and a sign of adolescent ambitions abandoned prematurely. In response to her day of "hard work," she allows herself the indulgence of retreating to the daydream of dancing.

The fantasy provides the opportunity for the video to formulate a conclusion that integrates both discovery and access signs. In the last sequence, the protagonist takes to a city boulevard as the dancer of her dreams and is quickly joined by a cadre of dancing women dressed in uniforms that denote a variety of traditionally female work classifications. A high angle shot shows the women literally taking up a city block, all the while stretching out their arms for more space. The choreography, like that which will appear later in Benatar's *Love Is a Battlefield*, includes aggressive chest and hip thrusts that mock the male spectator like a tribal dance of insult. *She Works Hard for the Money* constructs discovery signs from the representation of female fantasy and pleasure, and integrates them with a call for access through the symbolic vehicle of the street, a melding that becomes a standard device in female-address video.

1983: Coalescence
Girls Just Want to Have Fun;
Love Is a Battlefield

The year 1983 marks a watershed in the history of female-address video. It is the year that certain issues and representations began to gain saliency and the textual strategies of female address began to coalesce. The popularity of two videos in particular, *Girls Just Want to Have Fun* (Cyndi Lauper) and *Love Is a Battlefield* (Pat Benatar), set the stage for textual permutations in subsequent years. Both videos play to a female-adolescent target audience by representing the problems and desires of girls, both appropriate strategically the image of the street and use dance as their symbolic mode of protest, and both locate solutions in portrayals of female camaraderie and action.

In *Girls Just Want to Have Fun*, "fun" is articulated as an expansive and politicized concept for girls. Fun is defined visually both in terms of doing what boys do—getting out of the house (and housework) and onto the street—and in terms of the kinds of activities and relationships girls devise in their attempts to create a complementary order of female fun. By including images of female roles and labor, the video exposes the socially constructed limitations placed on girls who want to have fun. What is clearly *not* fun, the video suggests, is assuming the duties of mother and housewife. As the video opens, Lauper's character is shown bounding home one morning after apparently staying out all night. Upon entering the house, she finds her mother (played by Lauper's own mother) hard at work preparing food in the kitchen. The lyric, "When you gonna live your life right?" speaks for the mother. Her distress over her daughter's flagrant disregard for appropriate feminine behavior is expressed as she breaks an egg over her heart. The emphasis is on the social expectations placed upon female adolescents, and on the assumptions that underlie the category of "problem girl." The tiff between mother and daughter illustrates generational differences in opportunities for leisure, while at the same time aligning woman and girl under the same social system of gender. The Lauper character's disobedience expands to outright defiance of her father's rule. Lou Albano, the burly ex-wrestler who plays Lauper's father, speaks the lyric, "What you gonna do with your life?" as Lauper is shown pinning his arm behind his back in a wrestling maneuver. The video takes advantage of the formal device in music videos whereby a lyrical phrase is lip-synched as if it were dialogue. The father's scolding voice is replaced with the daughter's voice in order to parody and undermine the father's authority and (by symbolic extension) patriarchy itself.

The bouncing Lauper exits her home to lead a band of her girlfriends through New York City streets in a frenzied snake dance that turns women's experience of foreboding streets upside-down in a carnival-like display. Their arms reaching out for more and more space, the women push through a group of male construction workers who function as symbols of female harassment on the street. The image of men cowering in the wake of the girls' dance epitomizes female fantasies of streets without danger or fear, and girls' desire for an unmitigated release from socially imposed restrictions on female physical behavior. Lauper's kinetic body movements frustrate the voyeur's gaze. Her choreographed performance fills the frame, gyrating arms and legs stealing space away from the men. The lyrical refrain, "Girls just want to have fun," acts as a powerful cry for access to the privileged realm of male-adolescent leisure and fun.

Discovery signs are articulated as Lauper and her girlfriends chat on the phone in photographic shots of luxuriously long duration. The shots celebrate a girl leisure practice that is usually ridiculed as a mindless activity. The video also summons up the pleasure that many girls find in choreographed movement with a shot of Lauper and friends in a line, swaying rhythmically to the music and wrapped in each other's arms. Dance is the mode through which Lauper and her female followers accomplish their symbolic take-back of the street. At the video's end, the threat posed by the men on the street is alleviated, and the girls bring the men back to the Lauper character's home to experience female fun: dancing with wild abandon to records in the bedroom.

Lauper's stylistic affectations add significantly to the video's address. Her display of odd color combinations in dress and hair, her gaudy fake jewelry and application of striped and sequined eye make-up mock socially appropriate modes of female attire and behavior. Her look presents a rebellious, antifeminine, "She's so unusual" image suggestive of what Barbara Hudson (1984) has described as a creative strategy some girls adopt to ally themselves with (male) adolescent discourse. Enacting an antifeminine style of appearance, Hudson (1984) argues, is one way girls attempt to counter the femininity discourse, the set of expectations that attempts to restrict girls' behavior and choices at the time of adolescence. It is this sense of bucking the norm that *Ms.* magazine applauded in Lauper by awarding her a "Woman of the Year" citation in 1985, characterizing her rebellious style as a feminist stance (Hornaday, 1985).

Benatar's *Love Is a Battlefield* video (1983) also turns the street motif into a celebration of sisterhood, openly representing a symbolic takeover of male patriarchal privilege. Like Lauper, Benatar plays a teenager who is on bad terms with her parents. Cast out of the house by her angry father, she settles back into a fantasy sequence that speaks directly to the experience of women in public space, the state of relationships between the sexes, and the desire for closer contact with women. As a homeless female teenager on the street, Benatar's character is confronted by male harassment and threats. Tension is created between the coded image of the prostitute and the representation of ordinary women's experience of walking alone on the street. Because the girl who Benatar portrays remains unassociated with the activities of male-adolescent street culture, she is associated with prostitution. The visual images comment directly on this suspicion by intercutting Benatar walking on the street at night with neon signs from storefronts advertising adult peep shows, "Girls, Girls, Girls." As the video unfolds, the street is recovered as a site for female camaraderie and displays of female style, redirecting expectations.

Benatar's character ends up in a bar, a representation of male space. She appears as one of several women, slow-dancing like a zombie, her head turned away from her various male partners in utter boredom, her absolute lack of pleasure is apparent. The turning point in the video is marked by the scream of a woman who is being physically reprimanded by her pimp. Her voice, unconventionally laid over the musical soundtrack, shrieks, "Leave me alone!" Thus, the call to access begins. As lyrics sung by Benatar are heard, "We are strong, no one can tell us we're wrong," Benatar and the other women in the bar burst forth with aggressive chest thrusts and kicks, forcing the pimp back against the bar. Dance becomes a symbolic vehicle for female militancy. Choreographed jabs and kicks combine a wild sexual energy with self-defense moves to mock and threaten the pimp figure. Benatar splashes a drink violently in the pimp's face, a moment that is formally prioritized by the addition of a sound effect. The bar sequence is reminiscent of Shirley Ardener's account of a ritual performed by the Bakweri women in Africa when a culturally specific insult against a woman is perpetrated by a male member of the tribe:

> Converging again upon the offender, [the women] demand immediate recantation and a recompense. . . . The culprit will be brought forward, and the charges laid. . . . The women then surround him and sing songs accompanied by obscene gestures. . . . Finally the women retire victoriously to divide [a] pig among themselves (Ardener 1975, p. 30).

The confrontation culminates as Benatar and her female companions retreat to the street to demonstrate their solidarity and celebrate their defeat of the male ego. Benatar turns and saunters down the street, at last its rightful owner.

1984: Continuity and Expansion
Borderline; Lucky Star; Like a Virgin; What's Love Got to Do with It?; Private Dancer; Time After Time; She Bop

In 1984, Madonna and Tina Turner videos began to appear on MTV. Madonna's youth made her an ideal candidate to expand on the female-adolescent address evident in the Lauper and Benatar videos of the previous year. Turner's age, race, prior music career, and publicized life experiences provided complexities that enabled her to speak for a more diverse female population.

Madonna's first major video, *Borderline* (1984), following

Lauper's lead, turned representations of adolescent leisure practice into an arena for gender politics. Ambitiously, it exploited MTV's formal innovations by knitting together many narrative fragments to constitute its whole. The technique served the female-address stance by providing a look at the contradictory and multiple experiences girls encounter. Madonna plays a rambunctious teenager immersed in male street-corner culture. She is shown street dancing, spraying graffiti on urban walls, and loitering on a street corner with female peers. She blows kisses and initiates flirtations with street boys, and leads her girlfriends into the male turf of the pool hall. In short, she appropriates activities and spaces typically associated with male adolescence. Many of the activities in which she engages place her squarely in the role of male-adolescent delinquency. She defaces public and private property, loiters in "bad neighborhoods," and hangs out in the pool hall. Such images confuse the iconography of the prostitute that is suggested by her street-corner lingering and flirtation and obviate the different social standards for male and female adolescent transgressions. Building a tension between the two implicitly questions how the code of prostitution is elaborated and possible ways to revise representations of women and girls on the street. Another narrative fragment identifies part of the problem of access as being the male-adolescent response to girls. A romantic involvement is suggested between Madonna and one of the street boys. When she is alone with him, away from his friends, away from "his" domain of the street, the boy is open and intimate with the girl. The visuals reinforce the couple's distance from the street and all it represents by placing the lovers on a rooftop. But later, on the street corner, in full assertion of her right to participate in male leisure culture, the girl approaches him and his friends outside the pool hall. Suddenly, he is coy and feigns indifference.

The video moves into discovery signs in its presentation

of the female fantasy of becoming a fashion model. A fashion photographer, during the first street dance scene, "discovers" the character played by Madonna. The girl participates in the excitement and pleasure of wearing glamourous clothes and make-up until the male photographer begins to assert his authority over her "look." Defiantly, she grabs back the hat he does not want her to wear. Desiring to manage her own image, she leaves the studio and returns to participate with boys in street culture. She finds her boyfriend has undergone a change of attitude. In the video's final shot, he is shown teaching her to play pool, helping her to achieve access to his world.

Madonna's other videos from 1984, *Lucky Star* and *Like a Virgin*, rely on style and gesture rather than plot devices to construct her image and ongoing character logic. The style of Madonna's appearance, her "look," is made to tell many stories. Most significant in these two videos is the mode of dance, costuming, hair style, and make-up, which work to develop a signature Madonna style that would be replicated by her female fans. Madonna's skin-tight lacey undergarments and her crucifixes, her casual (yet calculated) use of wedding attire add up to a blasphemous "bad girl" affectation, particularly when worn by a woman who, as told in the promotional press, hated the uniforms at her Catholic school. She combines contradictory accoutrements of a feminine presentation with the affected attitude of a cinematic vamp. Her bleached blonde hair proudly displays its dark roots, self-consciously referencing the artifice of her visual representation.

The look provides the flip side to Lauper's politic of style. Madonna's visual image engages with and extravagantly exaggerates the discourse of femininity, enacting what Hudson (1984) asserts is another tactic girls use to undermine the discourse of femininity. At least part of the appeal of Madonna's overtly sexual image for adolescent girls lies in the way it can be used to counter feminine ideals of dependency and reserve.

Whereas behaviors and styles associated with the discourse of adolescence may be accepted as a "phase" or "status a teenager is moving out of," signs that feminine values are not being incorporated are far more threatening because "femininity is what a girl is supposed to be acquiring" (Hudson 1984, p. 44). Often admonished by feminist critics for making a sexual spectacle of herself, Madonna's "slut" affectation is in actuality marred by the indifference she projects toward men and the self-assurance she displays as an image of her own creation. The wild and sensual dancing she performs in many of her videos operates along the same lines, breaking with the socially mandated reserve over body movement and becoming a key sign of her allegiance to girl culture. Her alternation of choreographed moves and improvisational dance (dancing with "abandon") touches on two popular forms of dance pleasure for girls.

Tina Turner enacts signs of access in the video *What's Love Got to Do with It?* (1984) by taking a long, slow walk down a New York City street. Unlike the Lauper and Benatar videos from 1983, Turner's does not amass a group of women or girls for a final scene of male-space appropriation. It is as if this has already happened. Rather, the video picks up where *Love Is a Battlefield* ends; Turner is alone on the street from the beginning, already at one with it. Proceeding down the avenue, she encounters the gaze of a male onlooker. Far from averting her eyes, Turner matches his gaze with one of her own, and they circle momentarily in an equal exchange of looking. She comes across a group of men shooting craps on the sidewalk, a representation of male street-corner culture. Pushing them aside, she recalls a similar action by Lauper in *Girls Just Want to Have Fun*. Magically, Turner has acquired the status and power to transcend the female experience of dangerous streets. A shot of girls doing the "double dutch" jump-rope pattern, textually complements the shot of men shooting craps, thus creating a discovery sign.

In *What's Love Got to Do with It?*, Turner challenges the prostitute code head on. Strutting down the street, her mini-skirt, show of leg, and spiked-heeled shoes could operate to code her as a spectacle of male desire. Instead, the image she projects struggles for a different signification. It's easier to imagine the spikes as an offensive weapon than as a sexual lure or allusion to her vulnerability. Turner's control over her own body and interactions with others in the video, particularly with men, encourages a revaluation of her revealing clothes and high heels from indices of her objectification to signs of her pleasure in herself.

Turner's second video, *Private Dancer*, also released in 1984, falls outside the female-address pattern of combining access and discovery signs, although it symbolically represents female experience in its presentation of victimization and alienation from men. The video recreates dance halls of the past in which soldiers, sailors, and other unescorted men could rent female dance partners for a nominal sum. Turner and the other women look much like Benatar and her companions in the bar scene of *Love Is a Battlefield* before they are prompted to action. Mechanically, the dancers in the Turner video go through the motions of dance without the slightest expression of emotion or desire. In *Private Dancer* the allusion to prostitution is even stronger; money is openly exchanged between the dance partners. But unlike *Love Is a Battlefield*, no cathartic upheaval redirects the vision. There is no take-over scene, no reclaiming of dance for women. The video is concerned with representing victimization rather than showing its triumphant demise. In the final scene, Turner's character, after prolonged suffering, simply leaves her male dance partner, having reached her fill of being the victim. Metaphorically, the scene matches Tina

Turner's departure from Ike Turner, thus contributing to the autobiographical stance assumed generally in her comeback promotion.

Following up on the success of *Girls Just Want to Have Fun*, Lauper's record company released two videos in 1984, both based on female-address themes: *Time after Time* and *She Bop*. *Time after Time* is a visual interpretation of the ballad that Lauper and Rick Chertoff wrote about their impression of the impact sex-role changes were having on romantic relationships. The opening scene finds Lauper immersed in the narrative of a televised movie romance. "I've made up my mind, I'm going away," says the male character. The female lead answers, "Then I shall be alone." The cinematic representation foreshadows, even appears to provoke, the story the video will tell. Contrary to the male lead's initiative to leave the woman in the film sequence, it is Lauper's character who leaves her male lover behind at the video's end. The motivation for the Lauper character's action is drawn visually through a series of flashback sequences that juggle narrative time to portray the girl's early relationship with her lover (played by Dave Wolff) and her mother, the second pivotal character in the video (played by Lauper's own mother).

Time shifts are negotiated through Lauper's costume changes and, significantly, through changes in her hair style. In fact, Lauper's bright orange–tinted hair, which her female fans imitate, assumes a plot function in the video's narrative, symbolizing the change the girl undergoes as she focuses her ambitions, and signaling the dissolution of her relationship with her lover. In the first flashback scene, Lauper, as the female protagonist, appears in a dowdy gray wig. The girl's lover arrives at the store where she works, and in a visual enactment of a marriage proposal, hands her a child's lunchbox painted with a picture of a bride and groom. Consistent with the childish (ideological) vision of romantic bliss, they set up house in an old aluminum trailor, but the relationship soon sours as the girl undergoes a fundamental change in perspective. As the lyric, "You're walking too far ahead," is heard over the soundtrack, she joins her lover and his friend in a neighborhood diner, dressed in the outlandish clothes that have become Lauper's signature. Taking off her hat, she reveals her new asymmetrical hairstyle. Outraged, the boy raises his arm as if to strike her and she runs outside, taking cover in a storefront alcove. A video effect brings her face-to-face with the image of her mother, who is absorbed in the task of sweeping the floor. It is as if the girl is reflecting on the female condition, relating it to the demise of her own romantic vision. A dissolve returns Lauper's character to the kitchen of her youth. The love she feels for her mother is illustrated through shots of them whispering secrets and sharing hugs. The video constructs an emotional moment as Lauper lip-synchs to her mother, "If you fall I will catch you," demonstrating her intense lifelong commitment to her mother in a scene that operates both narratively and autobiographically.

Access signs revolve around the girl's initiative to leave her home and her lover. Defying the movie representation at the video's beginning, it is the girl who resolves to leave the boy behind, the female protagonist who looks to enter the vast public space beyond the domestic arena. Discovery signs function to catalyze her decision. Changes in style and appearance are precursory to changes in lifestyle and consciousness. Her identification with her mother and their unconditional love propels her to search for alternatives in her own life.

Lauper's second video of 1984, *She Bop*, presents a hilarious visual rendition of the song that the Parents' Music Resource Center (PMRC) placed on its "hit list" because of its allusions to female masturbation (The Women Behind the Movement, 1985). In the video, Lauper assumes the traditionally male role of voyeur, leafing through pages of male bodybuilders in *"Beef-*

cake magazine." Her "beefcake" is a motorcycle rider (played by Wolff), but her interest in him is diverted by her fascination with the vibrating body of his motorbike. In a scenario ironically suggestive of female attitudes toward sexual pleasure, man is replaced by machine. In a female-address comedy routine, Lauper can't keep her hands off the "vibrator." Reaching across the rider, she grabs the motorcycle's handle and revs the motor. The scene cuts to a game-show set where Lauper is shown winning handily at "Uncle Siggy's [Sigmund Freud] Masterbingo," her sexual arousal and climax portrayed as a bingo game—a masterful metaphor for female sexuality.

The video narrative is not without its complication. Lauper's preoccupation with the vibrating machine elicits the wrath of a "S.W.A.T. team" (Suburban Wives Against Transgressions), who arrive in an army jeep, wearing combat helmets wrapped in pink hair curlers, wielding rolling pins and pineapples as their weapons, and prepared to hunt down Lauper and bring her to justice. The scene dissolves into an animated chase sequence with the S.W.A.T. team hot on the heels of the "beefcake's" motorcycle, in which Lauper rides the sidecar. Out of gasoline, the biker stops at a service station to refill, a moment that allows the video the opportunity to elaborate further resonances with female sexuality. The biker pulls up to the "full service" machines and inserts the phallic nozzle of the pump into the bike's body. In contrast, Lauper gazes longingly at the "self-service" island and the three pumps that read, "Good," "Better," and "Nirvana." They set off again, but the enlarged, collective arm of S.W.A.T. plucks Lauper from the bike (and the animation sequence) and presents her to the police magistrate, "The Big Bopper." As the lyrics assert, "No, I won't worry, and I won't fret—ain't no law against it yet," Lauper raises her arms and breaks free from the chains that bind her. The last scene, all bright and white, is more ambiguous. It features Lauper and Wolff in sunglasses (allusion to the admonition against masturbation, "You'll go blind."), dancing with a top hat and cane (a male dance style) as they ascend a grand staircase and leave the photographic frame (allowed entrance to heaven after all—masturbation is *not* a sin). The video's comic and heavily symbolic rendition of the social regulation of female sexuality and female choice allows MTV to air the risky commentary, but only because the development of female address in previous years had paved the way.

1985: Self-Reflection
Material Girl; Sex as a Weapon

In 1985, Sire Records financed video promotion for the release of Madonna's single, "Material Girl," from her second album, *Like a Virgin*. The video works on a number of different interpretive levels, and its complexity allows for broad audience appeal while maintaining the focus on female address. Its subject matter raises issues and problems related to creative authorship, stardom, text and image construction, and interpretation, making it particularly analogous to Madonna's specific situation as a burgeoning star. In fact, there are several ways the video's content can be said to form a response to criticisms of Madonna made by the press and certain segments of the public during the period of its production.

The majority of screen time in the video is given over to a performance sequence in which Madonna sings "Material Girl" while replicating the staging of Marilyn Monroe's musical number "Diamonds Are a Girl's Best Friend" from the movie *Gentlemen Prefer Blondes*. Lessons in textual construction and authorship arise from the video's creation of a fictional scenario about the act of producing the performance sequence. In the opening scene, two men view and discuss the "dailies" from the performance shoot. Their roles in the production remain ambiguous, although by talking about the director they reveal that neither one of them operates in that capacity. The absence of the director from the screening room makes textual authorship itself a point of ambiguity and raises the possibility that the star is in control of her representation. The one man says to the other in exaggerated "Hollywood-ese", "The director's hot, he's hip, he's here. He's going to be doing all kinds of things. He's going to change the color of the set." But the expendability of the director has already been alluded to by the pre-existence of the performance footage, and this is reinforced by the other man's reply, "Don't change a thing! . . . I want to meet her." His emphatic statement suggests that he is the producer of the film, someone in a position of power, but this does not detract from his deference to the star as author, nor is it meant to raise the issue of his authority. Instead, his comments function to establish him as the romantic lead of the narrative. The implied creative impotence of the unseen male director becomes a gender-specific joke for fans (and scholars) who are aware that the video was directed by a woman, Mary Lambert.

The performance sequence is designated as fictional, and its performer made into a character, through narrative fragments that tell the story of the young female star of the performance footage (played by Madonna). The narrative traces how the girl's textual persona, her image, determines how she is treated by male admirers in her offscreen life. Onscreen, performing as the "Material Girl," she acts out a desire for conspicuous consumption and adopts an anti-romantic stance by asserting that men's cash holdings are to be prized over and above their sincere affection. The girl's suitors in real life, believing her image to be a reflection of her true personality, try to impress her with expensive gifts. The narrative demonstrates their mistake by showing us that the girl is really attracted to simpler pleasures—to love, not money.

A discovery sign communicates the information most crucial to the storyline, the difference between the young star's image and her actual identity. In a (synch-sound) telephone conversation with a girlfriend, the girl reveals her displeasure with boys who buy her expensive objects, mistakenly thinking she must want what the "Material Girl" wants. She updates her friend on the latest antics of a male suitor who is "still after [her]," turning the details of his courtship into pieces of telephone gossip. "He thinks he can impress me with expensive gifts," she explains, fingering the diamond necklace he has given her. The girl even offers the necklace to her girl-friend: "It's nice. Do you want it?" This gesture affirms for the audience the girls' connection and the sincerity of the Madonna character's desire for simple expressions of love. The conversation is overheard by the "producer," who despite his knowledge of the textual construction process also believes in the star's textual persona. He has been waiting outside her dressing room door with his own expensive gift, but having been enlightened by the girl's chatter about her requirements in a suitor, he throws his gift away and opts instead for a simple bouquet of daisies, which "wins" her at the video's end.

Significantly, the star is misunderstood by boys, but not by girls. A girlfriend offers her the only real instance of connection and understanding. The video leaves open the possibility that the girl's male suitors are actually *misinterpreting* her textual address, unable to recognize that it is a symbolic description of how she is treated and objectified by men. There is sufficient ambiguity built into the narrative to suggest that what is at issue is *not* the existence of a complete opposition between the girl's image and her identity, but the narrow, literal interpretation of the girl's textual address by male critics and male audience members.

The video works to counter two prominent criticisms of Madonna made in *Rolling Stone*'s 1984 cover story: first, that her image violates the ideology of authenticity; and second, that she exploited men to attain her career position (Connelly, 1984). By dwelling on the textual construction process, and the differences between textuality and reality, *Material Girl* creates a corollary to the ideology of authenticity. It operates in the ambiguous spaces between image and identity, representation and interpretation to illustrate Madonna's own position on composing textual personas: "Those characters are only *Extensions* of me" (Gilmore 1987, p. 87). The performance number's anti-romance stance, its attitude toward men, appropriates the accusation that Madonna is an exploiter of men and uses it as a sign of female access to male sources of power—wealth, recognition, and privilege. By referencing the legend of Marilyn Monroe, the appropriation is turned into an opportunity to reflect on the actual historical role of men in the careers of female culture producers—the role of enforcer and guardian of gender inequality.

Monroe enters the field of meaning as a historical, popular-culture figure who was victimized by her star image and the narrow interpretation given it by both Hollywood employers and the public. She epitomizes the passive model of a "discovered" star, her apparent suicide standing as evidence of her inability to speak about or to change the conditions of her stardom. Monroe was unable to control the consequences of her fame or the effect of the restrictive standard of female representation on her personal life and identity. *Material Girl* reflexively expresses Madonna's experiences as a representation and a star, and extends the reflection backwards in time to Monroe's condition. Madonna plays off the similarities and differences in their circumstances. Unlike Monroe, she represents an ambitious, aggressive, self-made and self-directed star, and the video's performance number closely evaluates and compares Madonna and Monroe. While similarities between the two are accentuated by the video's duplication of the *Gentlemen Prefer Blondes* performance number, there are many calculated differences. Monroe's film character needs a man to provide her with the financial security she lacks. Madonna's video character is already rich and is, therefore, interested in men who don't need *her* money. Mary Ellen Brown and John Fiske (1987, p. 70) identify the subtle differences in textual actions that distinguish the two performance numbers and give Madonna a more aggressive role, pointing out that Madonna "[takes] money not offered" and "[knocks] down a chorus boy." In this way, the performance number spotlights the historical progress of female performers and the changing modes of female textual address.

Also debuted in 1985 was Benatar's *Sex as a Weapon*, a video promoting the first single from her seventh album, *Seven the Hard Way*. The video departs from the narrative, story-telling form of Benatar's earlier videos, relying instead on montage as a formal device. Images are juxtaposed and layered in ways that create a visual critique of efforts to sell products by using sexualized female representations, and the work expresses concern over the way music video is used to sell female musicians, including Benatar herself. The first image-fragment pictures "Eve" dressed in tight black leather and holding the apple that, according to the biblical account, she accepted from the serpent and gave to Adam, thereby condemning all of humanity to pain and hardship. A scrawled subtitle reads, "Paradise: the first act of hard sell." The image is used to introduce metaphorically the historical use of women and women's images for the purpose of selling ideas and products (from the beginning of time!).

The montage progresses to establish complicated visual links between male rule and female sexual and representational subordination. An image of a man, dressed in a tuxedo and loading a gun, appears next to the subtitle, "Sex, violence and the worship of machismo." In the far lefthand corner, a series of colorful lipsticks stand in a row, looking like bullets. Through animation techniques, the lipsticks are replaced by images of different women dressed in sexual outfits—revealing bathing suits, bunny costumes, and maid outfits—that reference the female role of sexual service to men. Benatar's black glove enters the frame, and grabs the man by his lapel. She shakes her finger at him, admonishing him with the lyric, "Stop using sex as a weapon," before relieving him of the gun. Jumping back into view, she points the weapon at the camera (and the video audience) in a photographic shot framed by the black lines of a camera aperture, serving as another sign of the video's focus on the issue of representation. She shoots the man with his own gun, and he falls wounded. His splattered blood is multicolored, the colors of the lipstick "bullets" that represented the women he has exploited. Benatar is the one who aims the gun and pulls the trigger, but the implication is that her actions speak for all exploited women. As the man dies, his head is replaced by a close-up shot of Benatar's lips, symbolizing her ascendant discourse of gender equality.

The critique is reinforced in the next sequence. Beside the blinking word "peep," several shots of male eyes appear, stacked vertically in the frame. On the other side of the frame, an image of a faceless blonde woman dressed entirely in black and missing small sections of her body rotates mechanically. The combination of images creates a vision of male voyeurism, of the institutionalized fetishism of female bodies, and its damaging effects on women. One of the men, whose eyes were among those featured, is filmed in medium shot wearing a hat and trenchcoat in the mode of a "dirty old man." He leers at Benatar. This time she does battle by executing defensive kicks to dispel his presence. Her kicking silhouette changes colors, again to enable her to act on behalf of other female victims of the male gaze.

Advertising comes under attack as the seductively dressed "lipstick" women pop back onto the screen to pose with commercial products: giant cans of soup and dogfood, cereal boxes, tubes of shaving cream. In the last shot of the sequence, one of the women holds up a box marked "Music Video," and as she tips it an image of Benatar herself pours forth. With this, the video moves to a more reflexive level to comment directly on MTV's promotional role and its attempt to perpetuate the standard of female representation through its preferred male address. Benatar glances at the upper righthand corner of the frame, where an early publicity still of herself appears, a photograph in which she wears a leotard, tights, and stiletto heels, and bends over suggestively in a pose previously struck by the video's "exploited women." The shot reveals the specific history of Benatar's representation as a sexual object of sale by her record company. The criticism of her "employer," coming within an employer-financed promotion, reveals the current state of her authorship and exposes a hard-won creative control over her representation and textual address. It also presents viewers with what is now her own dilemma, how to promote records without succumbing to sexist representations.

1986: Second-Wave Fragmentation
Typical Male; Papa Don't Preach; Open Your Heart; True Colors

The end of 1985 marked a turning point for each of the four musicians under study. Benatar's *Sex as a Weapon* video promoted a new album release; but Lauper, Turner, and Madonna had all completed video promotion for their first albums by 1986 (and quickly released second album in Madonna's case). Turner reserved time in 1985 to act with Mel Gibson in the third "Mad Max" movie, *Mad Max—Beyond Thunderdome*. In her role as "Aunty Entity," the villain ruler of Bartertown, Turner found a vehicle for at least some of the traits she had established in her comeback image. Aunty Entity's survivorship in a hostile post-nuclear civilization primarily founded on male standards of brute strength and cut-throat opportunism paralleled symbolically Turner's own battle for survival against wife abuse and bad professional management. The movie role allowed her to carry the publicized details of her own life into a fantastic fiction.

In 1986, Turner released her second solo album and with it *Typical Male*, a video that contributed little to her stance of female address. It was an apparently low-budget, uninspired video that made only minimal stabs at using the nuances of Turner's performance style and the system of visual signs defining her address in *What's Love Got to Do with It?* The video's director chose to represent metaphorically the "typical male" of the song's lyrics with an oversized prop, a man's class-coded "spat" shoe, which may have been designed to appeal to Turner's considerable British audience. But the prop never manages to take on symbolic weight; it is not associated with any visual system of representation that would allow it to resonate with meaning. Furthermore, the size of the shoe required Turner to be filmed in long-shot and often from a high angle, techniques that did not flatter her body, nor allow her facial expressions to contribute to the song's rendition. Centering shots around the big shoe did not provide the opportunity for freely motivated body movement on her part either, resulting in the reduction of her dance moves to meaningless spectacle. A young, white (possibly British) man appears in the video as the object of Turner's onscreen affections, but no context is provided for his or her desire. The song's focus on the category of "typical male" creates great potential for female address, but this is weakened by the badly crafted and ill-conceived video.

In 1985, with *Material Girl*, Madonna wrapped up a continuous stream of video promotion for her rapidly released *Madonna* and *Like a Virgin* albums. Largely on the basis of her performance in *Material Girl*, she was chosen to co-star in Susan Seidelman's film, *Desperately Seeking Susan*, a box-office hit that enabled her to pursue additional cinematic work. Nevertheless, Madonna managed work on a third album, *True Blue*, and on the eve of its 1986 release, the track "Papa Don't Preach" had already been vigorously promoted with a video on MTV. *Papa Don't Preach* uses a textual strategy employed in earlier Madonna videos, the representation of "two looks," and "two lives." *Material Girl* explored the tensions between onscreen and offscreen personae, between star and "ordinary" person. *Borderline* presented an early version of the same device, the "girl of the street" versus the "photography model," two looks that contrasted the eclectic style of the adolescent girl and the polished, glamourous look of the fashion professional. In *Papa Don't Preach*, Madonna's two looks are even more extremely at odds. One look is developed in a narrative character portrayal—the schoolgirl who has fallen in love and apparently become pregnant.[3] The other look is revealed in dance performance sequences that cut into the narrative at moments when the song directly addresses the father character with the admonition, "Papa, don't preach."

The schoolgirl appears simply and fully clad in blue jeans and a striped top. Her hair is almost white, short and cropped, unstyled and boyish. Her facial make-up is plain. Natural light from location shooting is used as a lighting source. Given the overtly sexual presentation in Madonna's earlier work, the look is shockingly pared down, de-sexualized, and ordinary. Her hair, always a potent signifier in Madonna videos (blonde with dark roots in *Borderline*, a platinum reproduction of Marilyn Monroe's hair in *Material Girl*) has again been altered dramatically from her last public appearance. Within the context of the narrative, the schoolgirl's look connotes youth and a lower-class social position. The school uniform she wears for part of the video aligns her with adolescence, Catholicism, and, as is developed in all of Madonna's work, a regime of sexual repression that must be resisted. The opposing look is overtly sexual and affected. Her hair is slickly styled, her made-up face lit by a key light. She wears an off-the-shoulder black bodystocking and performs a sexually coded dance. Although formally set apart from the narrative flow, the sexual look joins with the desexualized character to construct two contradictory aspects of female adolescence and, specifically, of the life of the story's girl. She is a schoolgirl bound by the moral and behavioral codes of class, religion, and adolescence, but she is also a fully sexual woman who is physically capable of attracting men and bearing a child.

The schoolgirl's affair with her young Italian lover is played out with a number of discerning reflections on the girl's social condition as a motivating factor and with a self-consciousness about her romantic fervor. From the opening montage sequence, which presents an immigrant's point of view of entering New York Harbor, the sexual encounter between the boy and girl is associated with the perpetuation of her Italian heritage. On hiatus from school, the girl loiters on the street in a T-shirt printed with the words "Italians Do It Better," a complicated and contradictory sign of her ideological resistance. The message brings together her pride in her class and ethnic heritage and her rebellion against their economic and moral constraints. It is the shirt that first attracts her lover's attention to her and results in the physical culmination of its contradictions. In the broader romantic context, sexual union is linked to travel, to departure from one's own condition. Postcards of distant places hang on the girl's bedroom walls. Her house, located in a lower-class suburb of New Jersey, overlooks the span of water that separates it from New York's cityscape, reinforcing the vision of her isolation from excitement and opportunity. When together, the lovers are shown next to the river's edge, or in the case of the ferryboat scene, in the watery space between suburb and city, one step closer to hope and ambition.

The video quite explicitly plays off the myth of hetero-sexual coupling as a means for young women to escape the drudgery of responsibilities at school and at home. The girl is shown in the role of a daughter who must take care of her spouseless father. In fact, more screen time is given to the rela-tionship between the girl and her father than to the girl and her boyfriend. Ostensibly, this is because the lyrical content mandates the girl's disclosure of her pregnancy to her father, but the relationship is far more complex visually. In the ellip-tic timeframe of music video narratives, the video traces the changes that occur between the girl and father as she grows up. The father cares for the girl when she is too young to care for herself, but as she grows older, the girl is expected to care for the father. Both father and boyfriend are in fact linked by the girl's "mothering" behavior toward them. In one scene, she leans over to kiss the boy, who rests his head in her lap; in another, she drops food in his mouth as he sits on a bench with his arms outstretched, waiting to be fed. Thus the dark side of the girl's romantic attitudes toward her preg-nancy is established—the perpetual caretaking activity that is her female destiny.

The girl's romantic fall, her absolute infatuation with the boy and their love, is the subject of many self-consciously acted gestures by Madonna. When the boy's blue-eyed gaze first meets that of the girl, it is obvious from her facial ex-pression that she has been smitten with love. The power of his gaze over her is suggested in scenes in which she appears oblivious to the warning signs of love's doom. A shot of the service station where the boy works could become a sign of his inability to support a wife and child, yet the image seems to fade away as the girl meets his gaze and his smile. On the ferry, the girl concentrates on his countenance, and Madonna's fluttering eyelashes contribute to her pose of utter abandon.

A subtle exchange of looks between the boy and a middle-aged man on board the ferry inserts a commentary on the system of male assumptions that underlies their courtship of women. The man, who is seated next to his wife, smiles at the boy and nods in the direction of the girl as if to acknowledge her as a "fine catch." The girl, clued in to the boy's distracted attention, looks over at the older couple and smiles broadly, reading in the older man's smile an affirmation of her love and its potential to supersede time. She interprets selectively from the man's expression of satisfaction, ignoring the implications of his wife's unhappy glare. The system of looks and glance/ object editing that construct the scene are so subtle as to be ambiguous and easily misread. Nevertheless, the satirical logic of the scene undercuts the aura of romance by pointing out the girl's own thoughtless immersion in it.

The video's nuance-filled critique of adolescent girls' romantic visions of love and teen pregnancy escaped its many adult critics. The *New York Times* (Dullea, 1986) in an article entitled "Madonna's New Beat Is a Hit, but Song's Message Rankles" reviewed the criticism the song and video sparked among adult special-interest groups upon its release. "Pro-choice" advocates (supporters of the right to abortion) believed the song discouraged girls in the audience from considering birth control and abortion, setting them up for lifelong poverty. Planned Parenthood's executive director, Alfred Moran, elaborating a direct-effects communication model, linked girls' imitation of Madonna's style (which he observed in Planned Parenthood offices in 1985) to the fear that girls would get themselves pregnant in an attempt to act out Madonna's song. "Pro-life" advocates (opponents of abortion rights) anxious to latch onto any and all mention of birth, heralded *Papa Don't Preach* as an anti-abortion statement.

But the contrast between the girl's innocence and naiveté and Madonna's usual portrayal of a sophisticated and street-wise character did not go unnoticed by those familiar with her many videos. Neither was the romanticism embedded in the fantasy of teen pregnancy allowed to go unexamined in the text. But the video's critique is handled in such a way as to permit viewers to be both critical and gratified. The lyrical content of the song, which has the girl standing up to the authority of the father and making her own decision about whether or not to continue her pregnancy, appeals to female-adolescent viewers' desire to exercise more control over their bodies and their lives.

In the second half of 1986, Sire Records released another controversial Madonna video. In *Open Your Heart*, Madonna appears as a sex-shop burlesque dancer, performing a floor show for male customers, who gaze at her through glass partitions from individual cubicles. She wears a scanty black "bustier" with sculpted breast cups that have gold tips and dangling tassels. The video presents an extreme version of visual motifs already pioneered by other female-address videos: the image of the paid female partner/dancer in Benatar's *Love Is a Battlefield* and in Turner's *Private Dancer*, and the image of male voyeurs in Benatar's *Sex as a Weapon*. In *Open Your Heart*, the presentation of a sex shop makes for a more explicit and dangerous portrait of male voyeurism by revealing its connection to pornography and the reinforcement of male social privilege through male sexual pleasure.

The video's resonance, its ability to act as a social commentary on the regimen of female representation, is tied to the cumulative text built by Madonna's previous video promotions and to her evolved status as a superstar. Her video of the previous year, *Material Girl*, established a distinction between a star's textual representation and actual persona; this distinction functions in *Open Your Heart* to discourage equations between the erotic dancer and Madonna's subjective view of herself. This allows her to become a critical narrator, to present the issues and problems of female representation without being completely enslaved by them.

As always with Madonna, her look becomes a mediator working to resolve the contradictions activated by her controversial representations of women. In the case of *Open Your Heart*, what is most obvious and shocking to Madonna fans is the changes she made to her body. Madonna's public had become accustomed to her regular alterations of hair style and color but this time were confronted by her thinner, more muscular figure. Her achievements in the weight room gave a new physical embodiment to the strength she had already acquired in the arenas of economic and creative control. The muscular physique draws as much attention to her body as the eroticized dance she performs, attentuating any impression of abject victimization. Madonna's dominion over her own representation compounds the complexity of her portrayal of a woman whose representation is largely a function of the male gaze. As Tama Janowitz (1987, pp. 56–57), writing for *Spin*, phrased it: "She is playing a role perhaps only she can afford to play. . . . This is because Madonna is not merely selling sex —she is representing power."

Narrative fragments frame the erotic performance section of the video to create a context for the erotic dancer's character, albeit in highly ambiguous terms. A young, preadolescent boy dawdles outside the sex parlor, wanting to go inside, but unable to convince the ticket master. The boy's motivations are not altogether clear, although his young age and inquisitive gestures suggest that his interest is *pre*-sexual. In his innocence, he is fascinated with the act of looking, and covers one of his eyes and then the other, exploring the boundaries of vision. He uses his hand to cover and uncover different parts of the naked woman pictured on a poster under the marquee, mimicking the black cutout that shields her breasts from view. His gaze emanates more from an identification sensibility than a sexual voyeurism, and is therefore linked to female rather than male spectatorship. He strikes poses and dances erotically in front of a distortion mirror for his own pleasure, an imitation impulse not unlike that of Madonna's female fans. The boy's presence sets up Madonna's requisite second look, (second life, second attitude) in the video. She re-enters the frame, dressed not as the erotic dancer, but in the clothes and hat of a boy— of the young boy who identifies with her. As she leans over to kiss him, the similarities in their faces, in their facial type, are apparent. His naive, playful fascination with sexual performance is void of the maliciousness and perversity implied in the adult-male consumers' pleasure, and it is with this wonderment that Madonna chooses to align herself. Madonna and the boy merge in a prepubescent existence in which gender inequality is held in abeyance. They dance together, mirroring each other's movements, play, and chase each other. Together they run away from the ticket master who calls out in Italian, "Come back, Madonna. We still need [are in need of] you." She abandons the role of adult erotic dancer, retreating to a vision of life in which gender is undelineated, and representation and performance uninformed by hierarchical regimes of looking. The contrast between prepubescent equality and entrenched adult inequality helps locate adolescence as a key time of gender formation.

Lauper was absent from public view in 1985 while she took time to write songs for her second album, *True Colors*, which was released late in 1986. The *True Colors* video (1986), produced to promote the album's title track proved to be significantly different from her 1983 and 1984 music videos. Seeking to update her image and differentiate her long-awaited second effort from her wildly successful first album, Lauper diversified her look and its referents. Although her previous videos relied heavily on narrative logic and explicit references to female-adolescent experience, *True Colors* is more ambiguous in form and context. The video presents a dreamy, surreal, psychological, and autobiographical backdrop for lyrical refrains about identity and self-worth (e.g., "Don't be afraid to show your true colors"). Jon Pareles (1986), writing for The *New York Times Magazine*, on apparent authority from Lauper and Pat Birch, her video director, described the mesh of intertextual allusions to art and popular culture that make up the video's visual motifs—images from paintings by Salvador Dali and Jean Cocteau's film, *Orpheus*, and fashions from the glamorous 1920s. Such details were undoubtedly designed to tap a more varied, culturally sophisticated, adult audience (leading Pareles to label Lauper's image the second time around as more "mature"), an effort to expand on the preteen girls who made up a large portion of her fans in 1983. But despite the additions to Lauper's look and visual repertoire, allusions to signs of access and discovery are apparent. Female-adolescent discourse was still an organizing sensibility.

The video's surrealistic imagery comes together around the figure of a prepubescent girl. It was Lauper and Birch's intention in the video, according to Pareles (1986), to evoke a sense of rites of passage and Lauper beats on African drums to lend the appropriate anthropological air as the video opens. She tosses a flower offscreen, which is picked up by the young girl in the following shot. As she walks to where the flower has come to rest, the girl becomes separated physically from the two young boys with whom she has been building a sand castle. The image of the preteen girl playing together with boys locates access in a preadolescent lifestage. She leaves the time of relaxed gender distinctions when she accepts an adult woman's symbol, Lauper's flower, possibly even a sign of the beginning of menstruation. The girl is singled out, identified as different because of the early move into adolescence that her biological make-up requires, a point reinforced visually by her departure from the two boys, who remain together.

The sand castle, which the girl was building with the boys, suddenly takes on life-size proportions, and she travels its halls, passing through time, presumably through years. She comes across a rowboat moored in the sand and has a vision of two women inside it, one white and one black. The two drink tea together, realizing the image of adult femininity encapsulated by the tea party, a play activity of young girls. Gender unifies the women, transcending their racial difference. Pareles' (1986) interpretation of the scene, apparently taken from the stated intention of Lauper and Birch, is that the girl, who represents Lauper herself, is shown in the process of growing into womanhood.

However, another system of reading presents itself to Lauper's girl fans, one in which the video is interpreted as a direct acknowledgment of female fan practices, and a demonstration of Lauper's desire to speak specifically to and about them. Many of Lauper's girl fans fall into the same age category as the girl represented in *True Colors*, essentially that of ten-year-olds. The girl is clearly costumed to provoke an association with Lauper's look: a multicolored plume on her head alludes to Lauper's dyed hair; the abundance of bracelets she wears are like those worn by Lauper. Rather than interpreting the girl as a metaphoric representation of Lauper's own persona, as Pareles (1986) does, the girl could easily be translated by fans into a representation of their dress-alike behavior, their imitation and adoration of Lauper. In this way, the video becomes more of a reflexive statement on Lauper's stardom and the role played by her female fans in its achievement, the kind of self-reflection that characterizes the Madonna and Benatar videos of 1985. When Lauper lays a flower at the feet of the girl in the video's opening scene, she reverses the pattern of gift-giving at her concerts, where girls flock to the front of the stage with flowers for her. On tour in Austin, Texas, to promote her new album, Lauper's singing of "True Colors" became a moment of collective celebration for female fans, young and old, who stood and sang the song in unison. The song's lyrics, "I see your true colors and that's why I love you," could very well be taken as her affirmation of her fans, an expression of trust and understanding of their female identities.

Perhaps the greatest contribution of female-address video is the discovery and articulation of female-adolescent subjectivity, although as we have seen in a number of later videos, the musicians were as concerned with articulating their insights into the problems of female authorship and artistry. Benatar's earliest videos provide a picture of the limited formal techniques, the absence of narrative devices, and the narrowness of female-musician promotion in the days prior to MTV (*You Better Run; I'm Gonna Follow You*). There is a poverty of representation and a prescription of poses evident in these early videos that foreshadowed the crisis over female-musician depiction that surfaced in the initial years of MTV. After MTV began, the videos turned to narrative styles, in keeping with the channel's innovation of the concept video, and Benatar prospered from evolving conventions that placed the singer in the role of protagonist (*Shadows of the Night; Lipstick Lies*). Her portrayal of young women working in traditionally male (and female working-class) environments created access signs, and became a vehicle for her to talk symbolically about her own position as a female rock musician. The introspective portraits isolated female experience and desire, creating the conditions for the development of discovery signs. Donna Summer made the important connection with the male-address sign system of the street, thus establishing the terms of textual appropriation for female address (*She Works Hard for the Money*).

In a previous chapter, four male-address videos from 1983 were analyzed, offering a glimpse of the state of MTV's preferred discourse in the year female address began to coalesce. Lauper (*Girls Just Want to Have Fun*) and Benatar (*Love Is a Battlefield*) responded to the entrenched male address by appropriating the coded images of male space and offering representations of female subjectivity and solidarity within a narrative line explicitly referencing female adolescence. Madonna added complexity and nuance to the vision of female adolescence (*Borderline; Lucky Star; Like a Virgin*) and Turner (*What's Love Got to Do with It?; Private Dancer*) broadened the parameters of the female-adolescent sensibility to implicate a system of gender difference functioning across social categories of age and race. Lauper contributed to the expansion of female address by reworking romance conventions (*Time after Time*) and by depicting the social hysteria over female sexual desire (*She Bop*). In 1985, Madonna and Benatar spoke of their experiences as female musicians, approaching the issues of how the public interprets a star's image (*Material Girl*) and how female bodies are made into commodities in advertising, including music videos (*Sex as a Weapon*). And in 1986, Madonna added depth to both the female-adolescent address and the critique of the ways that female artists are interpreted and used as objects to support patriarchal values (*Papa Don't Preach; Open Your Heart*), while Lauper explored the use of female-adolescence address as subtext (*True Colors*). Turner wavered in the promotion of her second album (*Typical Male*), but continued to assert her rock musicianship through live concert touring. Benatar, having established her track record with the success of seven albums in seven years, negotiated with her record company for time off in order that she and Neil Geraldo could care for their new baby.

SEVEN

FANDOM, LIVED EXPERIENCE, AND TEXTUAL USE

$\mathbf{F}$ANS PROVIDE some of the most visible and intense evidence of the existence of motivated textual interpretation and textual use in everyday life. As highly interested, active textual participants, fans create self-proclaimed interpretive communities and define their activities in relation to specific texts. In fact, fans demonstrate their response to an artist's productions by generating their own texts and performance acts (Fiske [1987, p. 108] calls them "tertiary texts"), which can be used as units of analysis. The activities of fandom incorporate a number of patterned responses and symbolic practices—these are shaped by fans into effective tools that enable them to express their relationship to specific textual products. By understanding how fandom, as a general cultural phenomenon, involves fans in textual and social experiences,[1] it is possible to move closer to understanding female-fan responses to female musicians and female-address video.

Many media critics have become trapped by the logic that audience interpretation of texts is essentially a mental process, complicated by unconscious impulses, and is therefore impossible to assess. Stuart Hall drew the connection between textual interpretation and social life when he described texts as "the ongoing product of people's appropriation of them in their attempts to represent their own experiences, to speak in their own voices rather than in hegemonic codes" (summarized by Grossberg 1984, p. 98). Involvement in cultural arenas such as popular music can change the life conditions of those participants who use their participation as a means of resisting oppressive social conditions.

When the female-address videos described in the preceding chapter appeared on MTV, women and girls recognized the representation of female experience, and responded to this historical moment of cultural ascendancy by seizing on female-address textuality as their own cultural expression. As textual readers, they brought a range of interests—cultural, psychological, sociological, and political—to bear on their interpretations of and affinities with female musicians and their texts, but gender experience became the common point of reference. Many women and girls contributed to the "moment of female address" by becoming fans, creating visible signs of female popularity. The girls who became intense fans did so not only because fandom was a way to show their avid support of their favorite female musician, but because fan activity enabled them to use female-address textuality in their everyday lives and to formulate their own responses to the experience of gender inequality.

Identity, Authority, and Community

Richard Dyer (1979) has noted that fan activity is most intense among social groups for whom role/identity conflicts are most acute. The members of these groups carry the baggage of socially marginal identities, and include adolescents, women, and participants in gay "ghetto culture"—in other words, those persons who deviate from the hegemonically empowered "norm" of the adult, male heterosexual. Fantasy identifications with textual personae provide an arena in which discourses on identity are activated, and through which one's own identity may be negotiated. Therefore, the appeal of stars is dependent on the extent to which their textual meanings accomplish "ideological work" for their fans (Dyer, 1979).

In adolescence, when involvement with fandom is common, conflicts over identity are particularly acute. While adolescence is ideologically defined as a time of making choices about one's future identity—what kind of job to do, what kind of relationships to become involved in, what kind of life-style to lead—a number of social factors actually work against free choice. This is doubly true for female adolescents, who find themselves subject to not only an entrenched system of compulsory heterosexuality (Rich, 1983), but a sexual division of leisure and the prospect of a future sexual division of labor. The desire for an alternative vision of gender identity becomes more intense as girls begin to face and understand the spectre of adult sex roles. Yet despite the fact that very real social contradictions lie at the root of female-adolescent conflicts over identity, the most popular perspective on female-fan identification with textual personae labels it as a "natural" manifestation of burgeoning (hetero)sexual desires. The possibility that fandom also can represent a resistive activity against socially prescribed identities is not considered.

When stars of the opposite sex are selected as objects of fan desire, heterosexual attraction is usually considered to be the generative mechanism. Girl-fan adoration of male rock stars is treated as an indication of desire for a heterosexual mate, an ideologically complicit response. Sue Steward and Sheryl Garratt (1984, p. 148) have written a critique along these lines: "Most of us dream of being a pop star's girlfriend: fame and recognition by proxy. Girls are taught to wait for men to give us what we want, rather than to get it ourselves." In such a formulation "identification with" male performers is subservient to "desire for"; the emphasis is on desire as defined by the heterosexual model of gender relations and not, for instance, as an expression of desire for social equality. Stars are considered attractive because they represent the dominant, socially approved modes of identity construction.

However, in their study of female-fan adoration behavior of the 1950s and 1960s, Barbara Ehrenreich, Elizabeth Hess, and Gloria Jacobs have uncovered evidence of female-fan resistance to dominant gender configurations. They have noted that the stars most actively adored by female adolescents were, in fact, the *least* suited to become actual heterosexual mates, according to the dominant ideological model:

> Part of the appeal of the male star—whether it was James Dean or Elvis Presley or Paul McCartney—was that you would NEVER marry him; the romance would never end in the tedium of marriage. Many girls expressed their adulation in conventional, monogamous terms, for example, picking their favorite Beatle and writing him a serious letter of proposal, or carrying placards saying, "John, Divorce Cynthia." But it was inconceivable that any fan would actually marry a Beatle or sleep with him (Ehrenreich, Hess, and Jacobs 1986, p. 27).

In their analysis, girls' enactment of a symbolic romance with a male star hinged on the *antithesis* of the romantic resolution —marriage.

Steward and Garratt (1984, p. 144) argued that androgynous rock stars find favor with female fans because they confuse the conventional image of male sexual attractiveness to women: "A touch of homosexuality seems to *enhance* a male star's popularity with women." Camp performances have been linked to a gay aesthetic by Jack Babuscio (1980), who believes the play on gender roles presented in such acts is appealing to homosexuals precisely because the performers do not conform to social expectations. Performance is often so central to the gay experience (e.g., passing for straight in a homophobic culture) that the theatricality embodied in camp is particularly significant for gay audiences. For girls, the sexual playfulness in the appearance of androgynous rock stars taps into similar experiences. Taught to define themselves in opposition to a masculine ideal, the example of blending feminine and masculine imagery presents girls with an attractive alternative vision.

Ehrenreich, Hess, and Jacobs also have suggested that female-fan displays of desire for male stars are part of a larger articulation of the desire for male social privilege. The authors interviewed former Beatles fans; one woman, who was thirteen years old when the Beatles visited her home city of Los Angeles, analyzed her pleasure in Beatles fandom with the hindsight of twenty years and discovered a more complex and intricate source of appeal than she had previously imagined:

> Now that I've thought about it, I think I identified with them, rather than as an object of them. I mean I liked their independence and sexuality and wanted those things for myself. . . . Girls didn't get to be that way when I was a teenager—we got to be the limp, passive object of some guy's fleeting sexual interest. We were so stifled, and they made us meek, giggly creatures think, oh, if only I could act that way, and be strong, sexy, and doing what you want (Ehrenreich, Hess, and Jacobs 1986, p. 36).

My experience as a child fan of *The Man from U.N.C.L.E.*, a television detective show, suggests that adoration of a male star may serve as a cover for significant affective practices with respect to gender identity. My girlfriend and I each chose one of the two male leads of the program as a fantasy boyfriend. Incessantly, we confided in our chosen character by means of ballpoint pen "transmitters." The love talk, however, was in many ways secondary to the real affective use that we made of the text—our involvement in the male domain of adventure. The most significant feature of our interest in the show was that the text provoked us to devise physical tests of strength and problem-solving in the form of neighborhood obstacle courses.

Ehrenreich, Hess, and Jacobs considered the "flooding out" behaviors exhibited by the Beatles' American girl fans—screaming, fainting, and crying—to be less a reaction to an individual male star than an excuse for abandoning control over their own sexuality, which girls at the time were socialized to maintain. In the mid-1960s, even "letting down one's guard," was tantamount to signaling a boy to step over the line of discreet courtship behavior, and bold sexual displays were out of the question:

> For the girls who participated in Beatlemania, sex was an obvious part of the excitement. . . . It was rebellious (especially for the very young fans) to lay claim to sexual feelings. It was even more rebellious to lay claim to the active, desiring side of a sexual attraction: The Beatles were the objects; the girls were their pursuers (Ehrenreich, Hess, and Jacobs 1986, p. 19).

Female fans' extreme, eroticized preoccupation with male stars facilitated the striking of "bad girl" poses to subvert socially imposed modalities of passive feminine behavior, and may even have been employed for girls' protection within the arena of real sexual relations (e.g., "I can't love you; I love Ringo").

The nuances of female fans' adoration of male stars are largely missing from the most popular image of female fans, the "groupie" (a fan who offers her body to the male subject/object of her affection). This characterization of the female fan has been vehemently opposed by the fan magazine *Bitch—The Women's Rock Newsletter with Bite*. Cheryl Cline (1986a, p. 13) shared with magazine readers her attempt to "determine the difference between a girl Rock fan and a groupie, according to common Rock wisdom," and concluded, "Boiled down to the simple bare bones, the answer is: There *is* no difference.

Everybody is a groupie." The propensity to label female fans as groupies, Cline (1986b, p. 13) told her readers, stems from a "strictly masculine daydream." She then described the more likely female fantasy, as reported by Lori Twersky (*Bitch*'s other prolific writer on the subject), who credited girls with a more creative and active stance:

> In the classic female sex rock fantasy, the heroine is a musician, a journalist, a photographer—not a groupie. As Twersky describes the logic of the fantasy, ". . . If I were one of these [girls], creeps couldn't say to me, 'No head, no backstage.' I'd have a legitimate reason for being backstage and could be part of the action without being treated as if I were wearing a sign saying, 'fuck me. . .'"
> Young girls conclude the fantasy with ". . . One day my hero will see my act/photos of him/poems and say, 'Here is the soul mate I've been searching for'" (Cline 1986b, p. 11).

Twersky (1986, p. 11) herself argued under the heading "On Non-Sexual Obsessions" that female fans' adoration of male rock stars results from a variety of motivations, including an interest in their "work." Indeed, professional female rock-and-roll musicians have begun to report on their own adulation of male rockers, and how their identification inspired them to the stage and to careers in music. Tina Turner has acknowledged her early identification with Mick Jagger and cited the opportunity to perform alongside Jagger at the 1985 "Live Aid" concert as the culmination of an early fan desire (Elliott, 1985).

Such accounts fly in the face of feminist psychoanalytic approaches to textual identification, in which the (cinematic) text is considered to be overdetermined by patriarchal designs.[2] Typical analyses argue that men in the audience identify with male stars as embodiments of the power that they themselves are afforded in the gender-divided experiential realm. Female spectators are left with a desire for the hero as the "other," which only magnifies their own lack of social status. In such a formulation, female heroic figures are completely absent, and female spectators' identification is limited to female textual personae and reduced to sharing the heroine's desire to be desired by the "other." The impossibility of female identification with a male *or* female heroic figure is a theme that also runs through appraisals of female fans' relations with music stars: "It is . . . difficult for a woman to actually fantasize about BEING her hero in the same way a man could. With so few role models to follow, to fantasize about being on stage as a FEMALE performer may be almost a contradiction in terms (Steward and Garratt 1984, p. 148). Steward and Garratt, who, despite such statements, are fundamentally committed to recouping female-fan expression, have acknowledged the need for more critical research into same-sex relationships between fans and stars. Historically, the relatively small number of female performers has increased the difficulty of specifically addressing the female response to female stars, at least in the world of popular music —where some of the most visible manifestations of female fandom occur. But as video promotion brings more girls into contact with female musicians, a new site for discourse over identity has opened, and the discovery of new modes of identification has become possible.

One of the ways in which fans evaluate the textual identity of stars is through accumulating knowledge about the favored star and the star's textual products. As fans acquire textual authority, they assume a greater confidence in their textual interpretations. Fans are drawn to both extra-textual and textual details. They want to know the intricacies of their favored star's personal and professional lives, and the defining conventions and finer features of their creative works. It is this acquired knowledge that separates them from more casually interested audiences and identifies and validates their fan status. They develop their store of extra-textual information through promotion and publicity texts; through interpersonal exchanges with fellow fans; and through *fanzines,* publications that specifically target and are sometimes produced by fans. If popular support for a text is great enough to allow a continuous play or to generate auxiliary texts, fans appoint themselves historians of the resulting textual accumulation.

Fans of long-running television shows, for instance, accumulate a memory of the program and its characters that they expect writers and producers of newer episodes to respect. The consistent internal logic and historical coherence of the British television serial "Dr. Who" has delighted fans for over twenty years. John Tulloch and Manuel Alvarado, who have studied the show's popularity, explained the fans' extended engagement with the text by using Sheila Johnston's (1981) terms for spectator pleasure in serial narrative:

> The primary source of pleasure is to be found not in the "closed and comforting symmetry" of narrative, but in the "long-arch" storyline, which allows the "creation and slow consolidation of a complex fictional world." . . . Yet, there is a "closed and comforting symmetry" none the less: for long-term fans the endless unfolding of the show's mythology is pleasurable only if the continuity of "Doctor Who" as institution is upheld (Tulloch and Alvarado 1983, p. 83).

Just as fans' education is accomplished through experience with popular-culture texts, so their historical expertise is manifested in the form of "popular memory": "Such knowledge may circulate, usually without amplification, in everyday talk and in personal comparisons and narratives. It may even be recorded in intimate cultural forms: letters, diaries, photograph albums and collections of things with past associations" (Johnson and Dawson 1982, p. 210). Fans often chronicle or "re-present" their histories of popular texts by creating scrapbook collections of reviews and photographs, on occasion supplementing them with "original" photos or autographs and documents of their involvement with a chosen celebrity (e.g., a concert ticket stub). Such collections are common among fans of rock stars. One fan of Elvis Presley, according to Jerry Hopkins' (1972, p. 166) account, produced sixty-two scrapbooks, and another, thirty thousand photographs. The Presley estate maintains an archive of the many scrapbooks sent to Presley by his fans and displays them at Graceland on a rotating basis.

Fans' custom of giving away the historical records that they have created affirms the distinction between the "popular memory" of fandom and the "official" practice of producing historical documents. A select number of fans are more self-conscious about the process of historical documentation and, recognizing their unique position as textual experts, have authored books on favored stars and texts. But for the most part, fan histories are generated and circulated in ways that do not garner social recognition. Fans popularize learning by becoming apprentices to popular texts, not by using academic training or accepted research methods. Their expertise in the minutiae of popular culture is usually deemed inconsequential, their fan knowledge regarded as "trivia." It is not hard to imagine a fan whose knowledge of the celebrity subject exceeds that of the academic critic, yet because the fan's knowledge is embedded in private channels of circulation, it remains unrecognized and unvalued.

This is not to say that fans lose out on an affective authoritative practice by avoiding "legitimate" routes of knowledge acquisition and production—quite the contrary. The construction of authority in the popular realm functions as an act of empowerment precisely because it establishes an alternative field of validation. To casual textual participants, the fan's recounting of textual and extra-textual knowledge can be an awe-inspiring event, and within the world of fandom itself, the expanse of a fan's cumulative knowledge is a mark of status.[3] A premium may be placed on having recognized the talent of an individual or the quality of a text from the earliest moment of his/her/its public life. To have lived out that early history in fandom may even position some fans at the top of an internal hierarchy. For adolescent fans, the construction of authority through fandom can function as a form of resistance to formal modes of education and the institutional framework of the school, thereby subverting one of the most active ideological fields at work on youth (Althusser, 1971). In informal peer-oriented forums, youths use popular authority to demonstrate intelligence and creativity.

Fan knowledge forms a basis for fans to communicate among themselves and join together in "communities of interest" (Bishop and Hoggett, 1986). In fact, fans are characterized not only by their intense relation to texts, but by intense relations with each other. Fan alliances vary in their degree of formality and may emerge either as informal ad hoc groups or large-scale organizations. Hopkins (1972, p. 167) has commented that in the 1960s there were Elvis Presley fan clubs "in every major city in the U.S." and described them as institutions that provided interpersonal benefits for members, "where any traveling fan is sure to have a place to stay the night." Events staged by Elvis fans range from casual, personal gatherings to large-scale, highly organized conventions.

> In honor of Elvis and Priscilla's third wedding anniversary, for example, Maureen Fricker planned an all-day celebration party that promised screenings of "Roustabout," "Follow That Dream" and selected short subjects including three Warner Pathe new films, one of them of Elvis's wedding. Additionally there was a "Question Half Hour" and a "Discussion Half Hour." . . . A larger Elvis "do" is the annual convention, now in its sixth year, organized by the *Monthly*, and usually held in London, but in 1970 all over Europe (Hopkins 1972, p. 169).

Fan events are not always the product of fan-club sponsorship, but this does not necessarily detract from fans' participation in them. Rock concerts, which are organized by record companies and often financed through commercial sponsorship, are occasions for fans to congregate and celebrate their fandom.

Fans develop modes of displaying their fandom in order to signal their membership in a larger fan community. This brings them into contact with commodity transactions, either in the form of interpersonal trade or marketplace purchasing. Merchandising campaigns provide many objects for fan consumption. Such production of goods *for* the fan market becomes a kind of production *by* the fan as merchandisers take their lead from fan commitments and popularity. But not all market transactions by fans involve the domain of public commerce. Fans frequently engage in the production of goods and services for their own community's enjoyment, a practice Bishop and Hoggett (1986), who studied group organization around leisure "enthusiasms," call "mutual aid." In these instances, fan interest groups bypass the institutional marketplace to create private mechanisms of exchange for their own products. Again, Hopkins' study of Elvis fans in the 1960s documented "mutual aid" activities:

> In Portland, Oregon, a college senior named Carl Obermeier was hastily filling orders for bumper stickers imprinted Elvis Master of Rock 'n' Roll (fifty cents), blue T-shirts with white letters that boast I'm an Elvis Fan (three dollars, plus twenty-five cents mailing), pencils with Forever King Elvis cut on the sides (six for a quarter), combs that say I'm an Elvis Fan Club Member (six, in assorted colors, for a dollar), and a wide range of rubber stamps for the fan to cover his or her correspondence with messages such as Music that Will Be New Tomorrow, Our Elvis Is Singing Today! and Yes, I'm an Elvis Fan and Proud of It! Carl says business is good (Hopkins 1972, pp. 162–163).

Newsletters produced and distributed by fan clubs are not only objects of exchange, but support the informal economy of fans by providing a place for individuals to advertise their wares for sale or trade. Items of collection (objects of a star's or text's history) enter this private exchange flow, as do goods produced expressly for fan consumption. Bishop and Hoggett have proclaimed such self-organized, private exchanges to be a means by which participants negotiate alternatives to dominant market practices:

> The values . . . are radically different from those embedded within the formal economy; they are values of reciprocity and interdependence as opposed to self-interest, collectivism as opposed to individualism, the importance of loyalty and a sense of "identity" or "belonging" as opposed to the principle of forming ties on the basis of calculation, monetary or otherwise (Bishop and Hoggett 1986, p. 53).

As collective bodies of consumers, fans also exercise control over the means of star and text production. Having fans in one's corner provides a performer with a kind of currency that can be cashed in for everything from creative control to additional work in their industry. Fan devotion is a tremendous professional boon, allowing performers to diversify into other kinds of textual production while maintaining a loyal following. Tulloch and Alvarado reported that fans of "Dr. Who" are considered a "bedrock" audience, necessary for the program's continued success. The producers who began working on the show in the middle of its run worried over maintaining their address to the show's fans before they considered initiating new appeals to nonfans, a group they explicitly referred to as a "bonus" audience (Tulloch and Alvarado, 1983). Fan support for particular stars and even genres of programming is exploited by media industries when they originate new programming. A notable example is the television "spin-off" series.

The case of fan involvement in the American television program "Cagney and Lacey" received wide publicity.[4] During its run, the program's staff mailed a newsletter to its fans and frequently solicited their input. Hopkins also painted a picture of the authority inscribed in fan-club membership when he described the attention given to Elvis Presley fan clubs by Presley's personal manager and his record label:

> The Colonel . . . has cultivated the fandom, regarding the clubs as the money in the bank they represent. The letters he sends the club presidents may be mimeographed, but they're full of news and come often; and RCA is instructed to send enough calendars, photographs and record catalogues for all the members. Whenever Elvis fans gather in convention, as they do in many parts of the world, the Colonel sends a telegram (Hopkins 1972, p. 164).

Management is not always so willing to admit to the role fans play as sustainers of textual industries, even when it is in their interest to do so. Dorothy Hobson (1982) has reported on the uproar that occurred when the producers of the British television serial "Crossroads" decided to snub its fans by firing the show's long-time leading actress. The fans had come to equate their role as long-term supporters of the show with program ownership, a scenario that ultimately caused a serious struggle for control of programming decisions. Steward and Garratt discussed the popular music industry's determination to underplay the importance of the female fan in the financial support of their endeavors. Female-adolescent fans, the authors asserted, have been crucial to the success of a number of record companies and male stars, yet "they're quick to sneer at the girls who helped make them in the first place. . . . Of course, the serious, thinking rock audience they want is mainly male" (Steward and Garratt 1984, p. 142).

Fans are themselves aware of and often vocal about the effects their fandom has on careers and culture production. *Bitch—The Rock Newsletter with Bite*, in a promotional piece on the International Fan Club Association, reminded its fan subscribers that "Fans *Do* Make a Difference":

> Keep in mind that there have been many instances where fans made a difference! Television networks are keenly aware of this

power. Shows such as Cagney & Lacey, Hill Street Blues, Miami Vice and Fame are just a few of the shows that were being considered for cancellation until the fans made their voices heard. The rest is history! ("Fans *Do* Make a Difference" 1986, p. 11)

For adolescent fans generally, the recognition of their role in supporting stars and industrial textual products must be exhilarating. They who are manipulated, regulated, scrutinized, and disempowered in everyday social interactions with parents and institutions find themselves to be participants in an industrial process in which even the powerful and moneyed can take an extremely big and public tumble.

While fan communities may organize effectively for control at the site of cultural production, as in the case of "Cagney and Lacey" and to an extent with "Crossroads,"[5] their affiliation can also take on meaning as a broader political action. Ehrenreich, Hess, and Jacobs described the overwhelming expression of female fandom during the 1964 Beatles tour of the United States in terms of an emergent feminist politic:

If it was not the "[women's] movement," or a clear-cut protest of any kind, Beatlemania was the first mass outburst of the sixties to feature women—in this case girls, who would not reach full adulthood until the seventies and the emergence of a genuinely political movement for women's liberation (Ehrenreich, Hess, and Jacobs 1986, p. 11).

Thus, fan communities that find common ground in their interpretation of texts can become organized groups united by experience and purpose.

Style Imitation: The Preferred Mode of Female Fan Expression

Some ways have been suggested through which female-address videos incorporated style and appearance manipulation to construct discovery signs that tapped into the uses and pleasures of girl culture. Style is also a mode that girls used to formulate their response to the videos and their associated female musicians—specifically, style imitation. Most notable and publicized were the Cyndi Lauper "dress-alikes," who transferred the star's colorful and kooky image to their own bodies and faces, and the Madonna "wanna-bes," older girls (usually) who reproduced the complex textual references available in Madonna's videos. Style imitation was also practiced by fans of Pat Benatar and Tina Turner, although not with the same intensity, visibility, or organized participation.[6] Lauper and Madonna both devoted attention to the creation of distinct visual styles and to integrating style into the female-address textuality of their videos, which probably accounts for the greater participation of their fans in style-imitation behavior.

Andrew Tudor (1974) recognized the imitation of stars as an audience response in his early classification of different same-sex star–spectator relationships arising from cinematic texts. His typology contains four degrees of identification: emotional affinity, self-identification, imitation, and projection. The first two behaviors are described as essentially mental processes of involvement. Imitation and projection, on the other hand, are practices of enactment, more actively integrated into fans' lives. Imitation is a visible modeling behavior that involves mimicry of the star, a response Tudor observed to be particularly prominent in young viewers. Projection is a more extreme form of behavior in which viewers became completely bound up with living the life of the star.

There is evidence that style imitation occurs on both sides of the gender line. Hopkins (1972), for instance, has provided vivid examples of male Elvis Presley imitators. But there is also some indication that the practice may be more pervasive among female fans. Although Tudor considered style imitation to be a manifestation of same-sex fan identification, girls are prone to imitate the styles of male stars as well. Steward and Garratt (1984) have even suggested that male rock stars are selected by girl fans partly on the basis of how well they provide a style that can be easily imitated. One department store manager reported that ready-to-wear fashions designed to resemble those worn by male stars tend to be more popular with girls, citing that the "Michael Jackson look," for example, sold much better among female consumers (W. Wilson 1984, Fall).

Style imitation is a practice consistent with the expression of fandom. By imitating the style of the favored musician, the "wanna-bes" and "dress-alikes" demonstrated their identification with the figure of the female star, represented the textual knowledge they had acquired as fans, and displayed their association with a community of female fans. But style imitation was also a specific response to a specific system of textual address. It was a way girls acknowledged and participated in creating the meanings of female address and, more broadly, the meanings of female social experience. For women, appearance is a fundamental means of constructing female identity and identifications. From birth, the imposition of a gender-specific appearance by parents (largely through clothing), signals the social recognition of sexual difference and marks the first step in the construction of gender identity. Playing "dress up" in their mothers' castoff clothing is an encouraged socialization activity for little girls, one that directs them toward a female-identified concept of self. Girls have been shown to engage in dress-up play to a greater extent than boys (Stone, 1965) and to develop a higher level of clothes awareness (Vener and Hoffer, 1965). Boys are even considered by one study to be "disadvantaged" by their lack of participation in dress-up play and by their reliance on commercially purchased costumes in place of their fathers' old clothing (Stone, 1965). Another interpretation could be that boys are under less social pressure to identify with the role of the father, whereas the role of the mother has been made central to female identity, and dress imitation is a means of ensuring its internalization.

The activities of purchasing and dressing up in feminine clothes accompany every major event in a girl's life from first communion to prom night—culminating in that most fussed-over ritual, the wedding, with its expensive and rigidly defined attire. Often, it is the regimen of dress codes and restrictions on hairstyle and make-up that first exposes girls to gender contradictions. Girls learn early that buying and wearing clothes is a highly charged activity that situates one's own desires against a host of social approval ideologies. A girl's desire to dress like a boy is an early form of resistance to the physical and mental restraints that gender definitions seek to impose on her. As girls grow older and experience physical body changes, they discover the relationships between modes of displaying the body and social response.

Barbara Hudson (1984) has described clothing and appearance manipulation by adolescent girls as an outgrowth of their conflicted social status. Girls resist the discourse of femininity by aligning themselves with male-adolescent style, or conversely, by exaggerating feminine dress in displays that cross over into unbounded sexual display. In a sense, girls make *themselves* into access signs or discovery signs in an attempt to strike symbolic resonances that will facilitate an impression of control and subjectivity. Hudson observed that schools can become an embittered site for symbolic battles over standards of female attire:

> Teachers respond positively to "feminine" girls, whilst they like to encourage the development of feminine traits; nevertheless, the school is not regarded as an appropriate arena for the display of unbounded femininity. The idea that femininity can be taken on and off by changing clothes explains a form of behavior that is common amongst teachers; if femininity is bestowed by dress,

then teachers can keep displays of femininity within bounds by insisting on a plain, de-individualized dress (Hudson 1984, p. 39).

The home is just as charged a location for "dress wars." In *Interview* magazine, Madonna described how, in her youth, she and a best girlfriend deliberately created a "sexual persona" in order to subvert their parents' authority, an image that, interestingly, was inspired by their identification with a female musician:

> *Madonna:* It was a private joke between my girlfriend and me, that we were floozies, because she used to get it from her mother all the time, too.
> [*Interviewer*]: So somewhere you did like the floozy look.
> *Madonna:* Only because we knew that our parents didn't like it. We thought it was fun. We got dressed to the nines. We got bras and stuffed them so our breasts were over-large and wore really tight sweaters—we were sweater girl floozies. We wore tons of lipstick and really badly applied makeup and huge beauty marks and did our hair up like Tammy Wynette (Stanton 1985, p. 60).

Madonna's comment suggests that she had a certain familiarity with and adoption of strategies of subversive self-presentation in her own adolescence.

People Magazine and *Newsweek* recorded Lauper describing her alienated adolescence, which was filled with quests for independence, rebellious behavior, and an appearance set against the conventions of femininity:

> In high school I fell out of step. Everything became unreal for me. I felt there just wasn't any room for me in this world. . . . I didn't fit in, didn't have nobody to do things with that I liked. I did them by myself (Jerome 1984a, p. 87).
>
> I was an oddball. . . . No matter how hard I tried to look normal there was always something that wasn't right (Miller et al. 1985, p. 50).

Fans, who are prone to seek out extra-textual information about the stars' lives, are bound to assimilate such statements with the musicians' textual presentations. Whether or not the two musicians used their personal experience of female adolescence to construct their stylistic attitudes, their subversive styles and roles in their video performances are open to interpretation as textual strategies of opposition. Their representation of female identity as a social arena of struggle is part of the "ideological work" (Dyer, 1979) that Madonna and Lauper accomplish for female fans.

Style imitation activates a cultivated female arena of knowledge. By poring over fashion magazines, girls learn how to read texts and to imitate and appropriate them for their own everyday activities, which include the practice of fandom. The act of purchasing clothes and "putting oneself together" is, for women and girls alike, a task predicated on having learned the difference between which looks are current and which looks are dated, which looks are conventional and which are daring. As a fan practice, style imitation brings together what female fans have learned through "clothes culture" about creating appearances and their desire to express what they know about favored texts. Female culture-based knowledge and textual knowledge join to create a field of authority that is both gender and fan specific.

Steward and Garratt described how differences in gender-specific standards of knowledge produce differences in male and female fans' knowledge of popular music:

> They listen to and appreciate pop music in completely different ways: boys talk about the music, they swap information and show off their knowledge (or pretended knowledge) about instruments and equipment; girls, on the other hand, tend to talk about the stars, looks, fashions, and the "feel" of the song—particularly the words and whether or not the music is good to dance to (Steward and Garratt 1984, pp. 110–111).

The differences in fan knowledge manifest both the historical condition of gender inequality in music (the denial of musical training and education to females) and the creation by girls and women of a separate sphere of cultural interest.

Self-presentation in the form of style and appearance affectation also frames much of girls' social activity with each other. Style is experienced as a cultural vehicle for female social bonding. Mother–daughter dresses are symbols of matrilineal identification and represent one of the few tolerated expressions of mother–daughter love within the hegemony of the oedipal construct. Dressing alike is a familiar practice in girlhood, the time at which same-sex friendships are most valued. Christine Griffin (1985, p. 61) described the expression of female "best friend" relationships as inexorably linked to wearing "*exactly* the same clothes, shoes, hairstyles, even jewelry." Female fans of female address extend the status of "best friend" to their favorite star by imitating her dress and mannerisms.

The best-friend relationship is sometimes expressed in the fan letters that musicians receive. Benatar has offered such an interpretation of her fan letters from girls:

> If anything, they're loving you not so much as a role model, but as a friend, a sister, a pal, someone they can relate to. It's not even so much that they want to be like you; they just like what you are and would like to be friends with you. I think it's a real camaraderie (Benatar, 1987).

Benatar's assessment deviates from the usual explanation of adolescent adoration practices, which holds that adolescents need to model themselves after someone who represents a superior role or social position. Instead, her comments suggest a reciprocity between the fan and the textual persona, a pattern of identification, a relationship not unlike girl friendships in which secrets and wishes are exchanged.

The practice of style imitation resembles the use of style

in subcultures as described by British youth-culture scholars. Style imitators generally exhibit the three features that Michael Brake (1985, p. 12) has identified as features of subcultures: (1) *image,* the projection of an identity through costuming, make-up, and other visual material; (2) *demeanor,* the mode of stance, pose, performance—in effect, the way the image is worn; and (3) *argot,* a special vocabulary and verbal delivery style. Among style imitators, dressing and moving like the star fit the categories of image and demeanor. The special vocabulary that style-imitators share tends to center on their shared knowledge of texts, although in the case of Madonna's fans there is a patterned enunciation of "wanting to be famous," "wanting to be looked at," "wanting to be like Madonna," which is the source of their "wanna-be" label.

Despite their similarities in form, female fandom and subcultures must be considered to be fundamentally different if one accepts the underlying assumptions about subcultural manifestations made by subculture analysts. The British literature on subculture places an emphasis on class as the determining social structure that dictates subcultural form and emphasizes, more implicitly, that subcultures are male arenas.[7] Yet female-fan response is derived from a gender condition and incorporates female forms of experience and expression. The subculture literature's theoretical focus on authenticity (similar to that of rock ideology) devalues the diffusion of subcultural style into mass-media representations and marketplace reproductions. But the spectacular response of Lauper and Madonna fans comes directly from member interaction with mass-media texts and consumer culture.

Style imitation by fans demonstrates how female musicians' strategies of style and female address can cohere with female viewers' experience of gender to create a powerful correspondence between text and audience. It also demonstrates how textual exchange carries over into everyday social practice. The style imitators push through the symbolic discourse of female culture for the recognition that boys receive. They demand access to male privileges of money, power, and authority (which they find embodied in celebrities), but at the same time, they refuse to dispose of the expressive forms provided by female culture. It is because female musicians have developed a sensitive and descriptive textual practice around the representation of gender experience that adolescent girls were given this opportunity to speak.

EIGHT

FIVE FAN EVENTS

In late spring of 1984, Cyndi Lauper's success was recognized with a *Rolling Stone* cover story (Loder, 1984a). That fall, she launched her first concert tour to promote her already extremely popular first album, which had been released the previous year. The fall of 1984 found Madonna completing a co-starring role in the Hollywood film *Desperately Seeking Susan* and receiving her first cover story in *Rolling Stone* as well (Connelly, 1984). Her film was released in March 1985 to critical and popular acclaim, and Madonna began her first concert tour later that spring, playing three nights at Radio City Music Hall to fans who had bought all 17,622 available seats in a record thirty-four minutes (Skow, Booth, and Worrell, 1985). In conjunction with Madonna's New York concert dates, Macy's Department Store sponsored its "Madonna Look-Alike Contest," and "ABC World News Tonight" ran a report about Madonna and her avid female fans. In 1986, both Lauper and Madonna released new albums—Lauper's second and Madonna's third. To promote her album's title track, "True Blue," Madonna and her record company sponsored "Madonna's 'Make My Video' Contest" in conjunction with MTV, calling on viewers to submit their own video rendition of the song. Lauper went back on the road for a second concert tour.

The events of the almost two-and-a-half-year period involved female Lauper and Madonna fans as both textual representations and textual producers, as audiences and as performers. Using style imitation as their preferred mode of response, the girl fans became highly visible at concerts and shopping malls, on movie and television screens, so much so that they became news on national television. And all the while they were speaking, with the language of fandom, about gender difference and gender inequality.

Cyndi Lauper and Madonna Live in Concert—Austin, Texas

The rock concert had its historical beginnings in male rock culture. Concerts were not only places for aficionados to congregate, they were also sites of male-adolescent license, where drugs, alcohol, and rebellious styles were paraded and shared. Lauper's address to girls who "want to have fun" helped open the rock concert venue to female fans and their displays of style imitation. Female musician concerts became events for the female-fan community and, particularly in the case of Lauper concerts, became a family affair. Girls attended not only with dates, but with a girlfriend or group of girlfriends, and mothers and fathers brought their very young children.

Like most concert arenas, the Frank Erwin Center in Austin, Texas, on the University of Texas campus, does not allow amateur photographers to bring cameras to its events, effectively preventing fans from taking (sanctioned) photographs of stars for their personal collections. It does, however, send its own photographer to the scene to take pictures of the musicians, and sometimes the fans, for reproduction in its monthly entertainment magazine, *Applause*. Photos of stars serve to promote tours, and photos of fans provide visible evidence that the concert hall is a cultural site of fun and excitement, a ploy to encourage ticket sales.

The photographs in this chapter were taken by Erwin Center photographer Craig Meurer. Photographs 1 through 5 feature female style imitators who were attending Madonna's May 5, 1985, concert during her "Virgin Tour." Photographs 6 and 7 are from Lauper's October 13, 1984, concert, which was part of a tour to promote her first album, *She's So Unusual.* Photographs 8 and 9 were taken January 10, 1987, at her return appearance for the "True Colors Tour." The fans who appear in the photographs are dressed according to their own sense of what was appropriate for concert attendance. In other words, they were not motivated by an organized competition, as was the case with Macy's "look-alike" contest, and in all likelihood had no expectation that anyone would ask to take their photograph (although some were clearly prepared to strike poses). They had dressed for themselves and for those attending the concert.

The concert photographs demonstrate a range of textual involvement in the fans' selection of apparel and accessories. Among the Madonna fans, the wearing of crucifixes, black clothing, neck chains, gloves, lace fabric, sunglasses, multiple bracelets, big earrings (especially star and crucifix designs), belts, tights, headwraps, and midriff blouses (listed in descending order of frequency) were chosen as signs of "Madonnaness." The clothing and jewelry in the photographs are trendy and appear to be from recent product lines. The youngest fan (subject 1A) strikes a Madonna pose by raising her arms above her head.

The Lauper fans' attire is more varied, more individually "put together" and includes clothing recycled from thrift stores (e.g., an old formal gown, hoop skirts) and objects borrowed from male dress (e.g., hats, neckties). These fans' clothes are

Photo Credit: Craig Meurer

1. A young Madonna concert goer poses for the camera.

2. Two Madonna Fans show varying degrees of style imitation.

3A   3B

Photo Credit: Craig Meurer

3. Black clothing, neck chains, sunglasses, tights, and crucifixes
are used by Madonna imitators.

Photo Credit: Craig Meurer

4. Black rubber bracelets and lace fabric are popular objects of
imitation among Madonna fans.

5. A couple of style imitators are captured on film at Madonna's May 5, 1985, "Virgin Tour" concert.

6A   6B

6. Two concert goers make Lauper-like grimaces for the camera.

7A   7B   7C   7D

7. Objects of imitation are draped over the clothes of these Lauper fans.

8. A dyed wig steps up the look of one Lauper imitator.

Photo Credit: Craig Meurer

9. A fan strikes a Lauper-like body pose.

more patterned and colorful; hats are present in abundance. Bracelets and necklaces are as popular with Lauper style imitators as they are with Madonna style imitators; both Lauper and Madonna have worn black rubber bracelets, which have found their way onto the wrists of their fans. The Lauper fans also copy the outlandish poses and movements of their star; subject 9A strikes a Lauper body pose, while subjects 6A and 6B show the photographer their Lauper-like grimaces.

Some fans in the photographs chose to recreate the star's style more fully, using more detail, than others. Madonna-imitator 2B has elaborately recreated the star's look, with tights around her head, "lucky star" earrings, sunglasses, layered midriff blouse of black lace, neck chain, belt, miniskirt, black cut-out gloves, and black lace leggings. Her girlfriend (subject 2A), on the other hand, added only a few Madonna accessories to her own clothing—the black-lace blouse overlay, one glove, neck chains, and crucifix earrings. Of all the Madonna fans photographed, she is the only one who carries a purse, an object thoroughly out of keeping with Madonna's look.

The degree of style imitation among those fans shown mimicking Lauper's theatrical body language (6A, 6B, and 9A) is more elaborate than that of the other Lauper fans, with the possible exception of subject 8A, whose dyed wig steps up her look. The four girlfriends in photo 7 appear, for the most part, to have draped objects of imitation over their own clothes. In general, the looks of the fans represented in the photographs support the notion that everyday fan practice involves a good deal of appropriation, the "stealing" of star style objects for use in the fans' own creative self-presentations, rather than straight imitation. Lauper and Madonna encourage multiple interpretations of their looks by making frequent changes in their own appearance.

A Madonna "Wanna-Be" Story on Film

In the spring of 1985, Madonna's debut Hollywood film *Desperately Seeking Susan* was released. Madonna co-starred with actor Rosanna Arquette in a narrative line that *Rolling Stone* likened to the Carole Lombard and Claudette Colbert "caper comedies" of the thirties:

> Arquette's bored housewife, Roberta, follows the trail of Madonna's gutterball schemer, Susan, into a slapdash murder mystery that scrambles suburbanites and hipsters into something between farce and dreamy fable (Schruers 1985, p. 30).

But a description of the film might also read like this:

> Rosanna Arquette plays the part of a Madonna "wanna-be." Unappreciated and unnoticed in her dreary and exploited life as a young middle-class wife, she turns her vague desire for recognition and adventure into a fantasy identification with a textual persona. Arquette's character, Roberta, follows the trail of Madonna, the woman of the text. Roberta is a voyeur who observes from afar and participates vicariously in the narrative of Madonna that she, in part, creates. She buys Madonna fashions, and dressing in them, becomes Madonna. Or rather, she becomes the image of what Madonna represents to her. As a result, she is suddenly noticed by strangers, and acquires a complex personality based on Madonna's reputation, a prior public knowledge of who she is and what she represents. In living out her fantasy, she moves in directions she was previously too inhibited to pursue. She performs on stage and is recognized for the first time as an individual with her own style and talents by the very people who were indifferent before. She gains the confidence to change her life, to change the conditions that hampered her ability to know herself, and to act on her desires.

The decision to hire Madonna for the role of Susan was in part a decision to make the Susan character into Madonna. What appears to have been unintentional was the way in which

Madonna's selection for the role of Susan made Arquette's character, Roberta, into a Madonna "wanna-be." The film's storyline about a young woman who impersonates another woman, whom she has come to adore as a textual persona, was written a number of years before Madonna's rise to fame, yet it wonderfully encapsulates the "wanna-be" impulse. Those who worked on the film were quick to point out that *Desperately Seeking Susan* is not "Madonna's film." Madonna played a character role in an ensemble cast, a role in a screenplay that circulated Hollywood for five years before being sold as a package to Orion Pictures, teaming Director Susan Seidelman with Rosanna Arquette as the starring actor. The film's publicist, Reid Rosefelt, has distinguished *Desperately Seeking Susan* from a "vehicle film," such as Prince's *Purple Rain*, in which the script and starring role are designed around a particular performer: "This was a part that Madonna could look at and say, 'I could play that!' And she could find things in her personality that could fit that, but that's not her. Susan's not Madonna" (Bego 1985, p. 116). Yet Seidelman has said that she cast Madonna over some two hundred actors who tested for the part because she believed her style and image provided elements suited to Susan's character:

> There was something about Madonna. I think it's just kind of her. . . . She's got a sort of a bad girl/good girl quality that I think is real interesting. She's a little tough, but not too tough. A little "street" but also, I think, real appealing. Earthy in a way that I thought was essential to the character. . . . I thought Madonna had a sort of authentic quality that would be really good to try to capture on film (Bego 1985, pp. 102–103).

In any event, the character of Susan clearly became blended with Madonna's star persona. A repertoire of intertextual references to Madonna blurred the lines between her film character and her already popularized image. Most obvious was the adoption of Madonna's style to create Susan's character. Fans of Madonna recognized the black bra straps, sunglasses, exposed midriff, crucifix and star jewelry, headbands fashioned from stockings, layered clothing, and stringy hair that had become Madonna signature marks in the several videos she had produced prior to the film. Reportedly, the film's costume designer, Santo Loquasto, originally conceived of Susan as having more of a "West Side old clothes and thrift-shop" look, but after Madonna's selection for the role, he decided to create an adaptation of her style and worked with her to recreate Susan's look (Bego 1985, p. 113). Costume pieces that serve as plot functions, such as Susan's pyramid-eye jacket and the rhinestone boots for which she trades the jacket, were combined with Madonna's own clothing (Bego, 1985). This touch makes Roberta's assumption of Susan's look in the film all the more susceptible to the reading that she represents a Madonna style imitator. A Madonna song also was used in one scene. Although apparently not written for the movie,[1] "Into the Groove" explicitly states the film's thematic content with its lyric, "Live out your fantasy here with me." The location chosen for the song's debut in the film was New York's Danceteria, a club Madonna fans know as the place that led to her first record contract. Footage from *Desperately Seeking Susan* was reorganized in the music video produced for "Into the Groove" and distributed by MTV, which had the intent and effect of attracting Madonna fans to the movie. But most striking of all are the character traits exhibited by Arquette's character, Roberta, the de facto "wanna-be." Roberta is oppressed by her gender condition and this motivates her to create an identification with Susan, whose unconventional life becomes an attraction. Roberta is media literate and (like a fan) actively uses her contact with media texts to formulate a response, indeed, to effect a positive change in her life.

In the film, Roberta is first shown in a beauty parlor,

where she is one among many suburban housewives getting their hair done. Shots of identically disposed women, with the manufactured uniformity of their looks, call attention to the similarity of their social condition and locate gender as a central theme. The song blaring over the scene, Carole King's "It's in His Kiss," associates the beauty "work" underway with the women's insecurities over their husbands' love (e.g., lyrics such as "Does he love me I want to know? How can I tell?") and identifies monogamous heterosexuality as their chief social doctrine. Roberta is accompanied by her sister-in-law Leslie, who has brought her to the shop for a new hairstyle. "This is your birthday, I want to give you something different," Leslie says to Roberta. The hairdresser chimes in, "Her husband will love it." The gesture of her sister-in-law's birthday present, a "new look" that Roberta does not want, but that her husband will love, demonstrates her effacement, and the general disregard for who she is as a person and for her potential as an individual. Later, we see Roberta's birthday celebrated by a party full of her husband's friends, at which she is obliged to play hostess. Her social position is summarized visually in a low-level photographic shot that severs her head from her body, leaving only her arms to serve hors d'oeuvres. Background lyrics of another King song float in as if in admonition, "You don't have to prove to me that you're beautiful." Roberta is portrayed as an appendage of her husband, a woman trapped within a female role and having very little sense of worth. Immersed in her middle-class values and female role, Roberta lives in fear of change and risk. When her hairdresser holds up a page from a hair fashion magazine and chortles, "The look is you," Roberta's reply is, "But I only want a trim." But as the film unfolds, Roberta's textual identifications, particularly with Susan, will change her into an active risk-taker.

Roberta's infatuation with the on-going correspondence between Susan and her boyfriend, Jim, in the personal ads of the newspaper appears initially to revolve around the intensity of Jim's romantic desire for his love, Susan. He beckons to her in dire tones through personals with the heading "Desperately Seeking Susan." But soon it becomes clear that it is Susan and what she represents, in short, everything that Roberta is not, but desires to be, that is the basis of her attraction. Susan is an adventurous spirit. She has style and purpose and is wildly desired, all of which makes her exhilarating to Roberta. Susan is introduced in the film self-confidently snapping Polaroid pictures of herself, a device that Seidelman used in her first film, *Smithereens*, but one that also neatly coincides with the figure of Madonna, who authored her own public image. Rather than fashioning herself after a photograph of a model, as Roberta does to achieve her new and "different" look, Susan has command of the photographic apparatus and her representation. She takes pictures of men (the man asleep in her hotel bed [not her boyfriend, Jim] and the bellboy who delivers a room-service meal), an activity that develops her as a character who reverses traditional gender roles and who assumes a dominant posture alongside men. Whereas Roberta is shown giving and serving in her scenes, Susan takes and is served. When she leaves the man in the hotel room, she takes his cash and the Egyptian earrings he has also stolen, thereby laying the foundation for his murder and her endangerment, the film's primary jeopardy.

In her first scene, Susan is dressed in the pyramid-eye jacket ("like on a dollar bill") that Roberta will later purchase and wear, beginning her assumption of Susan's life. She exudes an idiosyncratic, personal style that is far distant from the commercial fashions through which Roberta's world seeks difference and change. Susan (like Madonna) *is* different, partly because she has her *own* style. The comparison the film makes between Roberta's fulfillment of gender expectations and Susan's breach of the same establishes gender oppression as a context for Roberta's identification with the textual persona of Susan. And Roberta's desire for attention, recognition, and excitement, qualities of life that she sees embodied in Susan, are basic components of the "wanna-be" impulse. Roberta's use of textual identification as a means to discover her own identity replays the girl-fan response to Madonna.

Although the film begins by showing Roberta's fantasy identification with Susan as a vague and passive longing for change, this stance expands as the film develops to give textual identification the power to motivate Roberta's actions, to launch her style-imitation behavior. She is inspired by a number of textual encounters to start making changes in her life. In the kitchen after her party, seated next to the remains of her birthday cake, Roberta watches the movie *Rebecca*. The clip shows a scene from late in the movie. Maximilian de Winter (Sir Laurence Olivier) is unburdening his guilty conscience to his wife (Joan Fontaine), "Gone forever, that funny young lost look I loved. It won't ever come back. I killed that when I told you about 'Rebecca.'" The description, "funny young lost look," fits Roberta's expression perfectly, and the film's narrative line, which speaks of a change undergone and a husband at fault, creates an alignment between the film and Roberta's story. The scene in the kitchen takes place early in the film, immediately before Roberta makes her first initiatory move, before she goes to Battery Park to watch Jim meet Susan. It is the act of watching *Rebecca* that provokes her to act on her fantasy attraction to Susan.

Another textual interaction immediately precedes Roberta's first move to contact Susan personally—in order to return the key Susan had left in the pyramid-eye jacket. Although Roberta has already purchased and begun to wear Susan's jacket, she has not as yet become completely committed to the imitation of her persona. Roberta rushes home, after remembering to pick up Gary's dry cleaning (but not his radio), to start dinner. She runs a Julia Child videotape on her kitchen VCR and begins to mimic each step the video cook makes. Julia breaks eggs, Roberta breaks eggs; Julia grates cheese, Roberta grates cheese. By imitating Julia Child's video image, she creates without being creative, makes a gourmet meal without being a gourmet cook. The video program symbolically establishes a solution for Roberta—by imitating Susan/Madonna, she will become her and thereby produce the changes in her life that she cannot seem to make of her own volition.

After Roberta sees Susan "in the flesh" at Battery Park (although it is her image that she sees through the mediating device of a coin-operated telescope), Susan's clothes come to embody for Roberta a world of adventure and independence. As Susan walks off down the street after meeting Jim in the park, Roberta is compelled to follow her. Susan tries on a pair of sunglasses and a hat from a street vendor. Roberta, at her heels, her "lost look" in place, repeats Susan's actions. She moves as if in a trance, as if immersed in a dream. All of Roberta's textual interactions are called up to constitute her motivation at this moment: her identification with the victimized wife in *Rebecca*, her imitation of Julia Child's video cookery, even her participation in re-creating the look of others through her new hairstyle. She moves into full style imitation of Susan and begins to live Susan's life. This moment in the film is one that style imitators in the audience would see as epiphanal, the moment Roberta decides (is driven) to be a style imitator. Madonna's "wanna-be" fans were already organizing around the practice of style imitation before principal shooting on the film was completed in November 1984. They were described in Madonna's first *Rolling Stone* cover story the same month: "The Madonna clones are ratting their hair, putting on rosaries and baring their bellies from coast to coast" (Connelly 1984, p. 81). For these fans, the film's portrayal of Roberta's identification with and style imitation of Susan was surely striking in its similarity to their own identification with and imitation of Madonna.

Desperately Seeking Susan organized a clearer, more accurate picture of the "wanna-be" connection to a textual persona than any produced by critics of actual "wanna-be" fans. Roberta never fully assumes the personality of Susan. But neither does she maintain the persona of Roberta, at least not the Roberta of "Gary's wife," which the film's audience comes to recognize was never who she really was in the first place. It is as if her imitation of Susan's style enables her to develop a personality all her own. This is crucial to understanding Roberta's response, particularly if it is proposed to extract from the film any insight into the imitative practice of Madonna "wanna-bes." More than a mindless reproduction of a star's clothing and hairstyle, style imitation operates as a medium that allows the discovery of creative impulses and the initiation of transformations.

In the world of the movie, assuming the identity of Susan produces a number of changes in Roberta. She leaves suburbia and discovers urban living. She leaves Gary and falls in love with another man. She ends her isolated existence as a housewife by getting a job in which she helps onstage to perform magic tricks for an audience. Even the murder adventure that Roberta inadvertently becomes involved in provides a contrast to her previous boring and staid existence. By the film's end, her husband, Gary, and sister-in-law, Leslie, are ready to admit, "She's really got style in a way; she's good," upon seeing Roberta's perfected stage act. Roberta also gets to meet Susan, her textual inspiration, in a scene in which they join forces to capture a murderous thug. In the last moment of the film, the two are shown hand-in-hand in a photograph on the cover of their beloved newspaper, being cited by the city for their efforts. The headline reads, "What a Pair!" Roberta has become what Susan represented to her initially, a textual figure worthy of recognition and perhaps worthy of yet another woman's identification.

Throughout the film, Susan serves as a guide through Roberta's dissatisfactions and fantasies. She discovers (in the not-so-hidden bedside chest of drawers) the books that are evidence of Roberta's intense involvement with textual products and her quest for relief from isolation in the home— *How to Be Your Own Best Friend*; *I'm OK, You're OK*; and *Dr. Ruth's Guide to Good Sex*. But it is Roberta's diary, which Susan unbashedly reads aloud, that reveals the intricacies of her fascination with the "text" of Susan: "He's looking for Susan again. She's late returning from Mexico. This is the fifth ad he's run. Why does he want to see her so badly? Who is she?" The exposure of Roberta's secret textual fantasy causes Gary and Leslie to ruminate wildly about her disappearance. They summon up fantastic scenarios about the secret lives of women. Perhaps she is a prostitute by day and returns to be a suburban housewife only in the evenings. But how to explain Roberta's selection of a woman, Susan, as her object of desire? Unable to fathom an identification rooted in social condition, they evoke the model of sexual attraction. She must be a lesbian, they conclude. The logic reproduces the common confusion over the same-sex star–fan identifications generated by Madonna's popularity with female audiences.

This confusion entered the dialogue of the movie's prerelease promotion. Two months before the film's release, *Rolling Stone* alluded to a parallel in the relationship between actors Arquette and Madonna and that of the characters they play in the film. The story, with an accompanying photograph, appeared in "Random Notes," a section that typically contains comments on a promotional photograph, using upbeat, gossipy prose while providing information on release dates or pertinent career moves of media stars. The headline reads,

"Two Lucky Stars Take a Shine to Each Other." In its use of the phrase "lucky stars" the headline makes reference to Madonna's hit video/song "Lucky Star." The phrase, however, uses the plural form of "star," thereby collapsing the two women together in "Madonna-ness." The headline suggests that the two actors have grown to like each other, to become something of a team, even friends, through the process of making *Desperately Seeking Susan*. The story's text emphasizes their closeness:

> In their co-starring movie, *Desperately Seeking Susan* (due in March), Rosanna Arquette takes on aspects of Madonna's personality—but who's borrowing whose style here? Well, both say they recognized similarities in each other right away. "We're like sisters—we've got lots of miseries in common, and boyfriend problems," says Madonna of her friend. "I love her," reciprocates Rosanna, "She's my long-lost sister." Now that they've found each other, the two intend to share social lives as much as possible (Ginsberg 1985, p. 6).

In the account, Madonna is quoted as calling Arquette her "sister." Arquette also refers to Madonna as a "sister," but with the additional inference of a "lover" ("I love her"). The author, Merle Ginsberg, uses the more neutral word "friend" to describe Arquette's relationship with Madonna, but at the text's end employs flowery descriptions more suited to lovers. Phrases in the last sentence, "now that they've found each other" and "share social lives as much as possible," are written in veiled language that could describe lovers.

The accompanying photograph is more ambiguous and provocative than the text in describing their relationship. Both women are dressed alike as Susan/Roberta–Madonna/Rosanna in pyramid-eye jackets. The jacket is more coded by Madonna's wearing of it than by its presence in the film, which had yet to be released. Both wear tights tied around their hair, the Madonna signature style that she brought to Susan's costuming. Arquette's leather pants, however, have no direct reference to the film's costume design. They are a sign of Arquette's own statement, and she wears them with the jacket in the mode of the female fans at Madonna's concerts, combining an item of star imitation with an item of personal clothing. The leather pants also contribute to the subtly sexual pose Arquette holds as she looks directly into the camera. The only visible key lighting is the sheen on her leather-clad hip. Although she is shown standing in profile, it is evident that her legs are parted. Madonna's pose is far more demonstrative, more dominant in its body language. Her right arm encircles Arquette's neck, and her left hand is placed so as to strengthen the hold. Her arm circles as if to choke—or is it to embrace? Arquette's right hand is placed over Madonna's elbow as if to pull her arm away—or is it to reciprocate the caress? Therein lies the core of the dilemma posed by the photograph: Is it hatred? Sexual love? Or is it friendship? Is the relationship reciprocal, or does Madonna dominate? The portrait must have intrigued fan viewers, planting a question in their minds: Did Arquette become a Madonna "wanna-be" during the making of *Desperately Seeking Susan*?

Macy's "Madonna Look-Alike Contest"

The shopping mall became one key site around which the Madonna and Lauper fan communities coalesced. "Madonna is everywhere," one biographer wrote. "There is even a mall in California that people have nicknamed 'the Madonna mall' because so many girls who shop there try to look just like her" (Matthews 1985, p. 8). Music video displays began popping up in "Juniorwear" departments at shopping malls across the country, the connection between MTV and girl culture having been recognized. While Lauper and Madonna videos were not the only ones shown in the displays, it was their clothing styles that the marketplace scrambled to emulate. Responding to the popularity of the two musicians, the fashion industry manufactured ready-to-wear fashion lines inspired by the stars' styles. *Seventeen* magazine ("Funky Frills," 1985) billing itself as "Young America's Favorite Magazine," disseminated word of Lauper-inspired fashion accessories: black rubber bracelets, twelve for $4; multicolored rhinestone bracelets, $9 each; black leather wristband with rhinestone cluster, $26; and gunmetal and rhinestone bracelets, $30 each. The Macy's Department Store in New York City created a whole department called "Madonnaland," devoted to cropped sweaters ($30), cropped pants ($21), and a variety of jewelry accessories such as crucifix earrings and outsized "pearl" necklaces ($4–$59) that resembled those worn by Madonna. The department became the location for the mobilization of Madonna fans in the summer of 1985, when Macy's sponsored a "Madonna Look-Alike Contest" to coincide with the star's New York concert date.

To encourage attendance, the store ran a full-page ad in the *Village Voice*, with text designed to capitalize on fan familiarity with Madonna's *Material Girl* video and the movie *Desperately Seeking Susan* (both released in 1985), in which she performed the song, "Into the Groove":

JRS!
DESPERATELY SEEKING MADONNA LOOK-ALIKES

Join our Madonna Day contest, Thurs., June 6 in Madonnaland on 4, Macy's Herald Square. If you're a brassy material girl, get into the groove and prove it (Village Voice, 1985).

Contestants presented themselves before judges (one of whom was Andy Warhol), who were seated beside a bank of video monitors that continuously played Madonna videos. A giant reproduction of Madonna's *Time* magazine cover (May

1985) presided over the event. The parade before the judges summoned up that ideological apogee of female competition, the beauty contest, but gave it a new context by involving girls who were united by membership in the same fan community. As a group, the contestants demonstrated a wide range of interpretations of Madonna's look. The differences were partly a product of Madonna's own cultivation of many looks, but they were also clearly a product of creative recombination. The fans balanced imitation of the star with the projection of self. On this instance, style imitation was, more accurately, style appropriation. Assuming the appearance of Madonna meant, in actuality, the dynamic taking-over of her style for their own personal and collective uses.

In sponsoring the contest, Macy's was clearly motivated by the desire to sell its "Madonnaland" clothes and accessories. The "Look-Alike" contest provided a direct incentive to peruse the department and purchase ensembles. But the fans' active participation in the store-sponsored contest also represented the fan community's selection of the store for its fan event. Style imitators involved stores as point of reference in an assertion of shopping and fashion as an authentic arena of female-adolescent culture.

The sexual division of labor and the regimen of female domesticity has long positioned women as the primary consumers in American society (Gardiner, 1979; Weinbaum and Bridges, 1979; Harris and Young, 1981). But stores came to be defined as female social space, as female cultural arenas, in the late nineteenth century. Leach (1984) has linked the rise of consumption culture before the turn of the century to a transformative effect on women's experience of gender. Centralized sites of consumption, in the form of department stores, offered middle-class women a socially acceptable way to escape the confines of the house and provided a richly imaginative culture in which to explore social possibilities. Leach's historical research provides details of how the department store also became an important center of women's political life. Newly cultivated advertising methods and modes of store display prompted suffragists of the period to adopt colorful, graphic forms of political expression. Stores were selected as sites from which suffrage activities were publicized and coordinated:

> Stores everywhere volunteered their windows and their interiors for suffrage advertising. In June 1916 Chicago's Carson, Pirie Scott [a department store] installed a wax figure of a suffragist in one of its windows, a herald of the coming convention of the Woman's Party in that city. At about the same time, Wanamaker's set a precedent by permitting all female employees to march in suffrage parades during working hours. In 1912 suffragists chose Macy's in New York as the headquarters for suffragette supplies, including marching gowns, bonnets, and hatpins (Leach 1984, pp. 338–339).

Culture critics have been reluctant to consider arenas of consumption as sites of cultural production. Characteristically, they express an aversion to all forms of commercial culture, coding the marketplace as the antithesis of authentic cultural expression and as essentially a mechanism of capitalist economic reproduction. Such assumptions create obstacles to the analytical treatment of consumer girl culture, operating to reduce girl participation in consumption to a kind of "false consciousness,"[2] of use only to the dominant order as a means to prepare girls for reproductive social roles. Carter (1984, p. 186) developed McRobbie's (1980) critique of male bias in theoretical work on youth subculture[3] by focusing on the way certain culture critics have blended commercialism and gender, deprecating both consumption and women simultaneously: "The analyses themselves are founded on a number of unspoken oppositions: conformity and resistance, harmony and rupture, passivity and activity, consumption and appropriation, femininity and masculinity."

In contemporary life, the shopping mall has come under the reign of teen and preteen girls. Consumer culture helps define and support female-adolescent leisure and culture practices. The mall is a popular female substitute for the streets of male adolescents. Its corridors offer active and semi-anonymous areas for adolescent loitering and peer gatherings, but within a more restricted and supervised setting. Girls at the mall have the option to retreat into stores, which provide the added attraction of shopping, an activity girls like to do together. Visiting the mall and shopping are not merely behaviors about the act of consumption, they are ways for girls to involve themselves in their own brand of adolescent culture, peer bonding, and the construction of style.

Both Madonna and Lauper adeptly created styles and video texts that acknowledged and celebrated adolescent girls' involvement in appearance and consumer girl culture. Madonna manipulated the "glamour" look and the codes of high fashion into appropriations and recombinations that tap into girls' fascination with fashion models and the ability of celebrities to direct trends. Lauper wore thrift store and boutique outfits that recirculated fashions from the past, calling attention to the circularity of consumption, pointing out ways to construct personal style on a budget, and suggesting how to exercise control over the terms of prevailing fashion. The styles of the two stars articulated the tensions between conforming to and resisting codes of gender-specific appearance, between following marketplace dictates and innovating fashion trends.

The overwhelming response to Macy's "Madonna Look-Alike Contest" by Madonna's fans was featured on both MTV and "ABC World News Tonight," where the "wanna-bes" reveled in their new-found fame. On camera, they gushed that they too "wanted to be famous" and "to be looked at" like their idol, Madonna. And for one magical moment, in front of ABC and MTV viewers, it came to pass.

"ABC World News Tonight" Presents
Madonna and Fans

Occasionally the timeliness and visible popularity of contemporary culture sends reporters scrambling to interpret popular culture phenomena. One such occasion was the "ABC World News Tonight" report (Aaron, 1985) on Madonna and her female fans, which followed Macy's "Look-Alike" contest and Madonna's concert tour and included film footage from both. The news story on Madonna and her style imitators was a fascinating moment in which journalism and popular culture were made to intersect. They were brought into what can only be described as an uneasy relationship; but it was a revealing one nonetheless, for a number of dominant approaches to popular culture were exposed in the process. And it was these ideological assumptions about popular culture that prevented a truly insightful report on Madonna's popularity and her fans' response.

"ABC World News Tonight" attempted to shape the report on Madonna and her fans to match the conventions of television news reporting, but both anchor Peter Jennings and reporter Betsy Aaron were faced with the problem of how to present objectively (in actual terms, *interpret*) an emergent popular culture event. In terms of journalistic assumptions, contemporary cultural phenomena suffer from a lack of history and context. Years of reporting on national or state news are useless to the reporter. For reports on emergent contemporary culture, there is no file footage. Popular culture is envisioned as a ship without port or anchor, sustained by its ability to float on the wave of fickle popularity. It was only the massive nature of Madonna's popularity, her and her fans' precocious visibility, that forced open the door to prime-time news, and even then gave them access to only the "kicker story" slot, the slot that closes out the newscast.

Jennings' opening remarks reveal the pervasive bias in favor of cultural events with a recognized history, those that have already been subjected to classification and evaluation, the "unnew": "And finally this evening: Madonna. If you think we are referring to the sweet expressions by the painter, Raphael, you clearly do not have a teenage daughter" (Aaron, 1985). His description of Raphael's paintings as "sweet expressions" evoked the historical, consensual evaluation of the dead artist's work. The reference to Raphael served to frame the upcoming story on popular culture in an oppositional relation to the normative standard of high art and high culture—a classic ideological scheme to devalue popular culture events.

Aaron's reportorial tactics were complicit, yet also more exploratory. Set adrift in the unfamiliar waters of popular culture, she was forced to formulate questions as well as answers in an attempt to avoid getting the story wrong. The result was the presence throughout the news story of alternating patterns of openness and closure, of exploration and convention. There was a lack of definitive analysis; at times a veritable catalog of possible angles on the story was presented alongside efforts to mold the story to news conventions and the ideology of popular culture.

In conventional reporting style, no fewer than four "experts" were called upon to give testimony, to define a context for the strong appeal Madonna holds for teenage girls—the "wanna-bes," whose images were strewn throughout the report. The choice of a reporter from *Rolling Stone* magazine was logical because Madonna's fame began in the world of popular music. But why did "ABC World News Tonight" select Merle Ginsberg, who had written very little in *Rolling Stone* on Madonna? Why weren't writers Christopher Connelly (1984) or Fred Schruers (1985) chosen, both of whom authored feature stories on Madonna? Perhaps it was because Merle Ginsberg is a woman. In fact, all four experts were female. But despite this, the gender critique of Madonna's popularity remained submerged, indeed suppressed, by Aaron's organization of the report.

Ginsberg's critique of Madonna—that she represents the "lowest common denominator of the American dream"—suggested that Madonna's appeal was to be understood as rooted in the fiber of American cultural values. Yet Ginsberg's amplification suggested another, more specific possibility: "She's got it all. She has a career, a love life, she's popular." These are the dreams of the *female* American striving to reconcile a desire for financial and spiritual attainment with the ideology of romantic love and the material realities of a sexual division of labor within the family. And what could be a more coded reference to female adolescence than the wish to be popular? But these were not the areas of desire that Aaron wanted to articulate or examine, despite the fact that they are the very building blocks of context that she needed for the sake of accuracy. The female fan respondent who appeared after Ginsberg's address offered a muted explanatory line. "I want to be famous like Madonna," she stated, speaking in the argot of Madonna "wanna-bes." Without a focus on gender inequality, which would have revealed the historical lack of recognition girls and women have received as cultural agents, the "wanna-be's" expression of desire for fame was reduced to the mire of popular culture ideology, where celebrity is a trivial flash in the pan. The historical background of the female-adolescent reader of Madonna's texts was denied and repositioned to disallow political effect.

But if there was to be no gender critique in the report, why was feminist Betty Friedan the second expert witness? Within Aaron's authorial command of the story, Friedan appeared as an instrument to support Aaron's efforts to discredit the major players of her report, Madonna and, by implication, those who identify with her. As she set up the transition to Friedan's segment, Aaron said of Madonna, "Her street-wise, funky, trashy look is not new. Her brand of teasing is not new," summoning up the classical treatise that popular culture is derivative, regurgitative, devoid of the originality and uniqueness that characterizes and defines high art. Each phrase Aaron uttered was accompanied by the line, "It doesn't matter," a veiled slur on the audiences who popularize Madonna. Friedan's voice was introduced in an attempt to confirm Aaron's analysis, saying, "She's a Marilyn Monroe look-alike." But again, as in the case of Ginsberg's remarks, the expert's comments spilled over the authority of the news reporter, contradicting Aaron, and setting a different agenda that had its foundation in female gender experience. "But she's not a victim," Friedan continued. "She's courageous and gutsy and individual." Friedan finally appeared on camera, saying, "I think her appeal is that she is feminine, she is herself, she is sexual, but she's strong." Despite the direction of Aaron's script, presenting Madonna's textual representations of female experience as mere recycling, Friedan's speech argued for their nuances, for the very genius of popular culture—its capacity for reworking deeply felt cultural contradictions. Friedan's comments also introduced the possibility of Madonna's feminism.

As if to mitigate Friedan's insights, she was the only expert who appeared without a defining, descriptive label keyed in with her name. Although she was photographed in the conventional, almost trite mode of expert witnesses—in a medium close-up shot, sitting in front of shelves of books—her unnamed position of authority was an awkward absence. It was as if naming her as a feminist authority, as the author of *The Feminine Mystique*, would have forced the report in a direction Aaron did not want it to take. The reporter's monologue aimed for closure, yet the addition of Friedan's analysis kept the options open, offering news viewers a choice of readership positions.

Expert number three, Elsye Addams, spokesperson for Unique Clothing, appeared in what was almost a parody of the usual "expert" shot, pictured not in front of books or magazines as was the case with Ginsberg and Friedan, but in front of racks of clothing. A sense of clothing and style as (female) knowledge and authority is precisely what "wanna-bes" draw on when they reproduce the styles of the star on their own bodies. In imitating Madonna's look, they demonstrate their adeptness at reading textual products. But Aaron's use of Addams was not designed to facilitate an entree into the issues of youth and style. Instead it served to introduce other popular culture ideologies. Addams commented, "It's fun, it's young, it's trendy, it's sexy, and sex sells."

In case viewers remained unconvinced by Aaron's previous suggestion that Madonna was "not new," Aaron produced another argument in an attempt to claw the story back to the conservative position that popular culture is unworthy: If Madonna's message *is* new, then it's merely *trendy*. To attach the label of trendiness to a cultural artifact is to disqualify, deride, and de-legitimize it, and in this news report, the label emerged as an apology, a wink to skeptical and quite possibly shocked news viewers who might be wincing in their La-Z-Boy chairs at the sight of so much sexual license displayed in their nightly newscast. The "trendy" classification was linked to another damning accusation, that Madonna's representations and the "wanna-bes'" responses were nothing more than consumerism run rampant, a merchandising ploy. The mention of consumerism is a traditional way to avoid crediting popular culture with political implications, as if the practice of consumption is thoroughly unmotivated by interest or directed use. Again, the contextual nuances of the Madonna story were missed—the historical intersection between female labor, female politics, and consumption practice. The real experts in the story were the "wanna-bes" themselves, who appeared in shots standing in front of Macy's department store, with their peers, and on the street, scenes that conveyed their expertise in female music culture to those viewers able to recognize it.

Interestingly, this was a moment in the newscast when Aaron became more exploratory and questioning. It was also at this point that her failure to establish a context for "wanna-be" activities became most glaring. Aaron had yet to connect the star's media representations to the style-imitation practices of her female adolescent fans, and time was running out. In stilted language, Aaron inventoried the affects of Madonna-ness: "The naked middles, the corsets, the lace, the jewelry, the crucifixes . . ." trailing off, without a rudder to direct her course. She called on a "wanna-be" for guidance, but her lack of investigation into the context of female adolescence, style-imitation fan practices, and girl culture meant that she hardly knew where to begin with her questions. She asked tentatively, "When you dress up like this, how do you feel?" To which the girl answered, "I feel wonderful." Moving to her most intelligent question, marking the news story's "third act," Aaron asked in rhetorical earnestness, "What are these kids really saying?" Had her story ended with the question, with the relatively open-ended descriptive survey of the components and opinions she has been pursuing, Aaron's work might have made a contribution to the public forum. But her journalistic training snapped her back to the need for a neat resolution.

The final word was provided by the fourth expert, Dr. Joyce Brothers, whose comments were of the least explanatory order. What these "kids" were really saying, according to the psychologist, was "I want to be a virgin, but I want to be a virgin who looks like I'm a slut." The social underpinnings of that apparent contradiction, the usefulness of the masquerade to teenage girls, remained completely unexplored. But the more misleading, deceptive comment was the one that followed:

"Once she becomes a flesh and blood person—then it's on to the next." Madonna, because she is a textual persona, can never become a flesh and blood person. She is a representation that imparts meaning through the readers' interpretation. It is they who approve and create her textual address, responding in kind with their own re-presentation of the text—the imitation of her style and performance modes. Yet Aaron accepted Brothers' prediction of Madonna's fall from grace as a given, stating in her wrap up, "If she is half the person her fans believe her to be, she'll handle it and so will they." However, regardless of Aaron's premature penciling-in of Madonna's demise and her orchestration of expert testimony, it is the relationship between the audience and the text that explains and still sustains the figure of Madonna. [4]

"Madonna's 'Make My Video' Contest" on MTV

In the fall of 1986, MTV put out a call to its viewers to submit their own video renditions of Madonna's new single release, "True Blue," whose promotion followed on the heels of "Papa Don't Preach." Sire Records produced a *True Blue* video for European distribution, but opted for a promotional device in the United States that would involve MTV's viewers in their own video production. The contest, billed as "Madonna's 'Make My Video' Contest," promised the winner a trip to MTV's New York studio, where Madonna would personally award a $25,000 check live on MTV. Thousands of viewers submitted tapes, many obviously using home-movie and consumer video equipment, and using themselves, their family, and their friends as talent (Danielson, 1986). According to MTV publicist, Peter Danielson, who personally viewed all of the submissions, many of the tapes included images of Madonna "wanna-bes," and many appeared to have been pro-

duced by teenagers (Danielson, 1986). The video entries were
shown in a continuous run on MTV, an unprecedented display
of the channel's stated commitment to viewer participation—
the same song over and over for twenty-four hours, but each
time with a unique visual interpretation. The event created a
kind of hermeneutic excess around the song and emphasized
Madonna's role as the purveyor of multiple audience readings.

MTV selected ten finalists, obviously chosen on the basis
of high production values, and viewers voted for their favorite
entry by calling a designated phone number. The final winner was chosen according to a standard of popularity, not
slickness of production or concept creativity. "Decide care-
fully," veejay Alan Hunter told viewers on the evening MTV
aired the finalists' tapes. "You could be deciding someone's
career." It appears that the finalist tapes were made by people
with at least some prior video or film production experience,
who probably did hope to add the contest video to their re-
sumes. One finalist tape was directed by a camera operator who
had experience shooting over two hundred music videos, but
whose ambition was to direct; but another was made by col-
lege students. The videos were not necessarily made with big
budgets; the winning production team spent less than $1,000.

The concepts used in the videos were wide ranging and
included a number of different strategies for interpreting the
elastic boundaries of the song's encoded systems of meaning.
Three of the ten finalist videos, including the winning entry
(Finalist 3), incorporated a nostalgic, fifties-style production
design in a nod to the song's musical and vocal qualities. The
song's lyrical narrative about "true love" formed the basis of
seven, possibly eight, of the videos, but was used in very different ways. The first video shown (Finalist 1) manipulated
home-movie footage of a wedding. The director, who appears
in the video working on his entry, was in his late twenties to
early thirties, as were the bride and groom. The video invokes

the cultural apex of "true love" by focusing on marriage, but within an age and generational context that lies outside of an adolescent address. This is in contrast to the winning entry (Finalist 3), which sweetly portrays the innocent infatuation of young lovers, although its setting in the 1950s distances the romance story from contemporary life. The third romantic rendition of the "true love" theme (Finalist 4) combined a nostalgic fifties vision of love with a more cynical, contemporary point of view. The female protagonist is in love with a sailor who is at sea (an interpretation of the lyric "I've sailed a thousand ships"). Her girlfriends, who apparently think she should not limit herself to one (absent) boyfriend, keep coaxing her to get out of the house and to begin dating other boys. At one point, they deliver several prospects to her house (actual "calendar boys" according to MTV's Alan Hunter) and parade them in front of her, pinching and fawning over them as they wait for her to choose. Another video (Finalist 8), produced by three male students from Vassar, shows a boyfriend and girlfriend together in various locations but has very little romantic tension. It focuses more on the male protagonist than the female, unlike the more romantic videos. The man is photographed often in slow motion in a form similar to the lusty shot of Madonna's Italian lover in *Papa Don't Preach*, but without the same allusion to the female gaze.

Another set of videos that works with the "true love" theme is more idiosyncratic, even aberrant.[5] One (Finalist 7) uses heterosexual love as a means to speak metaphorically about the threat of nuclear war between the United States and the Soviet Union. In the fantasy that the video constructs, two lovers become the respective leaders of the two countries, making them unsusceptible to their advisors' war mentalities. Another video (Finalist 10) shows a teenage girl preparing for a date with her "true love," but at the video's end, it is her father who arrives to take her out, not a male peer. Still another video

(Finalist 9) uses the heterosexual love theme but reverses the romantic assumptions to show the couple arguing and fighting with each other. Lyrical justification for the rendition is located in the lyrics "I've heard all the lines, I've cried, oh, so many times," which occur immediately before the more romantic stanza, "Those tear drops they won't fall again, I'm so excited 'cause you're my best friend." Traditional romanticism is further undercut by the video's use of a black female protagonist and an urban, ethnic setting. Whereas a number of the romantic videos are dotted with colorful and expensive sports cars, this antiromantic video shows the girl in a Volkswagen.

Two videos resist creating a narrative about true love. The first (Finalist 2), directed by the ambitious camera operator, and by far the slickest production, relies on elaborate fifties-style staging and choreography for visual interest. Although there is plenty of suggestion of heterosexual attraction, it is of the generic variety; no male or female protagonist is singled out. The second (Finalist 5), the only entry directed solely by a woman, operates within a more abstract, video-art tradition. The director, her oversized head matted onto an out-of-proportion body, lip-synchs to the song in the foreground as various images appear in the background. The images coincide with their lyrical referent—pictures of lips and ships are shown when the words "lips" and "ships" are sung. Rather than structuring the video around a narrative line, the director adopted a kind of literal montage technique.

Although most of the videos list male directors,[6] a female point of view was implied in a number of them. This was facilitated by the song's first-person address by a female vocalist, the pop music beat, and the romance theme, but also by the context of female address on MTV and Madonna's authorship. The winning entry (Finalist 3) shows the female protagonist supported and guided by a group of girlfriends, a common discovery sign. They serve as intermediaries and make contact with the boy for her, and they encourage her to go to his door with a flower, reversing the usual gender-directed pattern of gift giving. The boy's character logic is determined by the female image of the "perfect boy." He is attentive, cute, playful like a friend (after the lyric, "You're my best friend"), and not sexual. The video contrasts him with a self-centered boy, who puts on his sunglasses, throws his leather jacket over one shoulder, and walks away from the girl.

The social world of girlfriends is also presented as being of great importance in the video (Finalist 4) about the love-struck girl who pines for her sailor. It is her girlfriends who care about her needs, not the seaman, who has left her behind. The entry (Finalist 7) that portrays U.S.–Soviet relations presents a decidedly female solution to the threat of nuclear war. The female protagonist becomes the president of the United States, and she and her lover, who has become the Soviet leader, ensure that the children of the world live in peace. The video encourages a consideration of children in an early scene in which a young boy and girl play together in the ocean, before their respective parents wrap them in the flags of their countries and separate them.

The video (Finalist 9) of the arguing couple is striking in its use of access signs. For much of the video, the girl walks the urban streets of downtown Los Angeles, leaving her boyfriend behind in their apartment. At one point she trails her fingers along the metal links of a chain-link fence in a shot that closely resembles Tina Turner's similar action in the video *What's Love Got to Do With It?* The girl has an individualistic style that incorporates several features of male clothing— black high-top boots, a velvet suit jacket, and torn jeans. The dance that she periodically breaks into on the street is not the synchronized choreography recorded in the fifties videos but a wildly individual street dance. Her arms and legs flail in a manner reminiscent of Lauper in *Girls Just Want to Have Fun*. The video incorporates a scene of conflict with a man, a textual strategy that occurs in a number of female-address videos (*Love Is a Battlefield; What's Love Got to Do With It?; Borderline*). The girl strikes her boyfriend with a pillow, spilling feathers everywhere. At the video's end, while walking down a busy sidewalk, the girl encounters a boy who stops her in an attempt to dance with her. At first she refuses, but then she gets caught up in his actions and begins to dance with him in a manner that suggests a new-found reciprocity and equality with boys. They circle each other, dancing a similar dance, and then depart arm-in-arm down the sidewalk. The action recalls Tina Turner's encounter with a man on the street in *What's Love Got to Do With It?* and prefigures Madonna's dance with the young boy in *Open Your Heart*.

Visual references to Madonna appear in four of the videos, although in two videos they are relatively veiled. In the wedding video (Finalist 1) the circumstances of Madonna's visualization reveal the male director's nonfan status. The home-movie sequence of the friend's wedding is framed by a reflexive introduction, in which the director watches Madonna promoting the video contest on MTV and then rushes out to buy the record before starting to work on his entry. At the end, he holds the *True Blue* album up to the camera and moves it back and forth while processing the image with video effects. His interest lies not with Madonna, he doesn't even own her album. It is his fascination with video production that has prompted his involvement with Madonna and the contest, a point he emphasizes by showing on camera his abundant supply of video equipment.

When references to Madonna appear in videos with female protagonists, they take a distinctly different form. Although the video about global peace (Finalist 7) appropriates the song for an idiosyncratic political statement, the female protagonist was apparently selected because she has a general resemblance to Madonna. It is she who becomes the president of the United States, according to the video's fantasy. The girl in the "daddy love" video (Finalist 10) does not look like Madonna, but she does don the white lace gloves, multiple neck chains, and heavy make-up that is associated with Madonna's look and a "wanna-be's" practice of style imitation. A photograph of Madonna's symbolic mentor, Marilyn Monroe, is stuck on her refrigerator door. The narrative resolution, in which she demonstrates her allegiance to her father, also aligns with the narrative concentration on a father figure in the previous Madonna video, *Papa Don't Preach*.

But the video (Finalist 6) that portrays the female-fan point of view on Madonna most concisely is the one that features the full-fledged style-imitation performance of a Madonna "wanna-be." Her performance represents "true love" from a female fan's perspective, the love of the star and her textual offerings. The video begins with a shot of three adolescent girls analyzing photographs of Madonna from her "Virgin Tour" concert program. From the gestures the girls make, it can be deduced that Madonna's facial expressions are under particular scrutiny. The blonde girl in the center is then featured in the rest of the video as a style imitator of Madonna.[7] Her reconstruction of Madonna's look, gestures, and dance is very close to Madonna's original video performances. One casual viewer to whom I showed the video mistakenly thought the woman *was* Madonna. Skillfully made-up and costumed to look like Madonna, the girl expertly depicts gestures and dance steps from virtually all of Madonna's videos and the film *Desperately Seeking Susan*. Madonna's street attire from *Borderline* is reproduced down to the "Boy Toy" belt buckle and the fought-over hat. Madonna's sexual look from *Papa Don't Preach* is duplicated in the impersonator's black body stocking, her dance moves, and her tossed-back head, while Madonna's school-girl look is represented by her T-shirt, which bears the phrase,

"Italians Do It Better." The girl becomes Susan from *Desperately Seeking Susan* by putting on reproductions of the sunglasses, pyramid-eye jacket, and jewelry that Madonna wore in the film, and by mimicking her postures and gestures. She writhes on the floor in a black dress and blue stockings similar to Madonna's movement and attire in *Like a Virgin*. Her hair is styled like Marilyn Monroe's and she wears a rhinestone necklace and a facsimile of the pink dress from *Gentlemen Prefer Blondes*, which Madonna herself imitates in *Material Girl*. She wears a flowered dress and holds her knees to her bent head in the style of Madonna's *Live to Tell* video.[8] The director contributes to the effect through locations, props, and camera work that evoke those in Madonna's videos. The girl shakes a can of spray paint in front of a wall covered by grafitti and appears next to a statue of a male nude, both allusions to *Borderline*. At one point, the camera pans and picks up the girl's gaze in a shot that recalls a similar camera movement in *Papa Don't Preach*.

The video revels in a textual competency that only a fan (and possibly a scholar) could attain. Rather than illustrating a sequential progression of Madonna's looks or video texts, which might enable casual viewers to "catch on" to what they are witnessing, the references to individual videos are mixed up, intercut with each other as if secretly coded for only the most avid of fans to interpret. As a representational motif, style imitation allows the contest video to take advantage of a fan's knowledge of the star's image and textual address, while providing for both production and narrative economy. Appearance changes and performance manipulations avoid the use of expensive sets, actors, props, and an original script, yet give texture and depth to the song's interpretation. The video commemorates Madonna as a figure of cultural agency, as a historical subject, therein empowering both the star and her fan advocate.

NINE

POLYSEMY, POPULARITY, AND POLITICS

ONE DRIVING force behind this book has been my desire to refute the charge that MTV's visual discourse constitutes an overwhelmingly and uniformly sexist address. As critical academic work on MTV and its texts has developed during the period of my research, the issue of sexism has become a recurring and insistent theme. A "jump-on-the-bandwagon" momentum has fashioned the assertion of sexism, for many of MTV's critics, into a basic analytical assumption.

In the popular arena, the Parents' Music Resource Center (PMRC), headed by wives of prominent government officials, organized to focus attention on so-called pornographic rock-music lyrics and album covers and persuaded Congress to hold hearings on the enactment of a system for rating records similar to the one used for rating movies. Male musicians and bands came under the most fire, although Cyndi Lauper made the list for "She Bop," her song about female autoeroticism (The Women Behind the Movement, 1985). The Parents' Choice Foundation distributed a review of sexism on MTV in its newsletter, lumping Pat Benatar's *Love Is a Battlefield* in with its "worst case" videos and describing it in the following terms: "One performer fights with her ornery parents, then leaves home to become a hooker" (S. Wilson 1984, p. 3). [1]

In the world of academic criticism, the arguments are more sophisticated, but frequently lead to the same charge. Jane Brown and Kenneth Campbell (1986) used content analysis to assert the lack of positive female images on MTV without ever addressing the issue of female musicianship. E. Ann Kaplan (1985, 1986, 1987) has pointed out "alternative" representations in some of the same videos analyzed in Chapter Six but, ultimately, argued for the overdetermination of male address: "Despite the thematic positioning of women in these videos, iconographically the female body is usually presented in the traditional patriarchal 'feminine.' We have another example of the constraints of working within commercial forms, which always insist upon the culturally defined 'ideal' feminine" (Kaplan 1985, p. 15). Kaplan further contended that the twenty-four-hour flow of MTV "de-centers" the spectator, rendering engagement with individual "alternative" texts impossible, a position fundamentally at odds with the practice of fandom. Her over-arching reliance on a "postmodern" critique turned the analysis against issues of signification and the creation of meaning by interested viewers.

My own discussion of MTV's textual nature identifies and analyzes a "preferred" system of male address on MTV, taking up the issue of "sexism-in-the-text," but in the broader terms of hegemonic preference as discussed by Stuart Hall (1980, 1982). Hall (1982) described a tendency for texts to contain the codes and systems of meaning that reproduce dominant political interests. Applying Antonio Gramsci's (1971) theory of hegemony to signification practices, Hall has argued that the power to signify, to control "the means by which collective social understandings are created" is fundamental to the ability of the ruling power to maintain consent over subordinates (Hall 1982, p. 70). In the case of male address on MTV, the hegemonic relations of gender inequality are manifested in the exclusion of girls from its system of male-adolescent discourse and in their coded and narrow textual representation.

This textual enactment of gender ideology and social discourse is what feminist and moralist critics are observing when they raise objections to sexual stereotyping and misogynic imagery on MTV. But this polemical criticism fails to consider the conditional and historical character of textual meaning and the role of human agency in signification practices. The charge of sexism is an important one because it places an emphasis on textual politics, but it also reduces complex textual and social processes to simplistic and one-dimensional characterizations of how meaning is generated and exchanged. Most crucially, it fails to recognize that social struggles for power are linked to textual struggles over meaning. By looking for textual examples of social reproduction on MTV, the critics overlook the contesting of social (gender) inequalities that take place in the text, and also fail to see the points at which textual and social practices intersect.

John Fiske has argued that television texts are by their very nature contradictory and polysemic. This condition, he suggests, is dictated in part by economic necessity: "In order to be popular, television must reach a wide diversity of audiences, and to be chosen by them, be an open text" (Fiske 1986, p. 392). Although producers attempt to emphasize their preferred codes, the polysemy of the text creates a "semiotic excess," which is then "available for the culturally subordinate to use for their own cultural-political interests" (Fiske 1986, p. 403). This surplus of meaning facilitates the undoing of the producing industry's preferred ideological address and creates the conditions for struggles over meaning.

My findings suggest that semiotic excess is structured strategically rather than uniformly to produce a textual address. It was this *selective* polysemy that sparked struggles over meaning on MTV. In its earliest years, MTV's male-adolescent address was so narrowly conceived that it catered almost exclusively to white male adolescents. Before gender became the object of struggle on MTV, the battlelines were drawn over the lack of a semiotic position for black youth in its adolescent address. Black musicians and their record companies hedged their bets by exploring alternative channels of distribution for their promotional videos, such as the cable channel Black Entertainment Television (BET). Under pressure, MTV expanded its textual discourse to include certain (popular) black-male forms of adolescent experience in videos such as Michael Jackson's *Beat It*. The controversy over the ethnic complexion of male-adolescent discourse produced a semiotic excess that helped ensure a more solidly entrenched male address. The pessimistic realism of male gang warfare in *Beat It* and the playful nostalgia of white-male juvenile delinquency presented in *Sexy and 17*, suggest differing, ethnically specific, visions of male adolescence, even as they fundamentally unite behind an ideology of male-adolescent superiority and privilege. Therefore, while MTV's male address was not wholly omnipotent or devoid of contradiction on questions of masculinity and adolescence, it still remained semiotically impoverished for female audiences.

MTV's male-adolescent address was relatively closed in the sense that it failed to provide textual points of identification for those explicitly outside its system of address—namely, girls. However, it was *possible* for girls to create a place for themselves in their reading of the videos' texts—for instance, by identifying with a male performer. For certain female viewers, the blatant exclusion of a female-subject position was undoubtedly a source of discomfort, and conceivably a source of consciousness raising. And, as comments by female fans and female musicians suggest, picturing one's female self on stage in place of a male rock-and-roll star would not require a great leap of imagination. Nevertheless, MTV's symbolic reproduction of the gender-differentiated social conditions in adolescence (in which female adolescence is a subordinate discourse) left girls with few interpretive options. MTV's male-oriented semiotic excesses made its lack of female address all the more apparent and highlighted the socially inferior position of girls.

In hegemonic social relations, ruling members of the social order remain in the upper echelon of an unequal distribution of power and wealth only so long as they successfully promote an ideology that makes their superior position appear somehow natural. But at any strategic moment, subordinates may mobilize effectively to dismantle the ideological apparatus, thus threatening the continuation of the dominant group's rule. Similarly, the meanings encoded into texts are likely to be structured by hegemonic dominance but audiences may refuse to consent to the dominant meaning system (Hall, 1982). The dependence of popular culture texts on audience approval means that audiences can organize their opinions to encourage new textual practices.

Most discussions of textual struggle revolve around the audience–text relationship. Both Hall (1982) and Fiske (1986) attempted to understand how preferred encodings might be superseded by new orders of meaning through focusing their research on the interpretive practices of audiences. Encoding itself is considered to be an overdetermined source of hegemonic discourse and, therefore, receives little consideration. Fiske (1986), for example, used an "author-in-the-text" model, which did not consider the individuals or organizations that produce texts and provided no discussion of how textual polysemy might enable encoders to strike resonances with particular audiences, highlight specific social contradictions, or give voice to resistive stances.

Of course, there are a number of good reasons why theorists must be careful when approaching issues of authorship—the tendency to over-romanticize the idea of creative artistry, the difficulty of isolating individual creators within an industrial production practice, the problems that commercial and ideological imperatives pose for the production of subjective voices. Yet my study suggests that the definitional struggles over authorship in academic and popular criticism may be related to the contested and dynamic process of authorship construction that exists within commercial textual production itself. Rock musicians working within the record industry must constantly negotiate the contradictory roles they hold as self-expressive artists and paid workers in an industrial mode of music production. Female rock musicians contend additionally with their subordinate position as female social subjects. In order to function as authors, they (like all cultural producers) must be able to generate a consensus over their authoring of a particular product, a particular encoding.

In the case of MTV, the political stakes activated by the channel's construction of a preferred male address lie not only with the exclusion of a subjective female textual position, but also with the attempt to deny female musicians an authorship vehicle. Increasing numbers of female musicians found that they were not accommodated by MTV's system of representation. The channel's semiotic disparagement of female subjectivity left female musicians without the means to express their own gender-specific subjectivity and did nothing to improve on the discriminatory modes of female musician promotion. It was this semiotic spareness (gap in the semiotic excess) that made MTV vulnerable economically and ideologically. The presence of both a female audience without a textual address and female musicians newly in place at the site of production and in search of an authorship vehicle created the conditions for struggle over the terms of the channel's textual system. In other words, the emergence of female address on MTV involved more than the realization of oppositional decodings, or audience interpretations of a necessarily polysemic text, as suggested by the theoretical models of Hall (1980) and Fiske (1986), respectively. Rather, it resulted from a complex and dynamic interaction between decoding *and* encoding practices. Audiences and authors became allied at the site of the text and cooperated to make textual changes that were in their own respective social interests.

The female musicians I have discussed waged a cultural struggle against MTV's disparagements by appropriating the symbols used in MTV's male address, creating *access signs,* which exposed the privileged nature of male adolescence. This system of representation allowed the musicians to maintain the integrity of MTV's chosen semiotic formula, while broadening its system of meaning for female audiences. They rearticulated the deprived sign of the female body (and grouped female bodies) through textual strategies designed to create semiotic excess. The subordinate, yet complementary, discourse of female adolescence was useful in this endeavor. As Angela McRobbie and Jenny Garber (1976), and McRobbie (1980, 1983, 1984) have detailed, girls create their own elaborate cultural practices and discursive formations as a consequence of gender difference. This different, complementary cultural discourse allows girls to negotiate the contradiction between adolescent entitlement and female gender disenfranchisement. Discovery signs articulated modes of female-adolescent experience and desire, thus producing semiotic excess at the site of female representation.

The increase in female-oriented semiotic excess accomplished in MTV as a result of female address was demonstrated, in Fiske's (1986) terms, by a surge of popularity on the part of female-adolescent audiences. But this popularity was not merely an acknowledgment of MTV's broader textual address, it also recognized female musicians' struggles for authorship in an industrial and textual system that prefers male musicians and male-adolescent discourse. Female audiences provided audience consent, the essential link in those authorship struggles, accepting the musicians as authors of a subjective textual voice. Fandom proved to be an effective vehicle for girl audiences to organize in support of female-musician authors and female-address textuality. The fans' intense displays of identification with the text, particularly in the preferred form of style imitation, created structures of popularity that extended the usual measure of textual success—ratings (for television) and product sales (for music). Through their fan practices, girls produced a surplus of popularity, a kind of "popularity excess," which functioned to win consent for female-musician authorship and the alternative system of meaning represented in female-address videos.

The audience's participation, then, involved more than the interpretation of meaning against a preferred address, it entailed an alliance with particular encoders over the means of signification. The struggle over meaning took material form as new texts were created to convey a new textual address. Female address satisfied three groups: female musicians, who had been searching for a more complex and subjective mode of self-representation; female audiences, who wanted a system of textual discourse comparable to the prominent male-adolescent discourse; and even MTV, whose primary prerequisite was the delivery of a youth audience to advertisers. As a result, the preferred encoding that constituted male address was unable to sustain its ideological dominance fully. The creation of an alternative female address strained the hegemony of male-adolescent discourse central to rock music and music video. The previous control over the entry of women to cultural production, both as authors and as audiences, was undermined by their engagement in struggles over meaning on MTV. In an argument that sometimes serves as a companion piece to the charge of sexism, some critics have suggested that the political activism of rock music in the 1960s and 1970s withered away in the 1980s. MTV is cited as an example, if not a reason why. But the struggle over how gender is represented on MTV indicates that rock music may now be opening up to girls and women as a vehicle for their own subjective expressions and views. Moreover, pop music has begun to be recouped as a meaningful and artistic cultural arena.

I have explored in some detail the historical conditions that led female musicians to the moment of struggle over meaning on MTV and have looked at how the social contexts of gender and adolescence provided a basis for the articulation of a counter-address. But I have not delved into the social history, in particular, the history of women organizing for gender equality, which contributed to making MTV and music video a site for social struggle over gender oppression in the 1980s. It is significant, I believe, that leisure time and activities figure so prominently as a site of gender politics in music video. In the 1970s, the women's movement organized around the issue of jobs for women, often inadequately considering the domestic arena of female labor. In the 1980s, the wide popularity among girls and women, of Lauper's refrain "Girls just want to have fun" suggests a need to broaden the agenda to include a critique of leisure culture. Leisure is a powerful concept in male-adolescent discourse, embodying patriarchal patterns of male authority, camaraderie, and attitudes toward women and girls. Youth leisure culture rehearses male adolescents in male privilege before they enter the adult workforce, and establishes practices that continue to support the social system of gender inequality after their youth has ended.

Also significant is the way that female address on MTV has recognized adolescence as a particularly important time for the formation of gender ideologies and practices. The women's movement prompted research into the origin of sex-role typing and modes of parenting and teaching young children. But no special effort was made within the movement to investigate female adolescence or to enlist girls in the work of liberation. In fact, as media and advertising came under attack, images of female youth and youthfulness began to take on negative connotations. Two girls, in their contribution to a collection of articles published by the British women's magazine *Spare Rib* characterized the neglect as "ageism in the women's liberation movement" and pleaded for recognition within their own circle of gender:

> The women's movement must now come to terms with the contradiction of needing young women to be part of it, and treating us as if we were smaller, inadequate and immature versions of older women in it. Obviously our experiences are different from yours. But that doesn't make them less valid. Aren't we all meant to be learning from each other, and sharing these experiences? We can never really be together until the oppression of ageism is recognised and worked on (Sally and Ilona 1982, p. 158).

The emergence of female-adolescent discourse on MTV is important politically because it has provided a vehicle for girls to speak about their experiences as female adolescents. But it is also important because it has expanded the consideration of gender inequality to include adolescence, thus beginning the much needed work of acknowledging the fact that oppressed women begin their lives as oppressed girls.

NOTES

INTRODUCTION

1. Stuart Hall's (1983) term.

CHAPTER ONE

1. An update on MTV's ownership has been provided by Frederic Dannen (1987, p. 46): "MTV began as the creation of Warner Amex Satellite Entertainment, the defunct joint venture of Warner Communications and American Express. In 1984, Warner Amex sold one third of MTVN (MTV Network) to the public. The network was then acquired by Viacom in 1986, after an abortive attempt to go private in a leveraged buyout."

2. For a discussion of qualitative methodology, see Clifford Christians and James Carey (1981).

CHAPTER TWO

1. WASEC conducted consumer lifestyle evaluations of potential MTV viewers to discover "the way the channel should feel, the

image, the style, what the veejays should wear" (Levy, 1983, p. 33).

2. Frankfort School is a shorthand designation for the theoretical perspectives that emanated from scholars associated with the Institute for Social Research opened in 1923 in Frankfort, Germany, as a center for Marxist scholarship, many of whom later relocated to the United States with the advent of fascism. Participating scholars such as Max Horkheimer, Herbert Marcuse, and Theodor Adorno concluded that under an advanced capitalist state, media was motivated by sheer economic determinism and resulted in the manipulation of consumers. See Bennett (1982) for a critical review of the Frankfort School perspective.

3. I use the term "patriarchy" in an informal sense, (as have other feminist critics) to describe an institutionalized system of male privilege and female subordination under capitalism, and not as a strict anthropological description.

4. An interesting comparison is the Spanish-language music-video program on the cable channel, SIN, described by Greg Easley and Lauren Rabinovitz (1988, p. 65): "*TNT*, the music video show that has replaced *Video Exitos* (1984–1987) in the same SIN time slot, has somewhat reconfigured the veejay while maintaining her same basic function. The new program features TWO female veejays in their early twenties, fashionably dressed in clothing provided by the youth-oriented, transnational Benetton, Inc. The women 'perform' on a set designed to simulate a typical (though large), up-to-date female teenager's bedroom. Dressed in lavender, yellow, pink and blue, the set is a high-tech, idealized interpretation of bourgeois teenage desires. The cluttered room is adorned with wall posters of pop stars, stuffed animals and dolls, soft, color-coordinated furniture, and, of course, the latest in audio-visual gadgetry, including a stereo, television and VCR."

CHAPTER THREE

1. Similar representations occur in Pat Benatar's *Love Is a Battle-field* and Tina Turner's *Private Dancer*.

CHAPTER FOUR

1. Tim O'Sullivan and associates (1983, p. 102) define hegemony as follows: "A concept developed by Gramsci (1971) and taken up in cultural studies, where it refers principally to the ability in certain historical periods of the dominant classes to exercise social and cultural leadership, and by these means—rather than by direct coercion of subordinate classes—to maintain their power over the economic, political and cultural direction of the nation. The crucial aspect of the notion of hegemony is that it operates not by forcing people against their conscious will or better judgement to concede power to the already-powerful, but that it describes a situation whereby our consent is actively sought for those ways of making sense of the world which 'happen' to fit in with the interests of the hegemonic alliance of classes, or 'power bloc.'"

2. Music teacher Elaine McCauley from Tucson, Arizona, has informed me that this classic mnemonic device for learning the position of notes on a musical staff has been updated by her male guitar students to "*E*mpty *G*arbage *B*efore *D*ad *F*lips," a phrase that perpetuates the original focus on boys and men by referencing a son's chore and a father's rule. With respect to the original, a simple alteration would correct the gender bias, "*E*very *G*irl (and) *B*oy *D*oes *F*ine."

3. See also Michelle Rosaldo (1980), in which Rosaldo critiques her previous work as well as the work of others who have relied heavily on a structural conceptual framework. While Rosaldo does not disavow her earlier work on the domestic/public split, she does critically dismantle the structuralist influence on it. In effect, Rosaldo has moved from the narrow, deterministic frame sometimes exhibited in her early work toward a multi-faceted approach to social relations, toward specificity, toward the individual actor, and toward understanding relationships between and among women *and* men.

4. For discussions in these areas see Robert Angus (1976), Mark Hickling (1981), Marc Kirkeby (1980), Steve Pond (1982), and Robert Wallace (1980).

CHAPTER FIVE

1. From "I Might Have Been Queen," recorded by Tina Turner (credited songwriters: Jennette Obstoj, Rupert Hine, Jamie West-Oram; 1984, Capitol Records).

2. "What's Love Got to Do with It?" recorded by Tina Turner (credited songwriters: Terry Britten, Graham Lyle; 1984, Capitol Records).

3. From "Takin' It Back," recorded by Pat Benatar (credited songwriters: Neil Geraldo and P. Giraldo; 1984, Chrysalis Records).

4. As told to the author by Pat Benatar, August 1988.

5. Tina Turner reports a similar motivation for her stage clothing: "Everything I've done for my act has really been so practical. I started wearing net stockings because the other stockings ran. . . . The leather came because I was looking for a material that didn't show perspiration. . . . Dirt doesn't show on leather, and it's good for traveling. It doesn't wrinkle, and it's durable. When I wore it, I didn't think people were going to think I was hot or tough" (Collins, 1986, pp. 106–108).

6. Steve Pond (1980, p. 13) quotes Pat Benatar as saying, "The shit the record company puts out is embarrassing. I came back from the last tour and found out they'd made a cardboard cutout of me in my little tights. What has that got to do with anything? They also took out an ad in *Billboard* and airbrushed part of my top off. They knew I'd never pose like that, so they took the cover of the new record, moved the bottom line up a bit and airbrushed it to look like I'm naked. If *that* is gonna sell records, then it's a really sorry thing."

7. From "One Track Mind," recorded by Cyndi Lauper (credited songwriters: Cyndi Lauper, Jimmy Bralower, Jeff Bova, Lennie Petzie; 1986, Portrait/CBS Records).

8. At this writing, Lauper and her manager have reportedly assumed a strictly business relationship.

9. Acting as the songs' publisher, Rick Chertoff probably stood to gain additional compensation over and above his cut as producer.

10. From "Girls Just Want to Have Fun," recorded by Cyndi Lauper (credited songwriter: Robert Hazard; 1983, Portrait/CBS Records).

11. From "Over and Over," recorded by Madonna (credited song-writers: Madonna and Steve Bray; 1984, Sire Records).

12. Mark Bego (1985) reports that Madonna's contract started out as a "singles" deal with an option for an album if the records sold well. Three singles were released before an album was produced: "Everybody" (which went to Number 3 on the dance music chart), "Burning Up," and "Physical Attraction."

13. See Christopher Connelly (1984) Fred Schruers (1985; and 1986), Mikal Gilmore (1987). *Rolling Stone*'s cover headline, "Madonna on Being a Star," is particularly evocative of pop discourse.

CHAPTER SIX

1. The original impetus behind my identification of these two categories of sign types came from my reading of Mica Nava's (1984) article on youth service provision to girls in Britain.

2. The term "woman-identified" is borrowed from Adrienne Rich (1983, p. 199), who characterizes "woman-identification" as "a source of energy, a potential springhead of female power."

3. The girl's preganancy is particularly ambiguous. There are limited visual signs of her pregnancy although in the soundtrack, the lyric line, "I'm keeping my baby," is more explicit. Research by Jane Brown and associates (1988) shows that audiences are split on the issue of whether the "baby" refers to her boyfriend or to a pregnancy.

CHAPTER SEVEN

1. Many of the authors who have contributed to the study of fans and fandom will appear in my forthcoming anthology, *The Adoring Audience: Fan Culture and Popular Media*, which will be published by Unwin Hyman, Winchester, Massachusetts.

2. See Jane Gaines (1985) for a review of feminist approaches to cinematic representation and identification.

3. MTV's music news segments perform such a function. The channel's originators decided to restrict news spots to reports on

rock stars and their careers with the full awareness that among fan groups, as Bob Pittman phrased it, "knowledge is status" (Levy 1983, p. 34).

4. See Julie D'Acci (1987) for an account of fan involvement with the television program, "Cagney and Lacey."

5. The actress was fired, but the way in which her character was written out of the program was influenced by fan protests according to Dorothy Hobson (1982).

6. The February 1986 edition of the British fashion magazine, *Tatler*, featured a cover photograph of "Yasmin as Tina Turner" (*Tatler*, 1986). David Gans (1983, p. 13) mentioned Benatar style imitators in his interview with Pat Benatar, "[Gans:] Witness the scene in [the movie] *Fast Times at Ridgemont High* in which two characters, taking note of the transitory nature of fashion, observe three girls affecting the 'Pat Benatar Look.' . . . Are there little Pat Benatars running around the suburbs? [Pat:] Yeah, you see them. But I think we see more little Go-Gos running around now." Benatar's response to Gans suggests that the female band the Go-Gos, popular with girls in 1983, also became subjects of style imitation.

7. For an elaborated critique on male-bias in the British subculture literature, see Angela McRobbie and Jenny Garber (1976) and McRobbie (1980).

CHAPTER EIGHT

1. The following excerpt from Madonna's interview with Harry Dean Stanton (1985, p. 66) for *Interview* discusses how "Into the Groove" found its way into the film: "The director, Susan Seidelman, said to me she was shooting a sequence where we needed a song that had a really good dance beat. She asked if we could just bring in the tape of the song that Steven Bray and I wrote. I said okay, and I brought in this tape we had been working on. Actually I wanted to test it out on all the extras who were dancing to it, to see if it was a good song. I had no intention of using it in the movie. So I brought it in and we played it, and we had to do take after take

and pretty soon everyone was starting to like the song and they were saying, 'What's this song, and where's it coming from?' I said, 'It's just a song,' and as the film got nearer to the end and they were doing the final cuts, Susan called me up and said, 'Look. . . .' Originally, I think they were going to use all songs that were already recorded in the soundtrack. I didn't go into this film thinking I'm going to get a hit song out of this, or an MTV video. No way! I think everybody wanted to turn the other cheek to that song and not bring it in because nobody wanted to make it that kind of a movie. So it was getting closer and closer and Susan Seidelman said to me, 'We're trying to find another song for that scene and we just think yours really works—it's a great song, the producers loved it, Orion loved it, everybody loved it.' I said, 'Okay, fine.' They synched the song to that sequence in the movie and showed it to me. I thought it was great and it didn't interfere with my character or what I was doing acting-wise, and we ended up using the original 8-track demo Steven and I had made. We never went into the recording studio and made a record out of it."

2. For a detailed discussion of Karl Marx and Frederick Engels' concept of ideology, and for comments on the context in which the term, "false consciousness" has been used, see Raymond Williams (1977).

3. Erica Carter (1984) cites the work of Richard Hoggart (1957), Phil Cohen (1972), Stuart Hall and Tony Jefferson (1976), Dick Hebdige (1979), and Paul Willis (1977) as examples.

4. *Rolling Stone*'s fifth cover story on Madonna, in its March 23rd, 1989, issue (Zehme, 1989), calls Madonna "the most famous woman in the world," making Madonna's featured comment in Betsy Aaron's 1985 newscast, "I want to conquer the world," the more accurate prediction (Aaron, 1985).

5. Tim O'Sullivan and associates (1983 p.1) define aberrant decoding as "a message that has been encoded according to one code [that] is decoded by means of another."

6. Directors of finalist videos are as follows: (1) Gary Pollard; (2) Eddie Barber; (3) Angel Gracia and Cliff Guest; (4) James Calciano; (5) B. Lee Papernik; (6) Louis Morneau; (7) Michael McAlex-

ander; (8) Bill Kent, Joe Messina, and Evan Wright; (9) Anthony Hoffman, Karen Petrosek, and Pamela Segall, (10) Jim Kubik and Ken Roy.

7. MTV announced the name of the style imitator as Denise Vlasis (phonetic spelling).

8. A video released in 1986 to publicize the song used in the movie, *At Close Range*, which co-starred Madonna's then husband, Sean Penn.

CHAPTER NINE

1. Examples of popular criticism that describe music video as sexist include Levy (1983) and Barol (1985).

AARON, BETSY. "ABC World News Tonight" report on Madonna. ABC News, New York, 1985.

ALLEN, ROBERT C. 1985. *Speaking of Soap Operas*. Chapel Hill and London: University of North Carolina Press.

ALTHUSSER, LOUIS. 1969. *For Marx*. London: Allen Lane.

———. 1971. "Ideology and Ideological State Apparatuses." In *Lenin and Philosophy*. London: New Left Books.

ANG, IEN. 1985. *Watching Dallas: Soap Opera and the Melodramatic Imagination*. London and New York: Methuen.

ANGUS, ROBERT. 1976. "Pirates, Prima Donnas, and Plain White Wrappers." *Hi Fidelity* (December), pp. 76–81.

ARDENER, SHIRLEY. 1975. "Sexual Insult and Female Militancy." In *Perceiving Women*. Edited by Shirley Ardener. New York: John Wiley Publishers, pp. 29–83.

BABUSCIO, JACK. 1980. "Camp and the Gay Sensibility." In *Gays and Film*. Edited by Richard Dyer. London: British Film Institute, pp. 40–57.

BAROL, BILL. 1985. "Women in a Video Cage." *Newsweek* (March 4), p. 54.

BEGO, MARK. 1985. *Madonna!* New York: Pinnacle Books.

BENATAR, PAT. Telephone interview with author, 25 February, 1987.

BENNETT, TONY. 1982. "Theories of the Media, Theories of Society." In *Culture, Society and the Media*. Edited by Michael Gurevitch,

Tony Bennett, James Curran, and Janet Woollacott. London and New York: Methuen, pp. 30–55.

BENNETT, TONY, and JANET WOOLLACOTT. 1987. *Bond and Beyond: The Political Career of a Popular Hero*. New York: Methuen.

BESSMAN, JIM. 1985. "How Clips Helped Break Cyndi." *Billboard* (March 9), p. 38.

BISHOP, JEFF, and PAUL HOGGETT. 1986. *Organizing around Enthusiasms: Mutual Aid in Leisure*. London: Comedia.

BOWERS, JANE, and JUDITH TICK, eds. 1986. *Women Making Music: The Western Art Tradition, 1150–1950*. Urbana: University of Illinois Press.

BRAKE, MICHAEL. 1985. *Comparative Youth Culture*. London: Routledge & Kegan Paul.

BRANDT, PAM. 1982. "At Last . . . Enough Women Rockers to Pick and Choose." *Ms.* (September), pp. 110–116.

BROWN, JANE D., and KENNETH C. CAMPBELL. 1986. "Race and Gender in Music Videos: The Same Beat but a Different Drummer." *Journal of Communication* 36, no. 1 (Winter), pp. 94–106.

BROWN, JANE D., LAURIE SCHULZE, KIM WALSH CHILDERS, and LIA NICKOPOLOU. "Race and Gender Differences in Interpretations of Sexuality in Music Videos." Paper presented at the American Studies Association Conference, Miami, October 1988.

BROWN, LES. 1971. *Television: The Business Behind the Box*. New York: Harcourt Brace Jovanovich.

BROWN, MARY ELLEN, and JOHN FISKE. 1987. "Romancing the Rock: Romance and Representation in Popular Music Videos." *One Two Three Four—A Rock 'n' Roll Quarterly* 5, pp. 61–73.

BROWNMILLER, SUSAN. 1984. *Femininity*. New York: Fawcett Columbine.

BRUNSDON, CHARLOTTE, and DAVID MORLEY. 1982. *Everyday Television: "Nationwide."* London: British Film Institute.

BURKE, JULIA. 1985. "Letters" column. *Ms.* (April), p. 5.

BUTCHER, PETER. Interview with author, Europa Recording Studios, Austin, Texas, March 1987.

CANTOR, MURIEL G. 1974. "Producing Television for Children." In *The TV Establishment: Programming for Power and Profit*. Edited by G. Tuchman. Englewood Cliffs, N.J.: Prentice Hall, pp. 103–118.

CARTER, ERICA. 1984. "Alice in the Consumer Wonderland." In *Gender and Generation*. Edited by Angela McRobbie and Mica Nava. London: Macmillan, pp. 185–214.

CAUGHIE, JOHN. 1981. *Theories of Authorship*. London: Routledge & Kegan Paul.

CHAMBERS, JAIN. 1985. *Urban Rhythms: Pop Music and Popular Culture*. New York: St. Martin's Press.

CHRISTIANS, CLIFFORD G., and JAMES W. CAREY. 1981. "The Logic and Aims of Qualitative Research." In *Research Methods in Mass Communication*. Edited by Guido Herman Stempel and Bruce H. Westley. Englewood Cliffs, N.J.: Prentice Hall, pp. 342–362.

CLINE, CHERYL. 1986a. "Rock Critics and Girl Fans—Part Two: Fans and Groupies." *Bitch—The Women's Rock Newsletter with Bite* (July), pp. 13–14.

———. 1986b. "Sexual Crushes on Rock Stars, or David Lee Roth—Threat or Menace?" *Bitch—The Women's Rock Newsletter with Bite* (March), pp. 9–14.

COHEN, PHIL. 1972. "Subcultural Conflict and Working-Class Community." *Working Papers in Cultural Studies* 2, Spring.

COLLINS, NANCY. 1986. "The *Rolling Stone* Interview: Tina Turner." *Rolling Stone* (October 23), pp. 46–52, 106–108.

CONNELLY, CHRISTOPHER. 1984. "Madonna Goes All the Way." *Rolling Stone* (November 22), pp. 14–20, 81.

COWARD, ROSALIND. 1983. *Patriarchal Precedents*. London: Routledge & Kegan Paul.

CRETCHER, JEFF. 1983. "Hard Up Was Hard to Do: The Production of a Rock Video." *American Cinematographer* (September), pp. 56–59, 108–113.

D'ACCI, JULIE. 1987. "The Case of Cagney and Lacey." In *Boxed In: Women and Television*. Edited by Helen Baehr and Gillian Dyer. London: Pandora Press, pp. 203–225.

DALSIMER, KATHERINE. 1986. *Female Adolescence: Psychoanalytic Reflections on Literature*. New Haven and London: Yale University Press.

DANIELSON, PETER. Telephone interview with author, 1986.

DANNEN, FREDRIC. 1987. "MTV's Great Leap Backward." *Channels* 7, no. 7, (July–August), pp. 45–47.

DE LAURETIS, TERESA. 1984. *Alice Doesn't: Feminism, Semiotics and Cinema*. Bloomington: Indiana University Press.

DULLEA, GEORGIA. 1986. "Madonna's New Beat Is a Hit, but Song's Message Rankles." *New York Times* (September 18), pp. B1, B9.

DYER, RICHARD. 1979. *Stars*. London: British Film Institute.

———. 1986. *Heavenly Bodies: Film Stars and Society*. New York: St. Martin's Press.

EASLEY, GREG, and LAUREN RABINOVITZ. 1988. "No Controls: Music Video and Cultural Difference." *Wide Angle*, 10, no. 2, pp. 62–69.

EHRENREICH, BARBARA, ELIZABETH HESS, and GLORIA JACOBS. 1986. "Beatlemania: Girls Just Want to Have Fun." In *Remaking Love: The Feminization of Sex*. Garden City, New York: Anchor Press/Doubleday, pp. 10–38.

ELLIOTT, RONA. 1985. Tina Turner interviewer for NBC Radio and the "Today Show."

Fans *Do* Make a Difference. 1986. *Bitch—The Women's Rock Newsletter with Bite* (March), p. 11.

FEUER, JANE, PAUL KERR and TISE VAHIMAGI. 1984. *MTM: "Quality TV."* London: British Film Institute.

FISKE, JOHN. 1986. "Television: Polysemy and Popularity." *Critical Studies in Mass Communication* 3, no. 4, pp. 391–408.

———. 1987. *Television Culture*. London: Methuen.

FISSINGER, LAURA. 1985. "Maybe She's Good—Ten Theories on How Madonna Got 'It.'" *Record* (March) 4, no. 5, pp. 30–36.

FOSTER, EUGENE S. 1982. *Understanding Broadcasting*. 2d ed. Reading, Mass.: Addison-Wesley Publishing, pp. 174–181.

FOUCAULT, MICHEL. 1981. "'What Is an Author?'" (extract). In *Theories of Authorship*. Edited by John Caughie. London: Routledge & Kegan Paul, pp. 282–291.

FRIEDAN, BETTY. 1974. *The Feminine Mystique*. 10th anniversary ed. New York: W.W. Norton.

FRITH, SIMON. 1981. *Sound Effects: Youth, Leisure, and the Politics of Rock 'n' Roll*. New York: Pantheon Books.

———. 1988. *Music for Pleasure*. New York: Routledge & Kegan Paul.

FRITH, SIMON, and ANGELA McROBBIE. 1978–1979. "Rock and Sexuality." *Screen Education* 29, pp. 3–19.

Funky Frills: Take Center Stage in Cyndi Lauper and Madonna-Inspired Extras. 1985. *Seventeen* (July), p. 34.

GAGNON, MONIKA. 1986. "Bella-donna: Madonna at a Glance and in Retrospect." *Borderlines* (Summer), pp. 4–5.

GAINES, JANE. 1985. "Women and Representation." *Jump Cut* 29, pp. 25–26.

GANS, DAVID. 1983. "Business as Usual, the Pat Benatar Way." *Record* (March), pp. 1, 12–13.

GARDINER, JEAN. 1979. "Women's Domestic Labor." In *Capitalist Patriarchy and the Case for Socialist Feminism*. Edited by Zillah Eisenstein. New York: Monthly Review Press, pp. 173–189.

GEERTZ, CLIFFORD. 1973. *The Interpretation of Cultures*. New York: Basic Books.

GILMORE, MIKAL. 1987. "The Madonna Mystique." *Rolling Stone* (September 10), pp. 36–38, 87–88.

GINSBERG, MERLE. 1985. "Two Lucky Stars Take a Shine to Each Other." *Rolling Stone* (January 17), p. 6.

GITLIN, TODD. 1985. *Inside Prime Time*. New York: Pantheon Books.

GRAMSCI, ANTONIO. 1971. *Selections from the Prison Notebooks*. Edited and translated by Quintin Hoare and Geoffrey Nowell-Smith. London: Lawrence and Wishart.

GRIFFIN, CHRISTINE. 1985. "Leisure: Deffing Out and Having a Laugh." In *Typical Girls? Young Women from School to the Job Market*. London: Routledge & Kegan Paul, pp. 58–71.

GRIFFIN, NANCY. 1985. "Tina: The Scorching Ms. Turner Chills Out at Home." *Life* (August), pp. 23–28.

GROSS, LYNNE SCHAFER. 1983. *Telecommunications: An Introduction to Radio, Television, and the Developing Media*. Dubuque, Iowa: Wm. C. Brown, pp. 144–151.

GROSSBERG, LAWRENCE. 1984. "I'd Rather Feel Bad Than Feel Anything at All: Rock and Roll, Pleasure and Power." *Enclitic* 8, no. 1–2, pp. 94–111.

HALL, STUART. 1980. "Encoding/Decoding." In *Culture, Media, Language*. Edited by Stuart Hall, Dorothy Hobson, Andrew Lowe, and Paul Willis. London: Hutchinson, pp. 128–138.

————. 1981. "Cultural Studies: Two Paradigms." In *Culture, Ideology and Social Process*. Edited by Tony Bennett, Graham Martin, Colin Mercer, and Janet Woollacott. London: Open University Press, pp. 19–28.

————. 1982. "The Rediscovery of 'Ideology': Return of the Repressed in Media Studies." In *Culture, Society and the Media*. Edited by Michael Gurevitch, Tony Bennett, James Curran, and Janet Woollacott. London: Methuen, pp. 56–90.

————. 1983. "The Problem with Ideology—Marxism without Guarantees." In *Marx 100 Years On*. Edited by Betty Matthews. London: Lawrence and Wishart, pp. 157–185.

HALL, STUART, and TONY JEFFERSON, eds. 1976. *Resistance through Rituals: Youth Subcultures in Post-War Britain*. London: Hutchinson.

HANEY, JAMES. "MTV: Beginning to Look a Lot Like Radio." Paper presented at the Speech Communication Association convention, Washington, D.C., November 1988.

HARRIS, OLIVIA, and KATE YOUNG. 1981. "Engendered Structures: Some Problems in the Analysis of Reproduction." In *The Anthropology of Pre-capitalist Societies*. Edited by Joel S. Kahn and Josep R. Llobera. London: Humanities Press, pp. 109–147.

HASKELL, MOLLY. 1974. *From Reverence to Rape: The Treatment of Women in the Movies*. Baltimore: Penguin Press.

HASLING, JOHN. 1980. *Fundamentals of Radio Broadcasting*. New York: McGraw-Hill Books.

HEBDIGE, DICK. 1979. *Subcultures: The Meaning of Style*. London: Methuen.

————. 1983. "Posing . . . Threats, Striking . . . Poses: Youth, Surveillance, and Display." *SubStance* 37/38, pp. 68–88.

HENKE, JAMES. 1982. "1981: Another Bad Year for the Record Industry." *Rolling Stone* (March 4), p. 51.

HENLEY, NANCY. 1977. *Body Politics*. Englewood Cliffs, N.J.: Prentice Hall.

HICKLING, MARK. 1981. "Record Sales Hold Steady with Last Year's." *Rolling Stone* (October 15), p. 52.

HOBSON, DOROTHY. 1982. *Crossroads: The Drama of a Soap Opera.* New York and London: Methuen.

HOFLER, ROBERT, and (photographer) BRUCE WEBER. 1986. "An Affair to Remember—Madonna Makes Love to the Camera." *Life* (December), pp. 50–62.

HOGGART, RICHARD. 1957. *Uses of Literacy: Changing Patterns in English Mass Culture.* Fair Lawn, N.J.: Essential Books.

HOLDSTEIN, DEBORAH H. 1985. "Music Video Messages and Structures." *Jump Cut* 29, no. 1, pp. 13–14.

HOPKINS, JERRY. 1972. "The Fans." In *Things in the Driver's Seat: Readings in Popular Culture.* Edited by Harry Russell Heubel. Chicago: Rand McNally, pp. 161–172.

HORNADAY, ANN. 1985. "Cyndi Lauper." *Ms.* (January), p. 47.

HUDSON, BARBARA. 1984. "Femininity and Adolescence." In *Gender and Generation.* Edited by Angela McRobbie and Mica Nava. London: Macmillan, pp. 31–53.

JANOWITZ, TAMA. 1987. "Sex as a Weapon." *Spin* (April), pp. 54–62.

JEROME, JIM. 1984a. "Cyndi Lauper." *People Weekly* (September 17), pp. 82–93.

———. 1984b. "They Film the Songs." *Gentleman's Quarterly* (March), pp. 90, 98, 100.

JOHNSON, RICHARD, and GRAHAM DAWSON for the Popular Memory Group. 1982. "Popular Memory: Theory, Politics, Method." In *Making Histories: Studies in History Writing and Politics.* Edited by Richard Johnson, Gregor McLennan, Bill Schwarz, and David Sutton. Minneapolis: University of Minnesota Press, pp. 205–252.

JOHNSTON, CLAIRE. 1972. "Women's Cinema as Counter-Cinema." *Screen*, Pamphlet no. 2, p. 28.

JOHNSTON, SHEILA. 1981. " 'Crossroads:' Approaches to Popular Television Fiction." Paper presented at British Film Institute Summer School.

KAPLAN, E. ANN. 1985. "A Post-Modern Play of the Signifier? Advertising, Pastiche and Schizophrenia in Music Television." In *Tele-*

vision in Transition. Edited by Phillip Drummond and Richard Paterson. London: British Film Institute, pp. 146–163.

————. 1986. "History, the Historical Spectator and Gender Address in Music Television." *Journal of Communication Inquiry* (Winter), pp. 3–14.

————. 1987. *Rocking around the Clock: Music Television, Postmodernism, and Consumer Culture*. New York: Methuen.

KATZ, CYNTHIA. 1982. "The Video Music Mix." *Videography* (May), pp. 28–35.

KIRKEBY, MARC. 1980. "The Pleasures of Home Taping." *Rolling Stone* (October 2), pp. 62–64.

KITAY, CYNTHIA. 1981. Interview with Bob Pittman, Vice-president of Programming, Warner Amex Satellite Entertainment Company (WASEC). *Programmer's Textbook*. New York: WASEC, unpaginated.

KONOPKA, GISELA. 1966. *The Adolescent Girl in Conflict*. Englewood Cliffs, New Jersey: Prentice Hall.

KUHN, ANNETTE. 1982. *Women's Pictures*. London: Routledge & Kegan Paul.

————. 1984. "Women's Genres." *Screen* 25, no. 1, pp. 18–28.

LAING, DAVE. 1985. *One Chord Wonders: Power and Meaning in Punk Rock*. Milton Keyes, England: Open University Press.

LEACH, WILLIAM R. 1984. "Transformations in a Culture of Consumption: Women and Department Stores, 1890–1925." *Journal of American History* 71, no. 2, pp. 319–342.

LEVY, STEVEN. 1983. "Ad Nauseaum: How MTV Sells Out Rock and Roll." *Rolling Stone* (December 8), pp. 30–37, 74–79.

LEWIS, LISA A. 1987a. "Consumer Girl Culture: How Music Video Appeals to Women." *One Two Three Four—A Rock 'n' Roll Quarterly* (Spring), no. 5, pp. 5–15.

————. 1987b. "Female Address in Music Video." *Journal of Communication Inquiry* 11, no. 1 (Winter), pp. 73–84.

————. 1987c. "Form and Female Authorship in Music Video." *Communication* 9, pp. 355–377.

————, ed. In press. *The Adoring Audience: Fan Culture and Popular Media*. Winchester, Massachusetts: Unwin Hyman.

LODER, KURT. 1984a. "Dream Girl." *Rolling Stone* (May 24), pp. 13–19, 60–63.

———. 1984b. "Sole Survivor." *Rolling Stone* (October 11), pp. 19–20, 57–60.

LODER, KURT, and STEVE POND. 1982. "Record Industry Nervous as Sales Drop Fifty Percent." *Rolling Stone* (September 30), pp. 69, 78–79.

LUNCH, LYDIA. 1985. "Lunch with Benatar." *Spin* (September), pp. 40–44.

McGUIGAN, CATHLEEN with PETER McALEVEY. 1984. "The Gracie Allen of Rock." *Newsweek* CIII, no. 13 (March 26), p. 80.

McROBBIE, ANGELA. 1980. "Settling Accounts with Subcultures: A Feminist Critique." *Screen Education* 34, pp. 37–49.

———. 1983. "Jackie: An Ideology of Adolescent Femininity." In *Mass Communication Review Yearbook*, vol. 4. Edited by Ellen Wartella and Charles D. Whitney. Beverly Hills: Sage, pp. 273–283.

———. 1984. "Dance and Social Fantasy." In *Gender and Generation*. Edited by Angela McRobbie and Mica Nava. London: Macmillan, pp. 130–161.

McROBBIE, ANGELA, and JENNY GARBER. 1976. "Girls and Subcultures." In *Resistance through Rituals: Youth Subcultures in Post War Britain*. Edited by Stuart Hall and Tony Jefferson. London: Hutchinson, pp. 209–22.

McROBBIE, ANGELA, and MICA NAVA, eds. 1984. *Gender and Generation*. London: Macmillan.

The Making of "Love Is a Battlefield." 1985. An interview with Pat Benatar in a commercially available Pat Benatar concert video.

MARC, DAVID. 1984. *Demographic Vistas*. Philadelphia: University of Pennsylvania Press.

MARX, KARL. 1972a. "The Eighteenth Brumaire of Louis Bonaparte." In *The Marx-Engels Reader*. Edited by R. C. Tucker. New York: W. W. Norton, pp. 436–525.

———. 1972b. "For a Ruthless Criticism of Everything Existing." In *The Marx-Engels Reader*. Edited by R. C. Tucker. New York: W. W. Norton, pp. 7–10.

————. 1972c. "The German Ideology (Part One)." In *The Marx-Engels Reader*. Edited by R. C. Tucker. New York: W. W. Norton, pp. 110–164.

MATTHEWS, GORDON. 1985. *Madonna*. New York: Wanderer Books/Simon & Schuster.

MAYNE, JUDITH. 1985. "Review Essay: Feminist Film Theory and Criticism." *Signs* 11, pp. 81–100.

MEEHAN, EILEEN R. 1986. "Conceptualizing Culture as Commodity: The Problem of Television." *Critical Studies in Mass Communication* 3, no. 4, pp. 448–457.

MEHLER, MARK. 1984. "Tina Turner's Still Shaking That Thing." *Record* (December), pp. 17–21.

Meldrum Tapes 1986. Video interview with Cyndi Lauper and David Wolff. New York: MTV.

MILLER, JEAN BAKER. 1973. "Introduction." In *Psychoanalysis and Women: Contributions to New Theory and Therapy*. Edited by Jean Baker Miller. New York: Brunner/Mazel, pp. v–viii.

MILLER, JIM, CATHLEEN McGUIGAN, MARK D. UEHLING, JANET HUCK, and PETER McALEVEY. 1985. "Rock's New Women." *Newsweek* (March 4), pp. 48–57.

MODLESKI, TANIA. 1984. *Loving with a Vengeance: Mass Produced Fantasies for Women*. New York and London: Methuen.

MORLEY, DAVID. 1980. *The "Nationwide" Audience*. London: British Film Institute.

————. 1986. "Family Television: Cultural Power and Domestic Leisure." Paper presented at the Second International Television Studies Conference, London (July).

MULVEY, LAURA. 1975. "Visual Pleasure and Narrative Cinema." *Screen* 16, pp. 6–18.

NAVA, MICA. 1984. "Youth Service Provision, Social Order and the Question of Girls." In *Gender and Generation*. Edited by Angela McRobbie and Mica Nava. London: Macmillan, pp. 1–30.

NEWCOMB, HORACE M. 1984. "On the Dialogic of Mass Communication." *Critical Studies in Mass Communication*, no. 1, pp. 34–50.

NEWCOMB, HORACE M., and ROBERT S. ALLEY. 1983. *The Producer's Medium: Conversations with America's Leading Television Producers*. London: Oxford University Press.

NEWCOMB, HORACE M., and PAUL M. HIRSCH. 1983. "Television as a Cultural Forum." *Quarterly Review of Film Studies* 8, no. 2, pp. 45–55.

O'BRIEN, CATHERINE. 1985. "Letters" column *Ms.* (April), p. 5.

ORTNER, SHERRY B. 1984. "Theory in Anthropology Since the Sixties." *Comparative Studies in Society and History* 26, pp. 126–165.

O'SULLIVAN, TIM, JOHN HARTLEY, DANNY SAUNDERS, and JOHN FISKE. 1983. *Key Concepts in Communication*. London: Methuen.

PARELES, JON. 1986. "The Return of Cyndi Lauper." *New York Times Magazine* (September 14), pp. 72, 76, 82–86.

PHILLIPS, LYNN. 1987. "Who's That Girl?" *American Film* 12, no. 9 (July/August), pp. 20–24.

POND, STEVE. 1980. "Pat Benatar—This Year's Model." *Rolling Stone* (October 16), pp. 12–15.

———. 1982. "Record Rental Stores Booming in U.S." *Rolling Stone* (September 2), pp. 37, 42–43.

RADWAY, JANICE A. 1984. *Reading the Romance*. Chapel Hill: University of North Carolina Press.

REITER, RAYNA RAPP. 1975. "Men and Women in the South of France: Public and Private Domains." In *Toward an Anthropology of Women*. Edited by Rayna Rapp Reiter. New York: Monthly Review Press, pp. 252–282.

RICH, ADRIENNE. 1983. "Compulsory Heterosexuality and Lesbian Existence." In *Powers of Desire*. Edited by Ann Snitow, Christine Stansell, and Sharon Thompson. New York: Monthly Review Press, pp. 177–205.

RIEGER, EVA. 1985. "'Dolce semplice'? On the Changing Role of Women in Music." In *Feminist Aesthetics*. Edited by Gisela Ecker. London: Women's Press, pp. 135–149.

ROCHLIN, MARGY. 1984. "Cyndi Lauper—The Surprising Mind Behind 'The Girl Who Just Wants to Have Fun.'" *Ms.* 13, no. 4 (October), pp. 72–75.

ROSALDO, MICHELLE Z. 1974. "Woman, Culture, and Society: A Theoretical Overview." In *Woman, Culture and Society*. Edited by Michelle Z. Rosaldo and Louise Lamphere. Stanford: Stanford University Press, pp. 17–42.

———. 1980. "The Use and Abuse of Anthropology: Reflections on Feminism and Cross-Cultural Understanding." *Journal of Women in Culture and Society* 5, no. 3, pp. 389–417.

ROSEN, MARJORIE. 1973. *Popcorn Venus: Women, Movies, and the American Dream*. New York: Coward McCann & Geoghegan.

ROSS, ELLEN, and RAYNA RAPP. 1981. "Sex and Society: A Research Note from Social History and Anthropology." In *Powers of Desire*. Edited by Ann Snitow, Christine Stansell, and Sharon Thompson. New York: Monthly Review Press, pp. 51–72.

ROWBOTHAM, SHEILA. 1973. *Hidden from History: 300 Years of Women's Oppression and the Fight against It*. London: Pluto Press.

RUBIN, GAYLE. 1975. "The Traffic in Women: Notes on the 'Political Economy' of Sex." In *Toward an Anthropology of Women*. Edited by Rayna Rapp Reiter. New York: Monthly Review Press, pp. 157–210.

RUBIN, LILLIAN BRESLOW. 1976. *Worlds of Pain: Life in the Working-Class Family*. New York: Basic Books.

SALLY and ILONA. 1982. "Ageism in the Women's Liberation Movement." In *Girls Are Powerful*. Edited by Susan Hemmings. London: Sheba Feminist Press, pp. 153–158.

SCHRUERS, FRED. 1985. "Lucky Stars." *Rolling Stone* (May 9), pp. 27–32.

———. 1986. "Can't Stop the Girl." *Rolling Stone* (June 5), pp. 28–60.

———. 1987. "How's That Girl?" *US* (September 17) 3, no. 58, pp. 12–17.

SHORE, MICHAEL. 1984. *The Rolling Stone Book of Rock Video*. New York: Rolling Stone Press.

SKOW, JOHN, with CATHY BOOTH, and DENISE WORRELL. 1985. "Madonna Rocks the Land." *Time* (May 27), pp. 74–77.

SOMMER, BRENDA. 1985. "At Home with Video." *The Austin Chronicle* (February 22), p. 9.

SPOTNITZ, FRANK. 1989. "Into the '90s: The Future of Talking Pictures. What Next?" *American Film* 14, no. 4 (January–February), pp. 28–30.

STANTON, HARRY DEAN. 1985. "Madonna." *Interview* (December), pp. 58–68.

State of the Industry: Part I: The Cable Numbers According to Broadcasting. 1981. *Broadcasting* (November 30), pp. 36–52.

STERLING, CHRISTOPHER H., and JOHN M. KITROSS. 1978. *Stay Tuned: A Concise History of American Broadcasting.* Belmont, California: Wadsworth Publishing.

STEWARD, SUE, and SHERYL GARRATT. 1984. *Signed, Sealed and Delivered: True Life Stories of Women in Pop.* London: Pluto Press.

STONE, GREGORY P. 1965. "Appearance and the Self." In *Dress, Adornment and the Social Order.* Edited by Mary Ellen Roach and Joanne B. Eicher. New York: John Wiley and Sons, pp. 216–245.

SUTHERLAND, SAM. 1980. "Record Business: The End of an Era." *Hi Fidelity* (May), p. 96.

SWARTLEY, ARIEL. 1982. "Girls! Live! On Stage!" *Mother Jones* (June), pp. 25–31.

Tatler (February), Cover. 1986. Yasmin as Tina Turner.

THOMPSON, E. P. 1963. *The Making of the English Working Class.* London: Gollancz.

TUDOR, ANDREW. 1974. *Image and Influence.* London: Allen & Unwin.

TULLOCH, JOHN, and MANUEL ALVARADO. 1983. *Doctor Who: The Unfolding Text.* London: Macmillan.

TURNER, TINA, with KURT LODER. 1986. *I, Tina.* New York: William Morrow.

TWERSKY, LORI. 1986. "On Non-sexual Obsessions." *Bitch—The Women's Rock Newsletter with Bite* (March), p. 11.

VENER, ARTHUR M., and CHARLES R. HOFFER. 1965. "Adolescent Orientations to Clothing." In *Dress, Adornment and the Social Order.* Edited by Mary Ellen Roach and Joanne B. Eicher. New York: John Wiley and Sons, pp. 76–81.

Village Voice. "JRS!" Advertisement for Macy's Department Store, 11 June 1985.

VOLOSINOV, V. N. 1973. *Marxism and the Philosophy of Language.* New York: Seminar Press.

WALKERDINE, VALERIE. 1984. "Some Day My Prince Will Come." In *Gender and Generation.* Edited by Angela McRobbie and Mica Nava. London: Macmillan, pp. 162–184.

WALLACE, ROBERT. 1980. "Crisis? What Crisis?" *Rolling Stone* (May 29), pp. 17, 28, 30–31.

WEINBAUM, BATYA and AMY BRIDGES. 1979. "The Other Side of the Paycheck: Monopoly Capital and the Structure of Consumption." In *Capitalist Patriarchy and the Case for Socialist Feminism.* Edited by Zillah R. Eisenstein. New York: Monthly Review Press, pp. 190–205.

WHITE, TIMOTHY. 1988. "Pat Benatar's Rock Dreams." *Program Guide* for Wide Awake Tour.

WILLIAMS, RAYMOND. 1975. *Television: Technology and Cultural Form.* New York: Schocken Books.

———. 1977. *Marxism and Literature.* Oxford: Oxford University Press.

———. 1981. "Analysis of Culture." In *Culture, Ideology and Social Process.* Edited by Tony Bennett, Graham Martin, Colin Mercer, and Janet Woollacott. London: Open University Press, pp. 43–52.

WILLIAMSON, JUDITH. 1985. "The Making of a Material Girl." *New Socialist* (October), pp. 46–47.

WILLIS, PAUL. 1977. *Learning to Labor: How Working Class Kids Get Working Class Jobs.* London: Saxon House.

WILSON, SUSAN. 1984. "So There It All Is: Rock TV 1984." *Parents' Choice*, pp. 3, 14.

WILSON, WANDA. Interview with author. Held at Scarborough's Department Store, Barton Creek Mall, Austin, Texas, Autumn 1984.

WOLCOTT, JAMES. 1985. "Let the Mascara Run." *Vanity Fair* (August), p. 71.

WOLFE, ARNOLD S. 1983. "Rock on Cable: On MTV: Music Television, the First Video Music Channel." *Popular Music and Society* 9, no. 1, pp. 41–60.

WOLFF, JANET. 1981. *The Social Production of Art.* London: Macmillan.

WOLMUTH, ROGER. 1983. "Rock'n'Roll'n'Video: MTV's Music Revolution." *People Magazine* (October 17), pp. 96, 99–104.

The Women behind the Movement. 1985. *Broadcasting* (July 15), p. 42.

WORRELL, DENISE. 1985. "Now: Madonna on Madonna." *Time*
(May 27), pp. 78–83.

WYNN, RON. 1985. *Tina: The Tina Turner Story*. New York: Collier
Books.

ZARETSKY, ELI. 1976. *Capitalism, the Family, and Personal Life*. New
York: Harper Colophon Books.

ZEHME, BILL. 1989. "Madonna." *Rolling Stone* (March 23), pp. 50–58,
180–182.

ZEMON DAVIS, NATALIE. 1965. "Reasons of Misrule." In *Society and
Culture in Early Modern France*. Stanford: Stanford University
Press, pp. 97–123.

INDEX

Aaron, Betsy: Madonna piece by, 200, 201–203, 204–205, 231n.4
"ABC World News Tonight": Madonna piece on, 200–206, 231n.4
Access signs, 109: in female-address videos, 110, 114, 120–121, 124; in videos, 210–211, 221
Addams, Elsye, 204
Adolescents, 8–9, 16, 199; as fans, 150, 151, 163, 171; female, 101, 109, 123–124, 147, 221; femininity of, 166–167; gender and, 34–38, 122, 218; ideology of, 8, 35–36, 123–124; male, 40–41, 50–52, 53, 122, 218; sexual relations of, 137–141; video depictions of, 44–53. *See also* Youth
Ageism, 223–224
Album-oriented rock (AOR), 25
Alvarado, Manuel, 157
Amateurism, 59
"American Bandstand," 16
American Express, 13, 14
Androgynous rock stars, 152–153

Andrzejewski, Patricia. *See* Benatar, Pat
AOR. *See* Album-oriented rock (AOR)
Ardener, Shirley, 121
Arquette, Rosanna: and role in *Desperately Seeking Susan*, 185, 186, 187–195
Audience, 29; fans as, 161–162; interpretation by, 149–150; MTV, 19–21, 26, 27; participation of, 221–222; research on, 27–28; targeting of, 5, 6, 15–19
Austin: rock concerts in, 174–175
Authority: fan, 156–159, 162; gang, 51–52; male–adolescent, 47–49; of performance, 80, 123
Authorship, 10, 95, 129, 219–220, 221; credit for, 64–65, 68; musical production and, 62–68; strategies of, 79, 94–96, 107; undermining, 88, 105

Babuscio, Jack, 152

Turner, Tina (*cont.*)
230n.6; movie role of, 135–136;
video symbolism of, 124–126. *See
also I, Tina*; Turner, Ike
Twersky, Lori, 155
Typical Male, 136, 147

Veejays, 25, 41, 226n.4
Viacom and Teleprompter, 14
Videos, 5, 6, 42, 173; eroticism in,
142–143; fantasy in, 112–117, 121–
123; female address in, 7, 44, 109–
116, 146–147, 209–210; female
roles in, 126–127, 129–133; femininity in, 123–124; girl culture in,
163–164; imagery in, 89–90, 98,
110–116; and "Madonna Look-
Alike Contest," 206–213; male
address in, 43–53, 111, 146–147;
promotion of, 71–72, 129; record
promotion and, 23, 25; sexual
roles in, 127–129, 133–135, 136, 137–
141; social symbols in, 117–120;
street culture in, 124–125; victimization in, 125–126; voyeurism in,
141–142
Violence: gang, 49–53; and sex,
133–134
"Virgin Tour," 175, 212
Vocalists, 58, 71, 82
Voyeurism: in videos, 48–49, 119,
127–128

Walkerdine, Valerie, 8
Walz, Ken, 98
Warner Amex Satellite Entertain-
ment Company (WASEC),
13–14, 18, 19, 20; and MTV programming, 21–22, 25, 225n.1; and
record sales, 23–24
Warner Cable, 13, 14
WASEC. *See* Warner Amex Satellite Entertainment Company
(WASEC)
What's Love Got to Do with It? 77,
147, 210; authorship of, 79–80;
reworking of, 78–79; symbolism
of, 124–125
Whites: rock bias toward, 32, 39, 51
Wolff, Dave, 93–94, 126; in videos,
94, 128–129
Wolff, Janet, 62
Women. *See* Females; Girls
Women's movement, 163; ageism
in, 223–224; influence of, 68–69,
100–101

You Better Run, 111, 146
Youth, 8; and culture formation,
37–38; female, 223–224; and rock,
32–33; sexual geography of, 35–37;
as target audience, 5, 16, 28. *See
also* Adolescents; Boys; Girls

ZZ Top, 46–47